Hospitality

A Cookbook
Celebrating Boston's
North Shore

SALEM HOSPITAL AID ASSOCIATION

Editor: Jean S. Connor
Graphic Design: Karen Gourley Lehman,
Steve Dariotis
Photography: Jim Scherer
Food Styling: Jami Barry

Cover illustration:
The Gardens at the House of Seven Gables
Salem, Massachusetts

House of Seven Gables Luncheon
Enjoy luncheon fare in the seaside gardens
of the famed House of Seven Gables in
Salem. The mansion, dating from 1668 and
luxurious for its time, became the setting
for Nathaniel Hawthorne's brooding classic
of the same name. The House of Seven
Gables is the only 17th century mansion
remaining in New England. Furnishings,
magnificent period gardens and a
panoramic view of Salem Harbor enhance
a visitor's experience. In 1908 the house
was bought and restored by philanthropist
Caroline Emmerton, a leader in the
settlement house movement in America.
Since 1910 proceeds from the historic site
have supported the community-based
programs of the House of the Seven Gables
Settlement, many of which enabled
immigrants to learn practical skills which
helped them adjust to the life and culture of
the United States.

Hospitality

Foreword

Hospitality! — The very name evokes a feeling of generosity and warmth. For more than fifty years the members of the Aid Association have been providing these important ingredients to the patients of Salem Hospital. *Hospitality: A Cookbook Celebrating Boston's North Shore* was conceived, nurtured and birthed by an Aid Association committee who willingly gave of their time to collect and test not only time-honored, but innovative and health-conscious recipes from friends all over the globe.

One of the first auxiliaries in the nation, the Salem Hospital Aid Association was formed in 1939, in the true New England spirit of caring. From the beginning, auxiliary members performed a variety of patient care services which included sewing, nursing and nutritional tasks and for many years the operation of a coffee shop for visitors.

Today the Aid Association numbers more than 650 men and women who voluntarily provide patient amenities, in addition to administrative and hospital fund-raising activities. Since its inception, this dedicated group has raised more than one million dollars to be used for the care of hospital patients.

Salem Hospital was founded in 1873 by sea captain John Bertram initially to care for sick and disabled seamen. Today this private, 580-bed not-for-profit medical center is the largest regional referral and acute care teaching facility north of Boston. In addition to Salem Hospital, the health care system includes North Shore Children's Hospital and Shaughnessy-Kaplan Rehabilitation Hospital. The fourth affiliate, the Home Care Group of the North Shore, provides discharge planning and home care services.

The medical center serves each of the 34 communities which comprise Essex County, approximately 500 square miles of breathtakingly beautiful seacoast and inland forests. The patient population extends well beyond the North Shore to many other towns to the south, north and west of the county as well, and as far as southern New Hampshire and Maine. Our rich cultural heritage in Essex County provided the framework for gathering culinary and historical information. Its archives are filled with names, events and places which helped shape the very structure of our nation. We are grateful to the historical societies in our county who shared their culinary and historical heritage and, in some cases, even their settings to be part of the pictorial focus of this project. Members of the Salem Hospital Aid Association invite you to enjoy *Hospitality.* In doing so, you help sustain our mission to provide access to uncompromising health care. Proceeds from *Hospitality* will provide diagnostic and life-saving patient equipment. We thank you for your support and hope you enjoy celebrating Boston's North Shore and the fruits of our labors.

The Committee

Chairwomen
Marilyn Canton
Sally Collier

Associate Chairwoman
Debbie MacLean

Editor
Jean S. Connor

Book Development
Joan Bacall
Judy Boal

Evie Baker
Diane Barbour
Kathie Bertrand
Martha Bridge
Nancy Bruett
Marilyn Campbell
Lee Carangelo
Joan Collins
Sandy Cross
Mary Donovan
Peggy Duncan
Ann Fratini
Nancy Geaney
Alice Goldsmith
Camille Goodby
Pat Healey
Janet Himmel
Judy Hood
Joan Johnson
D.L. Kaulbach
Joan Leonard
Jan Norris
Jan Phillips
Peggy Reiley
Mary Ann Schultz
Mary Tully

Contents

Appetizers and Hors d'Oeuvres   2

Soups   20

Salads   34

Brunch   46

Poultry   56

Meat   74

Fish and Seafood   88

Pasta and Rice   116

Vegetables   126

Breads   142

Desserts and Sweets   156

Trimmings   196

Index   204

Appetizers

Crab, Artichoke and Jalapeño Dip

1 green pepper, chopped

1 Tablespoon vegetable oil

2 14-ounce cans artichoke hearts, drained and finely chopped

½ cup bottled pimento, drained and chopped

1 cup freshly grated Parmesan cheese

2 cups mayonnaise

½ cup sliced scallions

1½ Tablespoons lemon juice

1 Tablespoon Worcestershire sauce

2 jalapeño peppers, pickled, seeded and chopped (wear rubber gloves)

1 teaspoon celery salt

1 pound crabmeat

⅓ cup sliced almonds, toasted lightly

▶ Pita Crisps:

8 large pita bread loaves

½ cup unsalted butter

- Preheat oven to 375°.
- Sauté green pepper in vegetable oil until soft. Cool.
- In a bowl combine green pepper, artichoke hearts, pimento, Parmesan cheese, mayonnaise, scallions, lemon juice, Worcestershire, jalapeño peppers and celery salt. Gently stir in crabmeat.
- Transfer mixture to a buttered baking dish and sprinkle with almonds.
- Bake 25-30 minutes, or until top is golden.

Pita Crisps:

- Cut each loaf into 8 wedges and separate each wedge into 2 triangles.
- Brush with butter and arrange triangles on a jelly roll pan. Salt lightly.
- Bake in the upper third of oven for 10-12 minutes, or until crisp. Cool. Store in an airtight container. Makes 128 triangles.
- Yield: 10 portions

Endive Leaves and Cherry Tomatoes with Crabmeat

1 pound fresh lump crabmeat

½ medium red pepper

½ medium yellow pepper

2 Tablespoons fresh dill, finely chopped

½ cup mayonnaise (approximately)

10 unblemished endives

chives

salt and freshly ground black pepper to taste

1 pint cherry tomatoes

- Clean and pick through the crabmeat, removing any cartilage.
- Dice red and yellow peppers as tiny as possible.
- Gently mix crab, pepper, dill, and enough mayonnaise to bind lightly. Season to taste with salt and pepper.
- Separate endives into leaves and use just the small inner leaves.
- Spoon crab mixture onto each leaf and garnish with chive strands and cherry tomatoes.
- Yield: 70 pieces

NOTE: Can also scoop out small portion of cherry tomato at the stem end and stuff with crabmeat mixture.

California Rolls

▶ Sushi Rice:
1½ cups short grain rice
1¾ cups cold water
¼ cup rice wine vinegar
2 Tablespoons sugar
1½ teaspoons salt
1 Tablespoon mirin or sherry

▶ California Rolls:
1 recipe for Sushi Rice
2 teaspoons wasabi powder
(available in Oriental
markets)
1 Tablespoon water
1 medium avocado, in ½" slices
4 sheets nori (dried seaweed)
6 ounces cooked fresh crabmeat
½ European cucumber, in ¼"
julienne strips
2 teaspoons sesame seeds
soy sauce

Sushi Rice:

- Rinse the rice, then mix it with cold water and let it stand 15 minutes.

- Bring the rice to a boil, covered. Reduce the heat and simmer about 15 minutes, until the water is absorbed. Let the rice stand 5 minutes.

- Mix the vinegar, sugar, salt and sherry. Pour over the rice on a non-metallic platter. Mix and cool.

California Rolls:

- Mix wasabi with water.

- Lay a sheet of nori on a work surface.

- With dampened hands, spread a cup of rice evenly over the nori, leaving a 1" strip along the top edge free.

- Using a quarter of the wasabi mixture, "paint" a stripe on rice 1" from the bottom edge.

- Arrange one quarter of the crabmeat over the stripe.

- Arrange one quarter of the avocado next to the crabmeat.

- Place one quarter of the cucumber slices next to the avocado.

- Sprinkle with ½ teaspoon of sesame seeds.

- Beginning at the bottom edge, carefully roll the nori up like a jelly roll.

- Moisten the top edge to seal.

- Repeat this method for the 3 remaining nori rolls.

- Slice into 2" segments.

- Serve with soy sauce.

- Yield: 20 rolls

Summer Crab Mold

¼ cup butter
¼ cup flour
1¼ cups milk
8 ounces cream cheese
1 envelope unflavored gelatin
3 Tablespoons water
¾ cup mayonnaise
½ cup chopped celery
1 cup crabmeat
1 small onion, peeled and grated
Beau Monde seasoning to taste
hot pepper sauce to taste

- Melt butter in a saucepan and whisk in flour. Cook, stirring constantly for one minute. Gradually whisk in milk. When thickened, stir in cream cheese.

- Soften gelatin in water and add to the hot mixture. Stir to dissolve gelatin and remove from heat.

- Stir in mayonnaise, celery, crab and onion. Add Beau Monde seasoning and hot pepper sauce.

- Rinse a 4-5 cup mold with cold water. Fill mold with crab mixture and chill until firm.

- Unmold and serve with crackers or melba rounds.

- Yield: 16-20 portions

Baba Ghanoush

2 pounds eggplant, about 2
    medium-sized
3 Tablespoons tahini paste
1 garlic clove, minced
¼ cup minced onion
4 Tablespoons low-fat yogurt
1 tomato, chopped
1 green pepper, chopped
¼ cup fresh lemon juice
salt and freshly ground pepper
    to taste
2 Tablespoons minced fresh
    parsley

- In a conventional oven: Cut the eggplant in half lengthwise and cut through the flesh, but not the skin, at 1" intervals. Place, skin side down, on an oiled cookie sheet and bake until charred and shriveled, 20-30 minutes.

- In a microwave oven (preferred): Prick the eggplant several times with a fork and place on paper towel in the microwave, on high for 12 minutes (in 650-700 watt oven). Cool and cut in half.

- When the eggplant is cool enough to handle, scoop flesh into a bowl and mash with tahini, garlic, and onion. Mix in yogurt, tomato, green pepper, lemon juice and seasonings.

- Just before serving, mound in a bowl and sprinkle with parsley.

- Serve with pita wedges or vegetable crudities.

- Yield: 2½ cups

Terrine de Trois Poissons

1 pound sole, puréed and chilled
1¼ cups heavy cream
1 egg white
¾ teaspoon salt
¼ teaspoon white pepper
1 Tablespoon chopped chives
1 pound scallops, puréed and chilled
1¼ cups heavy cream
¾ teaspoon salt
½ teaspoon white pepper
1 Tablespoon chopped parsley
1 pound salmon fillets cut into strips

- Transfer chilled sole to a stainless steel bowl. Whisk in cream.
- Beat egg whites until frothy and add to mixture.
- Add chives.
- Season to taste. Chill again.
- Repeat this process in a separate bowl with the scallops. Chill.
- Lightly oil a loaf pan or terrine mold, 9x5".
- Line the base with the sole mixture.
- Carefully add strips of salmon, packing them neatly together.
- Cover with the scallop mixture.
- Cover the terrine with foil. Set in a shallow roasting pan. Add boiling water up to 2" on the sides of the terrine.
- Bake 1 hour in a preheated 300° oven.
- Cool several hours and chill.
- To serve, run a sharp knife around the edges of the mold and invert on a platter.
- Slice mousse using a sharp, damp knife.
- Serve with mayonnaise of choice or a fresh tomato sauce.
- Yield: 8-12 portions

Smoked Salmon Pâté

4 ounces cream cheese
½ ounce capers
1 ounce red onion, finely diced
½ teaspoon lemon juice
½ teaspoon Pernod
dash Worcestershire sauce
¾ teaspoon Dijon mustard
1 whole egg
2 ounces ground smoked salmon
2 ounces fresh salmon, poached

- Whip the cream cheese until soft. Then incorporate all the liquid ingredients until well mixed. Fold in the capers and onion.
- Combine ground smoked salmon and fresh salmon and mix with cream cheese dressing to desired consistency.
- Serve on rye toast points or water crackers.
- Provide fresh lemon and garnish with parsley.
- Yield: 4 portions

This celebrity recipe was submitted by
Grill 23 and Bar
Boston, MA

Tartare of Marinated Salmon with Cucumber Salad

1 pound salmon fillet

2 Tablespoons fresh dill, chopped

zest of 1 lemon, finely chopped

1 Tablespoon sugar

1 teaspoon salt

freshly ground black pepper

1 Tablespoon sour cream

▶ Cucumber Salad:

2 cucumbers

4 teaspoons salt

4 teaspoons white wine vinegar

4 Tablespoons vegetable oil

1 teaspoon sugar

▶ To garnish and serve:

dill

1 lemon

2 Tablespoons sour cream

Marinating the Salmon:

- Skin and remove any bones from the fillet. Place a piece of plastic wrap that is large enough to totally wrap the salmon on a work surface. Place the fillet on it. Mix the dill, lemon zest, sugar, salt and pepper and press it firmly over the fish.

- Wrap the fillet up tightly, refrigerate and leave it to marinate for 12 hours.

- After this time, unwrap it, gently rinse off the dill mixture, and pat the fish dry.

- Cut the salmon into thin slices and blend it with the sour cream.

Cucumber Salad:

- Peel the cucumbers and slice them thinly. Sprinkle salt over them and mix thoroughly. Leave to drain for 1 hour. After this time, squeeze them out and place in a bowl with vinegar, sugar and oil. This can be done 1 hour in advance.

- Serve the salmon tartare in mounds by putting each portion into a biscuit cutter, leveling the top and removing the cutter. Serve with extra sour cream, cucumber salad and lemons.

- Yield: 6 portions

Scampi alla Griglia

16 large shrimp, shelled and deveined

½ cup cognac

16 thin slices prosciutto or ham

½ cup breadcrumbs, optional

16 fresh sage leaves, or 16 fresh bay leaves, or a combination of both

pepper to taste

1 Tablespoon fresh lemon juice

- Marinate shrimp 1 hour in cognac.

- Drain shrimp and wrap in prosciutto, which has been dipped in cognac as a marinade. Roll in breadcrumbs, if you choose, to make shrimp crunchy.

- Place on skewers alternately with sage or bay leaves.

- Sprinkle with pepper and place 3" from broiler.

- Broil 3 minutes on each side.

- Squeeze on lemon juice and serve hot.

- Discard leaves.

- Yield: 4-6 portions as an appetizer

NOTE: This can be an hors d'oeuvre, a first course, or served on top of barely cooked spinach tossed with a little olive oil, melted butter and minced garlic as an entrée.

Shrimp and Artichoke Log

3 Tablespoons butter

1 package frozen artichoke hearts, drained and halved

½ pound fresh mushrooms, sliced

2 Tablespoons minced fresh parsley

1 clove garlic, minced

salt and pepper

1 sheet frozen puff pastry, thawed

8-10 ounces Swiss cheese, thinly sliced

12 jumbo shrimp, cooked, shelled and deveined

1 egg, beaten

1 Tablespoon minced fresh parsley

- Melt butter and add artichokes, mushrooms, parsley, garlic, salt and pepper. Sauté until mushrooms are tender. Drain well.

- Preheat oven 475°. Roll out puff pastry to a 10x15" rectangle.

- Butter a jelly roll pan and place dough on it.

- Arrange cheese slices on the lower half of the pastry, leaving a border all around. Spread sautéed vegetables over cheese and add shrimp. Brush the edges with beaten egg and fold the top half over the ingredients and seal edges well.

- Brush top with egg and sprinkle with parsley. Bake at 475° for 15 minutes, then lower heat to 375° for 15 minutes.

- Yield: 4-6 portions

Spicy Shrimp with Snow Peas

▶ Marinade:

2 cloves garlic

1 Tablespoon dried ground cumin

1 Tablespoon ground coriander

1 teaspoon ground cardamom

1 teaspoon cayenne

1 teaspoon cracked black pepper

4 scallions, tops only, finely chopped

¼ cup finely chopped parsley

1 teaspoon salt

1 Tablespoon grated lemon zest

1 cup olive oil

1 teaspoon grated ginger

3 pounds large shrimp, about 20 per pound, shelled and deveined

about 20 snow peas for garnish, blanched

- Chop garlic finely and mash into paste by using a little salt and pressing down with the flat blade of a knife.

- Mix with remaining marinade ingredients in a non-corrosive bowl.

- Add the raw shrimp and marinate at least 4 hours in the refrigerator, turning the shrimp with your hands from time to time.

- In a non-stick pan, sauté the shrimp and marinade in small batches over moderate heat with very little oil. Be careful to let the shrimp color gradually. Turn the shrimp and sauté until just cooked.

- Cool to room temperature and fold in pea pods.

- Skewer shrimp on toothpicks.

- Yield: 60 shrimp

Hen Cove Scallops

1 quart bay scallops (at least 2 pounds)

1 cup dry white wine

1½ cups water

▶ Marinade:

⅔ cup lime juice

2⅔ Tablespoons dry white wine

⅔ Tablespoon grated lemon rind

4 Tablespoons finely chopped black olives

4 Tablespoons finely chopped leeks

4 Tablespoons finely chopped green pepper

1 small clove garlic, minced

dash cayenne pepper

dash nutmeg

3 Tablespoons chopped fresh parsley

- In a saucepan, poach bay scallops in white wine and water for 5 minutes. Drain the scallops.

- Mix together all the ingredients for the marinade and pour over scallops.

- Refrigerate for 6 hours.

- Serve on a bed of lettuce and garnish with lime wedges sprinkled with paprika.

- Yield: 8 portions

Lemon Cup Scallops

3 large lemons

¼ cup dry white wine

1 pound sea scallops, quartered

1 cup butter or margarine

1 small clove garlic, crushed

1 Tablespoon minced fresh parsley

3 tomatoes, peeled, seeded and chopped

- Halve the lemons. Squeeze the juice to measure ½ cup. Remove all pulp. Remove a thin slice from the bottom of each lemon to make it stand level.

- In a stainless saucepan, blend ¼ cup of the lemon juice with the wine. Add scallops and simmer, covered, 5 minutes. Set scallops and liquid aside.

- In the same pan, melt the butter. Add ½ cup of lemon juice and garlic. Heat gently.

- Remove from heat, add scallops and tomatoes, tossing carefully.

- Fill shells with the mixture. Put under the broiler for 2 minutes to brown lightly.

- Sprinkle with parsley and serve immediately. Serve on lettuce leaves with French bread to soak up the delicious sauce.

- Yield: 6 portions

World's Best Clams Casino

1 red bell pepper, seeded and chopped

1 green bell pepper, seeded and chopped

1 medium onion, peeled and chopped

1 large garlic clove, minced

12 Tablespoons butter or margarine

freshly ground pepper to taste

several shakes of hot pepper sauce to taste

4 cups buttery cracker crumbs

1/3 cup grated Parmesan cheese

5 dozen small clams on the half shell

1 pound raw bacon in 1" slices

- Sauté peppers, onion and garlic in butter over low heat until soft. Remove from heat.

- Add ground pepper, hot pepper sauce and cracker crumbs.

- Mix well and add Parmesan cheese.

- Be sure to cut clam free from shell, but leave in the shell, before topping with 1 tablespoon of crumb mixture.

- Place raw bacon slice on top and bake in preheated 350° oven for 15 minutes. The stuffing should bubble.

- Place 3" from broiler and broil for 1 minute to brown the bacon.

- Yield: 5 dozen clams

NOTE: For added convenience, the crumb mixture can be made ahead and frozen. Roll it into a "tube-shape" with wax paper and twist the ends. When needed, slice in silver dollar-sized pieces. Place one slice on top of each clam. Top with bacon and bake as usual.

Smoked Oyster Log

1 medium clove garlic, crushed

1 Tablespoon finely chopped onion

16 ounces cream cheese, softened

1 Tablespoon mayonnaise

1 Tablespoon milk

2 teaspoons Worcestershire sauce

1/4 teaspoon salt

1/8 teaspoon white pepper

2 3/4-ounce cans smoked oysters, drained

1/2 cup finely chopped pecans, walnuts or pistachios

- In a food processor, mix together all the ingredients except the oysters and nuts until well blended. Spread into an 8 x 10" rectangle on a foil-lined baking sheet.

- In the same bowl, purée oysters. Spread over cream cheese mixture. Cover loosely with plastic wrap. Refrigerate several hours or overnight.

- Using a long, narrow spatula to help release the cheese from the foil, roll up like a jelly roll. It does not matter if it cracks. Shape into a long log. May be refrigerated wrapped in plastic wrap for 3 days. Roll in nuts.

- Garnish with sprigs of parsley and pimento tips. Serve with crackers.

- Yield: 8-10 portions

Oysters on the Half Shell au Skiff

½ cup vinegar

8 scallions, chopped, including a little green

24 cold oysters on the half shell which have been detached from the shell

2 large avocados, peeled, optional

1 pint sour cream

1 can or small jar of either black or red caviar

- Bring vinegar to a boil in a small pan and blanch scallions for 10 seconds. Drain.
- Spoon a few scallions on top of each oyster.
- Place two small, thin slices of avocado on top.
- Next put a dollop (teaspoon) of sour cream and sprinkle ¼ teaspoon caviar over sour cream. Eat right from the shell.
- Yield: 2 dozen oysters

Baked Caponata

2 medium eggplants, peeled and diced into 1" cubes

salt

28-ounce can Italian tomatoes, drained, seeded and chopped

2 large red peppers, seeded and cut into 1" pieces

3 medium zucchini, washed and cut into ¼" slices

2 medium large onions, peeled and sliced very thinly

4 garlic cloves, coarsely chopped

2 heaping Tablespoons capers, rinsed

1 bay leaf

½ teaspoon fresh thyme leaves

salt and freshly ground black pepper to taste

¼ cup dry white wine, sherry, or 1½ teaspoons sugar

1-3 Tablespoons olive oil

chopped fresh parsley

- Place the eggplant in a colander and sprinkle generously with salt. Put a plate on top of the eggplant and a weight (such as a pan of water) on top of the plate. Let it sit for 1 hour while you prepare the other ingredients.
- Heat the tomatoes with a pinch of salt in a heavy-bottomed skillet or saucepan. Simmer over low heat for 15 minutes. Mash with the back of a wooden spoon.
- Preheat oven to 350°. Generously oil a large roasting pan, large enough to hold all the vegetables.
- Rinse the eggplant thoroughly and pat dry with kitchen towels. Toss together in the casserole with all the other vegetables, garlic, capers, bay leaf and thyme. Sprinkle with salt and pepper to taste.
- Heat the vinegar and sugar together in a saucepan just until the sugar melts. Toss with the vegetables. Add onions and toss again.
- Cover the baking dish tightly with foil and place in the oven. Bake 1½-2 hours, turning the vegetables every 30 minutes. When they are cooked through and fragrant, the caponata is done. Remove from the heat and allow to cool.
- Transfer to an attractive serving platter, cover and refrigerate overnight. Serve at room temperature.
- Yield: 6-8 portions

Chicken and Vegetable Terrine

▶ **Terrine:**

¾ **pound boneless, skinless chicken breasts**

2 egg whites

2 ounces very thin green beans

½ **pound slender carrots**

½ **pound broccoli broken into small florets**

½ **pound baby zucchini sliced lengthwise**

1½ **cups heavy cream**

▶ **Tomato Sauce:**

4 pounds ripe tomatoes, peeled and chopped

1 teaspoon salt

1 teaspoon sugar

2 Tablespoons tomato paste

¼ **cup freshly chopped basil leaves**

freshly ground black pepper

Terrine:

- Process chicken in a food processor for 1 minute. Add egg whites and blend for 2 minutes. Turn mixture into a bowl and place in the freezer until half-frozen.

- Prepare vegetables separately by blanching each for 2 minutes and then refreshing them under cold water. Dry carefully on paper towels.

- Put chicken back into the food processor. Add half the cream, process for 2 minutes, then add the remainder of the cream and process for 30 seconds.

- Line a terrine or a 9x5" loaf pan with foil.

- Begin by spreading the base with a layer of chicken mousse. Add a layer of beans, then alternate layers of mousse and individual vegetables, ending with the mousse.

- Bake in a preheated 375° oven for 90 minutes. Cool and refrigerate for 12 hours.

- Turn out and slice. Serve on individual plates with fresh tomato sauce.

Tomato Sauce:

- Place all the ingredients in a saucepan and gently bring to a boil.

- Simmer for 10 minutes.

- Purée and pour through a strainer.

- Yield: 8-10 portions

Green Chile Won Tons

8 ounces grated Monterey Jack cheese

1 4-ounce can green chilies, chopped

1 package won ton skins

vegetable oil

- Mix cheese and chilies.

- Place 1 teaspoon of this mixture on a won ton skin and fold up like an envelope.

- Fry in 2" of hot oil until brown, turning once. Drain.

- Serve with salsa or guacamole.

- Yield: 30 won tons

Spinach Wrapped Chicken with Oriental Dip

2 whole chicken breasts
1¾ cups chicken broth
¼ cup soy sauce
1 Tablespoon Worcestershire sauce
1 pound fresh spinach
lettuce leaves

▶ **Oriental Dip:**
1 cup sour cream
2 teaspoons toasted sesame seeds
½ teaspoon ground ginger
4 teaspoons soy sauce
2 teaspoons Worcestershire sauce

- In a 3-quart saucepan, simmer the chicken breasts in the chicken broth, ¼ cup soy sauce, and 1 tablespoon Worcestershire until tender, about 15-20 minutes. Remove the chicken breasts from the broth and cool.

- Thoroughly wash and remove the stems from the spinach leaves. Reserve smaller spinach leaves for another use, and pour 2-3 quarts of boiling water over the larger ones. Completely drain and set the spinach aside to cool.

- When the chicken breasts are cool, discard the bones and skin. Cut the meat into 1" cubes.

- To assemble, place a chicken cube at the stem end of a spinach leaf. Roll over once, fold leaf in on both sides, and continue rolling around the chicken piece. Secure the end of the leaf with a toothpick and chill in the refrigerator.

- Cover a serving plate with lettuce leaves. Place Oriental Dip in a small bowl in the center and surround it with the spinach-wrapped chicken pieces.

- To prepare the dip, in a small serving bowl, combine the sour cream, sesame seeds, ground ginger, remaining soy sauce and Worcestershire. Stir gently to combine the ingredients. Chill 4 hours in the refrigerator.

- Yield: 3-4 dozen

Seasoned Oriental Mushrooms

2 cups dried Oriental mushrooms
2 Tablespoons peanut oil
1-2 Tablespoons soy sauce
2 teaspoons sugar
1 teaspoon fresh ginger root, minced

- Soak black mushrooms in 3-4 cups of boiling water and cover for 15 minutes. Then trim stems, squeeze out the water, and cut mushrooms into even bite-sized pieces.

- Mix soy sauce, sugar and ginger in a bowl and set aside.

- Put oil in a skillet or wok over medium high heat. Add mushrooms. Turn and brown both sides. Stir in ginger and soy sauce mixture. After a few stirrings, lower the heat and stir until mushrooms absorb soy sauce evenly.

- Serve warm or cold as an hors d'oeuvre.

- Yield: 2 cups

NOTE: Bamboo shoots may also be included. May be made ahead and refrigerated.

Pork Won Tons

¾ pound ground pork
1½ teaspoons dry white wine
½ teaspoon salt
1 teaspoon garlic, minced
1 cup chopped Chinese vegetables
¼ cup chopped mushrooms
½-¼ teaspoon sugar
1½ teaspoons soy sauce
¼ cup minced onion
1 package won ton skins
vegetable oil

- Brown pork and drain well.
- Sauté onions in a little pork fat.
- Combine all ingredients except won ton skins and oil.
- Place a spoonful of pork mixture on a won ton skin and fold up like an envelope.
- Fry in 2" of hot oil until brown, turning once. Drain.
- Serve with soy sauce.
- Yield: 30 won tons

Indonesian Satay with Peanut Sauce

7 Tablespoons lemon juice
2 large cloves, minced
4 Tablespoons tomato sauce
¾ teaspoon salt
1½ pounds lean boneless pork, cut into ¾" cubes

▶ Peanut Sauce:
  2 Tablespoons creamy peanut butter
  1 Tablespoon butter
  ½ teaspoon sugar
  ½ teaspoon hot red pepper sauce
  ¼ cup half and half

- Combine 6 tablespoons lemon juice, garlic, 3 tablespoons tomato sauce and salt.
- Pour over pork cubes and marinate for 3-4 hours, turning occasionally.
- Remove pork and thread on skewers.
- In a saucepan, combine the reserved marinade, 1 tablespoon lemon juice, 1 tablespoon tomato sauce, peanut butter, butter, sugar and pepper sauce over low heat. Stir until thickened. Remove from heat and add the half and half.
- Broil skewered pork for about 15 minutes, turning once until done.
- Serve with warm peanut sauce.
- Yield: 6-8 portions

Pâté Maison Diamond

1 pound fresh chicken livers

1 pound lean fresh pork

1 pound good sausage meat

1 Tablespoon shallots or chives, finely chopped

2 Tablespoons parsley, finely chopped

2 teaspoons coarsely ground black pepper

½ teaspoon ground ginger

½ teaspoon ground cinnamon

2½ teaspoons salt

2 Tablespoons brandy

2 Tablespoons dry sherry or Madeira

1 pound raw bacon slices

- Ask your butcher to grind livers, pork and sausage together. Mix with all the other ingredients, except the bacon.

- Line an 8x4" loaf pan with bacon slices, and fill with mixture.

- Top with slices of bacon.

- Bake at 350° for 2 hours. If it browns too quickly, cover with foil.

- Cool loaf under pressure by putting another pan on top with a stone or a brick in it.

- Chill and slice.

- Serve with baguettes or toast as an appetizer.

- Yield: 8-12 portions

Tomato Concassé

1½ pounds tomatoes, peeled, seeded and chopped into small cubes

10 green pitted olives, chopped into small cubes

½ cup fresh basil leaves, chopped

salt and pepper to taste

2 ounces toasted pine nuts

vinaigrette

- Put chopped tomato, olives and basil into a bowl. Season with pepper but do not add salt at this stage as it will make the tomatoes watery.

- When ready to serve, adjust the seasonings and add salt to taste.

- To serve, place a round biscuit cutter in the center of each plate. Fill it with the tomato mixture, pressing the mixture down to form a mold. Carefully remove the biscuit cutter.

- Sprinkle toasted pine nuts around the edge of each plate. Decorate top of mold with a sprig of basil and drizzle the plate with vinaigrette.

- Yield: 4 portions

Savory Cheesecake Variations

⅓ cup fine breadcrumbs

¼ cup freshly grated Parmesan cheese

28 ounces cream cheese

4 large eggs

½ cup heavy cream

▶ **Variation I: Saga and Bacon**

1 cup chopped onion

½ pound bacon

½ Tablespoon bacon drippings

½ pound saga blue cheese

2-3 drops hot pepper sauce

salt and pepper to taste

French bread in ¼" slices

▶ **Variation II: Smoked Salmon and Leeks**

1 cup chopped leeks

1 cup chopped green pepper, optional

½ pound smoked salmon, finely chopped

1-2 Tablespoons butter

2 ounces freshly grated Gruyère cheese

2-3 dashes white pepper

salt to taste

French bread in ¼" slices

To begin for both:

- Sprinkle breadcrumbs and Parmesan cheese in a buttered, watertight 8" round springform pan. Set aside.

- Combine cream cheese, eggs, and cream in a mixer.

Variation I:

- Sauté bacon until crisp. Drain and chop finely.

- Reserve 1 tablespoon of drippings and sauté onion until clear.

- Add onion, bacon, blue cheese, salt and pepper to taste, and hot pepper sauce to the cream cheese mixture made above.

Variation II:

- Sauté leeks (and optional green pepper) in butter until clear and tender.

- Add onion, smoked salmon, Gruyère cheese, white pepper, and salt to the cream cheese mixture made above.

- For either variation, pour the cream cheese mixture into the prepared pan.

- Set the pan inside a larger pan and pour boiling water 3" deep into the larger pan.

- Bake 1 hour and 40 minutes in a preheated 300° oven. Turn the oven off and let the cake set for 1 hour in the oven.

- Remove the pan from its water bath and let cool for 2 hours before serving.

- Serve with sliced French bread or crackers.

- The smoked salmon and leek cheesecake can also be cut into wedges and served as an appetizer.

- Yield: 8-10 portions or more

Baguette Toppings

2 French bread baguettes, cut into ½" slices

▶ **Pesto with Mozzarella:**

1 cup pesto

1 pound fresh mozzarella, thinly sliced

10 sun-dried tomatoes, oil packed, drained and sliced

▶ **Curried Crab:**

1 cup mayonnaise

½ cup grated onion

1 cup shredded cheddar cheese

6 drops hot pepper sauce

¼ teaspoon curry powder

7 ounces crabmeat

- Preheat oven to 500°.

Pesto with Mozzarella:

- Spread French bread slices with pesto mixture. Place mozzarella slice on top. Top with a slice of sun-dried tomato.

- Bake on cookie sheets 4 minutes.

Curried Crab:

- Combine mayonnaise, grated onion, cheddar cheese, hot pepper sauce, curry powder and crabmeat.

- Spread mixture on bread rounds and broil until golden.

- Yields: 50 slices

Leek, Sun-Dried Tomato and Goat Cheese Spread

3 shallots, peeled and chopped

3-5 Tablespoons extra virgin olive oil

3 large leeks, chopped

8 Tablespoons butter

3-5 Tablespoons sun-dried tomatoes packed in oil, chopped

1 Tablespoon capers

salt and pepper to taste

2 logs of fresh goat cheese in ¼" slices

toasted French bread slices

- Sauté shallots in oil, 1-2 minutes. Add leeks and butter. Sauté over medium heat until tender, adding more oil and butter, as needed.

- Add chopped sun-dried tomatoes and capers.

- Arrange sliced goat cheese overlapping in a semi-circle on one half of a serving platter.

- Heat in microwave oven 20 seconds to soften slightly.

- Mound leeks and sun-dried tomato mixture in the center of the serving platter.

- Arrange French bread toasts in a semi-circle on the other side of the platter.

- To serve, spread goat cheese on toasted bread rounds and top with leek mixture.

- Yield: 6-8 portions

Basil Torta

1¼ pounds cream cheese, at room temperature

¾ cup unsalted butter, at room temperature

5 ounces Montrachet goat cheese, at room temperature

1 pound sliced provolone cheese

1 cup pesto

12 sun-dried tomatoes, packed in oil, drained and chopped

½ cup pine nuts, toasted

- Line a 9x5" loaf pan with a double thickness of damp cheesecloth.
- Beat cream cheese, butter and goat cheese until smooth. Divide into thirds.
- To assemble, arrange a layer of provolone on the bottom of the pan. Spread a layer of cheese on top with a spatula. Top with a layer of pesto and then a layer of provolone. Add a layer of sun-dried tomatoes and pine nuts. Continue to layer the ingredients ending with a layer of provolone.
- Cover the top with damp cheesecloth and gently press down on the torta to compress the layers. Refrigerate overnight.
- To serve, remove cheesecloth from to and unmold on a serving platter. Remove cheesecloth liner.
- Serve with crackers or slices of French bread.
- Yield: 20 portions

Mozzarella Milano

12 ounce package all-cream mozzarella

1 egg, beaten

1 cup breadcrumbs

peanut oil

▶ Sauce:

4-6 skinned tomatoes, chopped

1 Tablespoon fresh basil

4 cloves garlic, minced

1 small onion, peeled and finely chopped

1 Tablespoon olive oil

salt and pepper to taste

6 anchovy fillets, optional, but desirable

- Cut mozzarella into ⅓" slices.
- Dip pieces of mozzarella into beaten egg.
- Roll pieces gently in breadcrumbs and let sit for few minutes to dry.
- Repeat dipping and breading to make sure cheese is well-coated and sealed on all sides.

Sauce:
- Sauté garlic and onion in oil.
- Add optional anchovies, mash and simmer until flavors are "married".
- Add tomatoes and basil and stir to create a sauce. Set aside.
- Fry cheese slices in peanut oil to golden brown.
- Keep warm, then serve and pass the sauce.
- Yield: 4 portions

Baked Brie with Figs and Raspberry Vinegar

1 pound whole ripe Brie cheese, round or wedge shape

6 dried figs, finely chopped, about ⅓ cup

¼ cup raspberry vinegar

fresh raspberries for garnish

water crackers

- Halve the Brie horizontally. Place halves skin side down on a microwave serving platter.

- Sprinkle top evenly with finely chopped figs. Evenly drizzle the vinegar over the cheese.

- Cook on medium heat in the microwave for 3 minutes, or until the cheese is just softened. Do not overcook. Cheese should not be runny.

- Cheese can also be baked in a conventional oven at 350° for 5-10 minutes.

- Garnish with fresh raspberries.

- Serve with water crackers.

- Yield: 8-10 portions

HAMILTON
Originally "the Hamlet" of Ipswich, the town became independently incorporated in 1793. Alexander Hamilton, prominent and popular statesman of the time, was honored in the adoption of his name for the new town. This wonderfully wooded and green community has always been primarily an agricultural community, but Hamilton is also known as the site of the fashionable Myopia Hunt Club. The colorful hunts still held are reminiscent of those in Merrie England, though no real fox is hunted. On summer weekends, polo matches open to the public take place on the grounds.

Baked Brie Frangelico

¼ pound butter

½ cup brown sugar

dash of cinnamon

dash of nutmeg

1 pound wheel of Brie cheese

¼ cup Frangelico liqueur

¼ cup slivered almonds

- Preheat oven to 350°.

- Cook the butter, sugar and spices in a saucepan until thick.

- Place Brie in a decorative baking dish with low sides.

- Pour sauce over the cheese. Sprinkle with Frangelico and then with almonds.

- Bake for 5-10 minutes, or until cheese is melted.

- Serve with thinly sliced French bread.

- Yield 8-10 portions

Soups

Lobster and Corn Chowder

2 1½ pound lobsters, cooked, shelled and chopped

4 teaspoons minced garlic

½ pound bacon, diced

4 Tablespoons butter

1 cup chopped onion

1 cup fresh, frozen or canned corn kernels

2 cups minced carrots

¼ cup minced celery

1¾ cups new potatoes, diced into ¼" pieces

¼ cup flour

2 cups dry white wine

8 ounce bottle clam juice

1 cup water

1½ teaspoons fresh thyme, or ½ teaspoon dried

¼ teaspoon freshly ground black pepper

⅛ teaspoon cayenne pepper, or to taste

½ teaspoon salt

1 quart half and half

¼ cup dry sherry or Madeira wine

2 Tablespoons minced parsley and/or fresh chives

- Sauté the bacon until crisp. Drain on paper towels.

- Melt the butter in a clear saucepan or stock pot. Add the onions, corn, carrots, celery and potatoes. Stir and sauté over medium high heat until the vegetables are slightly browned.

- Add the flour, cook and stir 3-4 minutes more.

- Add the white wine, clam juice, water, thyme, pepper, cayenne, salt and bacon.

- Bring to a boil, reduce heat, cover and cook 10 minutes, or until potatoes are soft. Add the lobster meat and half and half. Bring to a boil.

- Stir in the sherry or Madeira and serve garnished with parsley or chives and common crackers.

- Yield: 3 quarts

Chowder Mexicano

2 cups sliced mushrooms
8 Tablespoons sweet butter
1 onion, chopped
1 small green pepper, chopped
1 teaspoon cumin
½ cup flour
¼ teaspoon cayenne
¼ teaspoon paprika
3½ cups chicken broth
¾ cup half and half
1 cup grated cheddar cheese
2 cups cooked corn kernels
¼ cup drained pimento
2 Tablespoons minced fresh
    parsley

- In a skillet, brown mushrooms in 2 tablespoons butter.
- In a kettle, cook onions, pepper and cumin in the remaining butter over moderate heat. Add flour, cayenne, and paprika and cook 3 minutes. Remove from heat.
- Add broth and cream and cook 2 minutes. Add mushrooms, cheddar cheese, corn and pimento and cook 2 minutes longer.
- Garnish with parsley and serve.
- Yield: 4-6 portions

Inaugural Fish Chowder

½ cup butter
3 cups diced onions
¼ cup finely grated carrots
2 teaspoons garlic, minced
½ cup flour
12 cups concentrated fish stock
4 pounds chowder fish fillets
    (such as 1 pound cod, 1 pound
    monkfish, and 1 pound cusk)
2 cups light cream
½ cup finely grated Monterey
    Jack cheese
salt and freshly ground black
    pepper to taste

- Heat the butter in a large saucepan until softened and sauté the onions, carrots, and garlic, stirring frequently, about 5 minutes. Add flour with a whisk.
- Return to the heat and cook, stirring for about 4 minutes.
- Meanwhile, begin heating the stock in a large pot.
- Add 1 cup stock to the flour mixture and then return it to the stock pot. Bring the stocks to a boil, whisking constantly, then reduce the heat and simmer for 10 minutes.
- Add the fish and simmer about 10 minutes longer. Stir in the cream and cheese; simmer until the cheese melts and is thoroughly incorporated into the chowder, about 5-8 minutes.
- Yield: About 3 quarts

This celebrity recipe was submitted by Chef Jean-Jacques Paimblanc Legal Seafoods Oyster Bar and Restaurant Cambridge, MA

NOTE: Reheat the chowder slowly to prevent the cream from boiling.

Massachusetts Seafood Chowder

4 slices bacon, chopped

1 large onion or more, as desired, peeled and chopped

4 medium potatoes or more, peeled and diced

salt and pepper to taste

1½ pints chopped fresh clams, with juice

1 pint sea scallops, cut in half, poached over medium heat, 2-3 minutes

1 pound scrod or cod

1 quart milk or light cream for a creamier chowder

2 Tablespoons butter or margarine

- Sauté bacon until crisp.

- Sauté onion in bacon fat until soft in a large pot.

- Add potatoes and clam juice to pot. Cook on medium heat about 10 minutes. Do not overcook and add water if necessary.

- Cut fish into large chunks and add to pot. Add clams and poached scallops.

- Add milk or cream, salt and pepper, to desired taste and thickness. Dot with butter. Heat thoroughly but do not boil.

- Yield: 6-8 portions

Pier 4 Clam Chowder

1½ pounds peeled and diced potatoes

1¾ quarts minced clams

½ quart clam juice

1½ ounces of powdered chicken soup base

salt and white pepper to taste

⅛ pound chopped onions

dashes of Worcestershire sauce

dashes of hot pepper sauce

⅛ pound salt pork, rendered

▶ Roux:

⅛ pound butter

⅛ pound margarine

flour to thicken

light cream

milk

- Rinse diced potatoes. Put potatoes, minced clams, clam juice, chicken soup base, salt and white pepper, onions, Worcestershire sauce, and hot pepper sauce in an 8-quart pot and bring to a boil.

- Simmer until the potatoes are almost but not thoroughly cooked through.

- Add rendered hot salt pork; add roux, and cook for 20 minutes. Cool.

- Make clam chowder in small batches by adding equal amounts of light cream and milk (1 cup cream/milk to 1 quart of stock).

- Heat over a very low heat and add salt and white pepper to taste.

- Yield: Makes 4 quarts or 32 servings

This celebrity recipe was submitted by Anthony's Pier 4 Restaurant Boston, MA

Mediterranean Fish Soup

7 carrots, thinly sliced

6 celery stalks, thinly sliced

3 potatoes, peeled and cut into ½" cubes

2 onions, coarsely chopped

16 ounce-can stewed tomatoes

¾ teaspoon freshly ground pepper

½ cup olive oil

1½ pounds haddock, or other firm white fish, cut into bite-sized pieces

- In a large kettle combine carrots, celery, potatoes, onions and tomatoes.

- Add pepper, oil, and 2½ quarts water. Bring to a boil; then simmer 20 minutes.

- Add fish and simmer 15-20 minutes.

- Yield: 12 portions

NOTE: Serve with crusty peasant bread.

Pasta e Fagioli (Pasta and Bean Soup)

¼ cup olive oil

1 cup coarsely chopped onion

1 cup coarsely chopped carrot

1 celery stalk with leaves, coarsely chopped

1 Tablespoon minced garlic

3 Tablespoons fresh basil or 1 Tablespoon dried basil

1 cup red or white canned beans, rinsed and drained

1 cup canned Italian plum tomatoes, chopped

7 cups chicken or vegetable broth

2 cups dried fettucine broken in pieces, or farfalle

grated Parmesan and/or Romano cheese

- Heat oil in a large heavy saucepan over moderately high heat. Add onions and sauté until they begin to turn golden.

- Add carrot, celery, garlic and basil and cook for a few more minutes, stirring occasionally.

- Add beans, tomatoes and broth. Turn heat to high and bring to a boil. Reduce heat to simmer and cook 30 minutes, or until vegetables are soft.

- Transfer 2 ladlesful of beans and their liquid to a food processor and purée. Return purée to soup.

- Fifteen minutes before serving, bring soup to boil and add pasta. Stir occasionally until pasta is cooked al dente.

- Remove from heat and season with salt and pepper.

- Ladle into soup bowls and sprinkle with Parmesan and/or Romano cheese and drizzle with olive oil.

- Yield: 8-10 portions

Zuppa Di Sposalizio/Abruzzi Wedding Soup

This celebrity recipe was
submitted by Bea Lazzaro

▶ **Basic Chicken Broth:**

1 roasting chicken, about 5
  pounds
2 cloves garlic
2 medium onions
2 whole carrots, peeled
2 celery stalks, with leaves

▶ **Mini Meatballs:**

2 slices bread
½ cup milk
1 pound ground beef
¼ pound ground pork
2 eggs
1 teaspoon garlic salt

▶ **Assembly:**

salt and pepper to taste
1 large head escarole
1 pound small pasta, optional
⅓ cup freshly grated pecorino
  cheese

Broth:

- Clean and cover chicken with about 4 quarts of water in a large pot.
- Add garlic and vegetables and cook until skin retracts from legs.
- Set aside to cool.
- Remove as much grease as possible from the broth.

Meatballs:

- In a bowl, wet the bread with the milk and squeeze dry.
- Add all the ingredients, working the mass with your fingers until well mixed.
- Form tiny meatballs the size of marbles.
- Taste the broth and adjust the seasonings.
- Remove the chicken and skin it. Bone and break the chicken into bite-sized pieces.
- Strain broth, discarding the vegetables.
- Wash the escarole well and towel dry it. Chop it into medium-sized pieces.
- Drop into broth and cook for several minutes.
- Add the meatballs.
- A small pasta may be added at this time, if desired.
- When all the ingredients are cooked, add the chicken pieces and heat for several minutes, just until the meat is warmed.
- Serve in pretty soup bowls with grated cheese.
- Yield: 8 portions

Won Ton Soup

▶ **Filling:**
½ **pound ground pork**
1 **scallion, sliced**
2 **teaspoons soy sauce**
½ **teaspoon cornstarch**
¼ **teaspoon ground ginger**
salt to taste
24 **won tons**

▶ **Broth:**
36 **ounces chicken broth**
24 **ounces water**
1 **Tablespoon soy sauce**
2 **scallions, sliced**

Filling:

- In a heavy skillet, cook pork and scallions until the pork is browned. Drain off the fat. Add to this mixture remaining filling ingredients except won tons. Place 1 teaspoon filling on center of won ton.

- Moisten the edges of the won ton with warm water (a little cornstarch may also be added to the water). Fold edges to form a triangle. Fold bottom 2 corners and squeeze together using the warm water.

Broth:

- Heat 5 cups of water in a large kettle to boiling. Slowly add filled won tons and bring water to boil again. Reduce heat, simmer uncovered for 2 minutes and drain water. (Be careful not to overcook won tons or they will split.)

- Heat broth, water, and soy sauce. Add sliced onions and heat for 15 minutes.

- Pour broth into serving bowls and add 3 won tons to each bowl and serve.

- Yield: 8 portions

Court Bouillon

3 **sprigs parsley**
1 **stalk celery**
1 **bay leaf**
1 **cup dry white wine**
bones and head of any white-meat fish
2 **quarts water**
10 **peppercorns, crushed**
pinch thyme
small onion, peeled and sliced
1 **carrot, peeled and coarsely chopped**
1 **teaspoon salt**

- With a piece of string, tie together the parsley, celery and the bay leaf.

- Combine all the ingredients in a deep saucepan and simmer, uncovered, 20 minutes.

- Strain the liquid using a double thickness of cheesecloth.

- Cool before using to poach fish or cook shellfish.

- Yield: 2 quarts

Sweet and Sour Soup

2 garlic cloves

3½ cups chicken stock

2½ Tablespoons white vinegar or fresh lemon juice

2 Tablespoons sugar

1¼ Tablespoons oyster or fish sauce

1 small onion, peeled and thinly sliced

1 medium carrot, thinly sliced

¾ cup sliced bamboo shoots

1 small zucchini, thinly sliced

¼ pound medium raw shrimp, peeled and deveined, sliced in half lengthwise

1 cup fresh mung bean sprouts

6-8 fresh mint leaves, minced

1 green chili pepper, seeded and thinly sliced (wear rubber gloves)

freshly ground black pepper to taste

- Rub the garlic cloves with oil and roast in a shallow pan at 400° until golden, about 15 minutes. Cool, peel and set aside.

- In a saucepan, heat the chicken stock with vinegar, sugar and oyster sauce. Just before it reaches the boiling point, add the onion, carrot, bamboo shoots, zucchini and shrimp. Simmer until the shrimp turns pink, about 3-4 minutes.

- Place the bean sprouts in warmed soup bowls and add the hot soup.

- Garnish with mint leaves, garlic and sliced chili pepper.

- Season with pepper to taste.

- Yield: 4 portions

Jarlsberg Vegetable Bisque

3 Tablespoons butter

3 Tablespoons flour

4 cups chicken broth

2 cups coarsely chopped broccoli

¾ cup chopped carrots

½ cup chopped celery

1 small onion, chopped

1 clove garlic, minced

½ teaspoon salt

⅛ teaspoon pepper

1 cup heavy cream, or half and half

1 egg yolk

1½ cups shredded Jarlsberg cheese

- In a large heavy saucepan, melt butter. Add flour and cook several minutes, stirring. Remove from heat.

- Gradually blend in broth and bring to a boil, stirring. Add next 8 ingredients. Cover and simmer 8 minutes until the vegetables are tender.

- Blend cream and egg yolk in a bowl. Blend tablespoons of soup mixture into egg and cream. Return this to the soup and stir until thickened.

- Blend in shredded cheese.

- Yield: 6-8 portions

Hearty Mushroom Barley Soup

1 ounce dried mushrooms

8 cups beef stock

3 or 4 Tablespoons medium barley

1 pound fresh mushrooms, sliced

2 Tablespoons butter or margarine

2 cups half and half or milk

fresh lemon juice to taste (about ½ lemon)

snipped fresh dill weed

- Soak dried mushrooms in 1 cup of hot water for 30 minutes.

- Heat 1 cup beef stock in a large pot. Add soaked mushrooms and their liquid, and simmer gently for 30 minutes.

- Purée mixture in a blender or food processor.

- Return puréed mixture to pot, add remaining beef stock and barley. Simmer 30-45 minutes, or until barley is very tender.

- Sauté sliced mushrooms in butter and add to beef stock mixture.

- Stir in half and half, lemon juice and dill. Bring to a boil, but do not boil.

- Yield: 12 portions

Parsnip and Onion Soup

1 large parsnip, peeled and sliced

1 large onion, peeled and sliced

2 Tablespoons butter

1 clove garlic, minced

1 Tablespoon flour

1 teaspoon curry powder

4 cups hot beef stock

salt and pepper to taste

2 Tablespoons light cream

croutons and fresh parsley for garnish

- Melt butter in a large pan. Add sliced vegetables and garlic. Mix well and cover with a tight lid.

- Simmer gently for 10 minutes, shaking the pan occasionally.

- Sprinkle on the flour and curry powder and mix well.

- Gradually add stock and simmer 20 minutes.

- Strain the soup. In a food processor, purée the vegetables and return them and the broth to a clean saucepan. Add salt and pepper and cream. Heat through, but do not boil.

- Serve with crisply fried croutons.

- Sprinkle with parsley.

- Yield: 4 portions

Russian Beet Borscht

2 quarts chicken stock

2 carrots, peeled and chopped

½ head white cabbage, chopped

2 potatoes, peeled and chopped

1 medium bunch beets, peeled and chopped

1 can tomato paste

salt and pepper to taste

1 teaspoon sugar

sour cream for garnish

- In a large kettle, place chicken stock and chopped vegetables. Boil until tender. Purée, if desired.

- Add tomato paste and seasonings.

- Serve with a dollop of sour cream.

- Yield: 4 portions

Boston's North Shore has always been identified with early and successful foreign trade, most notably with China, India and the East Indies. However, the story of the Baltic Trade is less well known. Trade with Tsarist Russia actually began in 1783. Ships from Manchester, Beverly and Salem were regularly exporting goods from St. Petersburg in 1815.

Zucchini Minestrone

3 Tablespoons olive oil

1½ cups coarsely chopped onions

1½ cups sliced celery

1 cup sliced carrots

½ cup chopped green pepper

5 cups sliced zucchini

1 28-ounce can Italian peeled tomatoes

1 4-ounce can tomato sauce

2 cups beef broth

¼ teaspoon freshly ground black pepper

½ cup elbow macaroni, uncooked

1 20-ounce can red kidney beans

½ teaspoon basil

½ teaspoon oregano

½ teaspoon thyme

1 bay leaf

1 pound cooked Italian sausage sliced into ½" slices, optional

Parmesan cheese as garnish

- Heat oil in a large pot. Add onion, celery, carrots and green pepper. Sauté until tender. Add zucchini, tomatoes, sauce, broth and pepper. Cover and simmer 45 minutes.

- Add macaroni, beans and herbs. (If using sausage, add it at this point.) Cover and simmer 15 minutes. Stir occasionally before serving. Sprinkle with Parmesan cheese.

- Yield: 8-10 portions

Sweet and Sour Tomato Basil Soup

2 cups finely chopped leeks (white part only), rinsed well and drained

4 ounces unsalted butter

10 cups beef or chicken broth

3 pounds tomatoes, peeled, seeded, and chopped (2½ cups), reserving and straining juice

5 Tablespoons red wine vinegar

¼ cup sugar

⅓ cup dry white wine

salt and pepper to taste

¼ cup cornstarch

1 cup firmly packed, chopped fresh basil leaves

- In a kettle, cook leeks in butter over moderate heat, stirring until softened.
- Add broth, tomatoes, vinegar, sugar, wine, salt and pepper. Bring to a boil and simmer partially covered for 25 minutes.
- In a small bowl, whisk together the reserved juice and cornstarch until smooth, then stir into soup.
- Bring soup to a boil and cook for 2 minutes. Stir in basil.
- Yield: 12 portions

Cream of Carrot Soup

2 pounds carrots, peeled and sliced

4 cups chicken stock

1 medium potato, peeled and sliced

1½ teaspoons salt

1 cup chopped onion

1-2 cloves garlic, minced

⅓ cup chopped almonds or cashews

2 Tablespoons butter

your choice of 1 of the following: 1 cup milk or 1 cup plain yogurt or ½ pint heavy cream or ⅔ cup sour cream

dash of nutmeg or cinnamon or mint or marjoram, as taste dictates

- In a large soup pot, place carrots, chicken stock, potato, and salt. Bring to a boil and continue boiling about 15-20 minutes until vegetables are tender.
- Sauté onions, garlic and nuts in butter 2-5 minutes.
- In a food processor purée vegetables as well as the onion and nut mixture.
- Add the dairy product of your choice and blend. Stir in a dash of seasoning.
- Serve warm or cold.
- Yield: 4-6 portions

Lafayette Onion Soup

4 Tablespoons butter or
  margarine

2 Tablespoons peanut oil

2 pounds sweet Bermuda or
  Spanish onions, thinly sliced

½ teaspoon basil

3 Tablespoons flour

½ cup cognac

2 quarts beef stock

salt and pepper to taste

loaf of French bread, cut into 1"
  slices

mozzarella cheese slices

Swiss cheese slices

freshly grated Parmesan cheese

- Melt oil and butter in a large kettle. Stir in onions and basil. Cook uncovered over low heat 30 minutes until light golden brown.

- Sprinkle flour over onions. Stir 2-3 minutes. Simmer stock separately in another pot.

- Combine both pots and simmer 30-40 minutes.

- Place 1 slice mozzarella and 1 slice Swiss cheese on each slice of French bread. Sprinkle with fresh Parmesan cheese and brown under broiler. Place 1 or 2 croutons on top of individual bowls of hot soup.

- Yield: 8 portions

Spicy Pumpkin Soup

¼ cup butter

1 cup chopped onion

1 garlic clove, minced

1 teaspoon curry powder

½ teaspoon salt

⅛-¼ teaspoon ground coriander

⅛ teaspoon crushed red pepper

3 cups chicken broth

1 16-ounce can of pumpkin

1 cup half and half

sour cream and chives, optional

- Melt butter in a large saucepan. Sauté onion and garlic until soft. Add curry, salt, coriander and red pepper. Cook 1 minute.

- Add broth and boil gently, uncovered, for 15-20 minutes. Stir in the pumpkin and half and half. Cook 5 additional minutes.

- Pour into a blender, cover, and blend until creamy.

- Serve warm, garnished with a dollop of sour cream and chopped chives, if desired.

- Yield: 6 cups

Tasty Lentil Soup

1 cup lentils
2 carrots, sliced crosswise
3 onions, chopped
1 15-ounce can tomatoes
1 small can tomato sauce
⅛ cup olive oil
⅛ cup red wine
1 teaspoon oregano
3 cloves garlic, chopped
salt and pepper to taste

- Boil lentils in water for 10 minutes. Strain. In fresh water boil lentils again for 30 minutes.
- Add remaining ingredients and 3 cups water. Simmer for 90 minutes, or until thickened and lentils are tender. More water may be added if needed during cooking.
- Yield: 6-8 portions

Celery and Stilton Soup

1 large head of celery, chopped
2 onions, chopped
1 clove garlic, chopped
1 chicken broth cube
1 large potato, peeled and
    chopped
pepper to taste
1 cup heavy cream
8 ounces Stilton cheese

- Boil first five ingredients in enough water to cover for 30 minutes.
- Purée, season with pepper and add cream. Chop cheese and add to soup. Reheat until cheese is melted, taking care not to boil.
- Garnish with small celery leaves.
- Serve with crusty French bread.
- Yield: 4-6 portions

Chilled Avocado and Grapefruit Soup

2 ripe avocados, peeled and
    sliced, to equal 3 cups
2 Tablespoons fresh coriander,
    minced or 2 teaspoons dried
    coriander
¾ teaspoon salt
2 cups grapefruit juice
1½ cups plain yogurt
1 jar red caviar for garnish

- In a large bowl, mash the avocado with coriander and salt.
- Beat in the grapefruit juice and yogurt, ½ cup at a time, combining the mixture well.
- Chill thoroughly.
- To serve, divide the chilled soup among 6 soup bowls and garnish each with a teaspoon of caviar.
- Yield: 6 portions

Chilled Strawberry and Wine Soup

2 cups strawberries
½ cup sugar
1 cup water
1½ Tablespoons fresh lemon juice
1 cup white wine such as white Zinfandel
1 teaspoon grated lemon peel
½ pint heavy cream, whipped

- Place strawberries, sugar and water in a blender. Cover and purée.
- Add wine, lemon juice and lemon peel.
- Fold in whipped cream.
- Chill and serve in glass bowls or stemmed goblets.
- Garnish with sprigs of mint.
- Yield: 6 portions

Is it possible that the ice made naturally in Wenham Lake was so pure that it was in world-wide demand? Indeed in the 1850s hotels advertised: "We serve Wenham Lake ice" and it was said to be a favorite of Queen Victoria. This special commodity was shipped as far away as India and Australia. Before the English settlers came in the 1630s, the land known as Wenham had been Algonquin Indian territory. The town was officially incorporated in 1643, the first to be set off from Salem.

NOTE: Can also be served as a light summer dessert.

Chilled Curried Apple Soup

1 shallot, peeled and sliced
1 large potato, peeled and sliced
1 clove garlic, minced
1½ cups chicken stock
3 Granny Smith apples, peeled, cored and sliced
½ cup milk
½ cup heavy cream
½ teaspoon curry powder
1 Tablespoon freshly snipped chives
salt to taste

- Place shallot and potato into a large saucepan with garlic and stock. Season with salt and bring to a boil.
- Add apples to pot and simmer 15-20 minutes. Cool mixture and purée in a food processor until completely smooth. Return to the pot.
- Combine milk, cream, curry powder and chives. Gradually add this mixture to the soup. Mix well and adjust seasoning.
- Chill 2 hours before serving.
- Yield: 4 portions

Salads

Seafood Salad Oriental

4 cups cooked long-grain rice

1 ripe avocado, peeled and cut into strips

2 tomatoes, peeled, seeded and cut into ¼" cubes

½ pound snow peas, trimmed and blanched

1 pound medium shrimp, peeled, deveined and cooked

½ pound cooked bay scallops

▶ Dressing:

¼ cup soy sauce

1 teaspoon salt

1 Tablespoon sugar

2 Tablespoons sesame oil

3 Tablespoons Chinese rice vinegar

1 Tablespoon rice wine

½ cup minced scallions

- Place the rice, avocado, tomatoes, snow peas, shrimp, and scallops in a large bowl. Blend ingredients.
- Prepare the dressing by combining the soy sauce, salt, sugar, sesame oil, rice vinegar, and rice wine.
- Add to the rice mixture and toss lightly.
- Sprinkle minced scallions on top.
- Yield: 6 portions

Dutch Herring Salad

2 jars herring tidbits in wine sauce, diced, with liquid reserved

2 cups unpeeled diced red Delicious apples

1 cup chopped onions

1½ cups sliced cooked potato

1½ cups diced cooked, or canned and drained beets

2 Tablespoons capers, rinsed

½ cup mayonnaise

½ cup sour cream

- In a large bowl, combine herring, apples, onions, potatoes, beets, capers, mayonnaise, sour cream and 2 tablespoons liquid from the herring jar.
- Mix well and refrigerate for at least 1 hour.
- Yield: 8 portions

Confetti Pasta Salad

▶ **Pasta:**

1 pound package dried rotini pasta

1 yellow pepper, diced

1 red pepper, diced

1 green pepper, diced

1 cup green peas

½ cup diced red onion

2 cups black olives, chopped

½ pound goat or feta cheese, crumbled

▶ **Mustard Herb Dressing:**

2 cups fresh herbs, such as parsley, basil, chives, etc.

2 Tablespoons Dijon mustard

2-3 cloves garlic, minced

½ cup red wine vinegar

1 cup olive oil

¼ freshly grated Parmesan cheese

- Cook pasta according to package directions until al dente. Drain and rinse in cold water to cool.
- Toss with vegetables.
- In a food processor, combine the dressing ingredients, excluding the olive oil and the Parmesan cheese. When everything is chopped, slowly add the oil through the feed tube until it is emulsified.
- Mix in the Parmesan cheese.
- Pour over the pasta and vegetables and toss.
- Top with crumbled cheese and garnish with fresh herbs.
- Yield: 8 portions

Rice Salad

2 cups converted white rice

¼ cup vegetable oil

⅓ cup white vinegar

½ teaspoon salt

¼ teaspoon pepper

¼ teaspoon dried tarragon

½ green pepper, finely minced

½ cup chopped scallions, including tops

½ cup minced fresh parsley

1 cup cooked green peas

1 pound cooked baby shrimp

½ cup sliced ripe olives

- Cook rice according to directions.
- While rice is still hot, place it in a large bowl with oil, vinegar, salt, pepper and tarragon. Toss lightly.
- Cool to room temperature, then add green pepper, scallions, parsley and peas. Mix well. Cover and refrigerate at least 2 hours.
- When serving, pile rice salad on a platter. Garnish with shrimp and ripe olives.
- Yield: 8 portions

Szechwan Lo Mein

3 Tablespoons red wine vinegar

1 large clove garlic

1 teaspoon ground ginger

¼ cup sesame oil

3 Tablespoons oyster sauce

1 teaspoon Chinese hot oil

3 Tablespoons soy sauce

2 Tablespoons medium-dry sherry

½ cup peanut oil

3 cups broccoli florets

2 cups pea pods

1 cup fresh mushrooms, sliced

1 cup mixed red and green peppers in julienne strips

1 cup sliced water chestnuts

1 pound linguine or Japanese noodles

- Blend first 9 ingredients in a food processor, adding the peanut oil last in a steady stream. Blend until well homogenized. Set aside.

- Cook noodles according to package directions. Drain.

- Combine noodles, vegetables and sauce. Toss well.

- Refrigerate overnight for best flavor. Serve cold on a large platter, garnished with toasted sesame seeds, if desired.

- Yield: 8-10 portions

Red and Black Bean Salad with Lime Vinaigrette

1 cup red kidney beans, soaked overnight

1 cup black beans, soaked overnight

¼ cup lime juice

pinch cayenne

1 teaspoon Dijon mustard

¼ teaspoon ground cumin

salt and pepper to taste

¼ cup olive oil

½ cup finely chopped red onion

1 red pepper, cored, seeded and chopped

1 stalk celery, finely chopped

handful Italian parsley sprigs, finely chopped

- Keep kidney and black beans separate while soaking. Drain each and place in two different saucepans with enough water to cover by 2 inches. Bring each to a boil and lower the heat. Cook the kidney beans 30 minutes or until tender, and the black beans 25 minutes or until tender.

- Drain beans and place in a common bowl.

- Whisk lime juice, cayenne, mustard, cumin, salt and pepper. Add oil, one spoonful at a time, until the dressing emulsifies.

- Pour dressing over beans. Add onions, red pepper, celery and parsley and stir gently.

- Taste and adjust seasonings.

- Allow to stand 30 minutes for flavors to mellow.

- Yield: 8-10 portions

NOTE: Wonderful with grilled chicken or salmon.

Chinese Sesame Noodle Salad

1 pound fresh thin Chinese noodles or linguine

2 Tablespoons dark sesame oil

▶ Peanut Butter Sauce:

¼ cup peanut butter

2 Tablespoons peanut oil

2 Tablespoons dark sesame oil

½ teaspoon coarse or kosher salt

4 teaspoons sugar

2 Tablespoons dark soy sauce

2 Tablespoons red wine vinegar

¼ cup cold water

2 teaspoons hot chili bean paste

▶ Soy Vinegar Sauce:

¼ cup dark soy sauce

¼ cup red wine vinegar

2 Tablespoons dark sesame oil

2 teaspoons sugar

▶ Garnish:

1 Tablespoon vegetable oil

1 teaspoon grated fresh ginger root

2 teaspoons finely chopped garlic

1 red pepper in julienne strips

1½-2 cups snow peas, trimmed and cut in half crosswise

4 scallions, thinly sliced

1 cup fresh bean sprouts

2 cups cucumber slices, cut in half and seeded

- Cook noodles according to package directions al dente. Drain noodles and rinse with cold water. Drain well.
- Place noodles in a large bowl and drizzle with sesame oil, tossing well. Cover bowl loosely with plastic wrap and set aside to cool.

Peanut Butter Sauce:

- Combine the peanut butter sauce ingredients in a bowl and whisk until well combined.
- Pour the sauce over the cool noodles, stirring gently. Cover again with plastic wrap and refrigerate one hour or more. The noodles may be refrigerated overnight.

Soy Vinegar Sauce:

- In a small bowl, mix together the soy vinegar sauce ingredients. Cover with plastic wrap and set aside.

Garnish:

- Heat vegetable oil in a skillet over medium-high heat. Add ginger and garlic and sauté 30 seconds.
- Add red pepper and snow peas and sauté 2 minutes. Remove from pan and cool. This may be done the night before serving and refrigerated, covered.
- Toss noodles with soy vinegar sauce.
- Arrange noodles on a large serving platter. Place the cucumber slices around the noodles. Top the noodles with the garlic, ginger, red pepper and snow pea mixture.
- Sprinkle with scallions and bean sprouts. Sprinkle with remaining soy vinegar sauce.
- Yield: 12 portions

Three Plum Island Salad

6 plums of three different colors
2 medium cucumbers
½ pound goat cheese
1 small clove garlic, minced
¼ cup red wine vinegar
2 dashes hot red pepper sauce
2 Tablespoons honey
½ cup vegetable oil
chopped walnuts for garnish
lettuce and radicchio

- Halve and pit the plums and slice them into very thin wedges.

- Peel the cucumbers, cut them in half, and scoop out the seeds. Slice thinly.

- Crumble the goat cheese.

- Mix plum slices, cucumber slices, and half the goat cheese. Toss lightly and place in the refrigerator.

- In a food processor or blender, combine the garlic, vinegar, pepper sauce, honey, oil and remaining goat cheese.

- Pour dressing over the plum-cucumber mixture until well coated.

- Garnish with chopped walnuts.

- Serve on bed of mixed lettuce and radicchio.

- Yield: 4 portions

California Chicken Salad

1 9-ounce package frozen artichoke hearts
½ cup plain yogurt
¼ cup mayonnaise
1 Tablespoon chopped fresh or 1 teaspoon dried tarragon
½ teaspoon salt
1 large avocado
2½ cups bite-sized chunks of cooked chicken
1 large red onion
1 cup alfalfa sprouts
freshly ground pepper

- Cook artichokes according to package directions. Drain well.

- In a large bowl, combine yogurt, mayonnaise, tarragon and salt.

- Peel the avocado and cut into large chunks. Add the avocado, chicken and artichoke hearts to the yogurt mixture. Toss gently to coat with dressing.

- Cut onion into paper-thin slices and separate onion slices into rings. Mince a few rings of onions. Arrange onion rings around the edge of a large serving platter.

- Place alfalfa sprouts on onion. Spoon chicken salad on top of alfalfa sprouts. Sprinkle chicken with minced onion. Grind black pepper on top.

- Yield: 4-6 portions

Fruited Herb Garden Chicken Salad with Orange Tarragon Dressing

6 boneless, skinless chicken breasts

¼ cup fresh orange juice

2 pounds fresh green beans, trimmed

1 ripe honeydew or cantaloupe melon

1 long or 2 regular sized cucumbers

½ cup freshly chopped mint leaves

3 Tablespoons finely grated orange zest

6 Tablespoons fresh orange juice

2 Tablespoons raspberry vinegar

½ cup olive oil

mixed salad greens, such as endive, red leaf lettuce, chicory, washed and trimmed

sliced red onions

salt and freshly ground black pepper to taste

fresh raspberries for garnish

▶ Orange Tarragon Dressing:

1 egg

2½ Tablespoons fresh orange juice

1 Tablespoon Dijon mustard

½ cup olive oil

½ cup corn oil

grated zest of 2 oranges

2 Tablespoons freshly chopped tarragon or mint leaves, or 2½ teaspoons dried

salt and freshly ground black pepper to taste

- Preheat the oven to 350°.

- Wash, pat dry and halve the chicken breasts lengthwise. Place in a single layer in a shallow baking dish. Drizzle with ¼ cup orange juice and cover pan tightly with foil. Bake 20-25 minutes, or until the chicken is cooked through. Set aside.

- Cook the green beans in boiling water for 4-5 minutes, or until crisp but tender. Drain beans, refresh under cold water and pat dry. Place in a large bowl.

- With a small melon baller, scoop the inside out of the melon and add to the beans.

- Peel the cucumber, halve it lengthwise and remove the seeds. Dice into ¼" pieces. Add the cucumber to the beans and melon. Toss in mint leaves and 2 tablespoons of orange zest. Cover and refrigerate salad until time to serve.

Orange Tarragon Dressing:

- Combine egg, orange juice and mustard in a food processor and process for 15 seconds.

- With the motor running, slowly pour the oils through the feed tube. Process until thick.

- Remove the cover and add orange zest and tarragon. Process for 10 seconds more. Remove to a bowl and season with salt and pepper. Cover and refrigerate at least 4 hours before serving.

- To assemble the salad, toss the assorted greens with half the vinaigrette.

- Slice each chicken breast half into diagonal slices. Arrange the greens on a salad plate and place the chicken slices on top in a fan shape. Spoon the melon mixture around the chicken.

- Place a tablespoon of Orange-Tarragon Dressing on top of each breast. Sprinkle with remaining orange zest and garnish with sprigs of tarragon and fresh raspberries. Serve extra dressing on the side.

- Yield: 12 portions

Mexican Bean Salad

▶ **Dressing:**
1 8-ounce can tomato sauce
¼ cup chili sauce
1 teaspoon hot mustard
2 teaspoons grated onion
2 Tablespoons horseradish
¼ teaspoon cayenne or hot red pepper sauce
½ teaspoon turmeric or chili powder
1 teaspoon dried basil
1 small garlic clove, minced
¼ cup vinegar
¼ teaspoon salt
2 Tablespoons mayonnaise or 1 Tablespoon olive oil

1 pound red kidney beans, soaked and cooked or 1 pound canned red kidney beans
1 cup shredded crisp lettuce, optional
black olives
scallions

- Combine tomato sauce, chili sauce, hot mustard, onion, horseradish, cayenne, turmeric, basil, garlic, vinegar and salt in a saucepan. Bring to a boil, then lower the heat and simmer 10 minutes.
- When cool, blend with mayonnaise or oil.
- Toss together with beans.
- Serve either in a dish alone or on a bed of shredded crisp lettuce.
- Sprinkle with chopped green onions and ripe black olives.
- Yield: 4-6 portions

NOTE: Julienned rare roast beef may also be added to the salad.

Tabouleh

8 ounces couscous
1 pound ripe tomatoes, diced
8 ounces Spanish onion, peeled and finely grated
6 Tablespoons oil
juice of 3 lemons
2 Tablespoons mint, minced
2 Tablespoons parsley, minced
salt and freshly ground black pepper to taste

- Place couscous in a salad bowl.
- Add diced tomatoes and their juices, onion, mint, parsley, salt and pepper.
- Add oil and lemon juice.
- Mix well and chill 3-4 hours.
- Yield: 6-8 portions

NOTE: Additions may include chick peas, chopped pickling cucumbers and/or chopped scallions. Wonderful as a side dish to barbequed meat or as a first course with French bread.

Moroccan Carrot Salad

2 pounds carrots, whole,
   scraped
1 large clove garlic, peeled
¼ teaspoon ground cinnamon
1 teaspoon ground cumin
1 teaspoon sweet paprika
¼ teaspoon cayenne
¼ cup lemon juice
¼ teaspoon sugar
½ teaspoon salt, or to taste
olive oil
1 Tablespoon freshly chopped
   parsley

- Cook carrots with garlic in a large pot until just tender. Drain water and discard garlic.
- Cut carrots into ½" pieces and set aside.
- Combine spices with lemon juice, sugar and salt in a mixing bowl. Blend well and pour over warm carrots. Toss to coat evenly.
- Cool to room temperature and chill until ready to serve.
- Just before serving, sprinkle with olive oil and toss to coat evenly. Adjust seasonings and sprinkle with parsley.
- Yield: 8-12 portions

Fiddlehead Ferns Vinaigrette

1 pound fiddlehead ferns

▶ Vinaigrette:
1 Tablespoon Dijon mustard
¼ cup red wine vinegar
¼ teaspoon sugar
1 teaspoon minced parsley
salt and freshly ground pepper
   to taste
½ cup olive oil

- Wash fiddleheads in several bowls of cold water. Cut off ends and remove any brown husks.
- Put in a large pot of salted, boiling water. Cook 2-3 minutes. Plunge into ice cold water to stop cooking and brighten color.
- Arrange ferns on a circular platter starting at the outer edge placing heads on the outside and overlapping. Make concentric circles of ferns.
- Whisk mustard, vinegar, sugar, parsley, salt and pepper together in a bowl.
- Drizzle in olive oil slowly while whisking. Whisk until thick and serve immediately.
- Yield: 4-6 portions

NOTE: Enjoy fiddleheads quickly as the season is short! About ⅓ cup of dressing is enough for 1 pound of fiddleheads.

Broccoli Salad

1 cup mayonnaise

2 Tablespoons vinegar

½ cup raisins

2 large bunches broccoli

12 slices bacon, fried to crisp and crumbled, or less to suit personal taste

1 medium onion, peeled and chopped

1 cup sunflower seeds

- Mix together mayonnaise and vinegar. Add raisins and set aside for 2 hours or more.
- Peel broccoli and blanch for 2-3 minutes in boiling water. Drain and rinse with cold water to stop cooking process. Chop into bite-sized pieces.
- Combine all ingredients and serve.
- Yield: 12 portions

NOTE: This can be made ahead; it keeps well.

Sesame Snow Pea Salad

▶ Dressing:

2 Tablespoons white wine vinegar

2 Tablespoons sugar

1½ teaspoons soy sauce

1 teaspoon freshly grated ginger

⅓ cup vegetable oil

1 Tablespoon sesame seeds

¾ pound snow peas, trimmed

1 cup mushrooms, sliced

4 ounces sliced water chestnuts

2 cups cherry tomatoes, halved

- Combine vinegar, sugar, soy sauce and ginger in a food processor. Add vegetable oil slowly through the feed tube.
- Toast sesame seeds in a skillet until lightly browned.
- Blanch snow peas in boiling water for 2 minutes. Drain and rinse under cold water.
- In a serving bowl, combine snow peas, tomatoes, mushrooms and water chestnuts. Sprinkle with toasted sesame seeds and toss with dressing.
- Yield: 4 portions

Potato Salad Française

3 pounds red potatoes

4 eggs, hard-boiled and chopped

4 celery stalks, chopped

¼ cup sliced ripe olives

2 5-ounce packages cream cheese with garlic and herbs

¾ cup olive oil

¼ cup lemon juice

salt and pepper to taste

1 cup freshly chopped parsley

- Cover potatoes with water. Heat to boiling and simmer until tender, about 25 minutes. Drain and slightly cool.
- Cut potatoes into bite-sized pieces and mix with eggs, celery and olives.
- Purée herbed cream cheese in a food processor. Add lemon juice, oil and salt and pepper.
- Mix dressing with potatoes and toss with parsley. Refrigerate until serving.
- Yield: 8 portions

Warm Goat Cheese Salad with Roasted Garlic Vinaigrette

▶ **Herb Coated Goat Cheese:**
  2 Tablespoons minced fresh chives
  2 Tablespoons minced fresh parsley
  ¾ teaspoon minced fresh oregano
  ½ teaspoon minced fresh thyme
  freshly ground black pepper to taste
  ½ pound milk goat cheese log

▶ **Roasted Garlic Vinaigrette:**
  5 large garlic cloves, skin on
  1 Tablespoon olive oil
  2 egg yolks
  ¼ cup wine vinegar
  2 Tablespoons minced shallots
  1 Tablespoon Dijon mustard
  ¾ cup safflower oil
  salt and pepper to taste
  assorted salad greens

- Mix together the herbs and pepper.

- Slice cheese into 6 portions. Coat the sides of each cheese portion with the herb mixture. Place on a baking sheet, cover with plastic wrap and refrigerate until needed.

- Preheat oven to 375°.

- Place garlic in an oven proof pan. Roll cloves in olive oil. Cover with foil. Roast for 15 minutes, or until soft. When cool, squeeze out garlic and discard skins.

- Mash garlic, add egg yolks, vinegar, shallots and mustard. Slowly whisk in safflower oil. Season to taste. Chill until needed.

- To serve, toss assorted salad greens with garlic vinaigrette. Place greens on 6 salad plates. Bake cheese rounds at 375° for 6-8 minutes to warm. Set cheese on top of dressed greens.

- Yield: 6 portions

This celebrity recipe was submitted by Chef Caprial Pence Seattle Sheraton Seattle, WA

Gruyère Salad

▶ **Dressing:**
  ¼ cup white wine vinegar
  2 Tablespoons Dijon mustard
  ¼ teaspoon salt
  freshly ground pepper
  ⅔ cup olive oil

▶ **Salad:**
  2 cups shredded Gruyère cheese
  1 cup celery, diced
  1 cup green pepper, diced
  1 cup ripe olives, sliced
  1 cup sliced fresh mushrooms
  ½ cup scallions, sliced
  4 cups fresh spinach, washed and torn

Dressing:

- Combine vinegar, mustard, salt, pepper and olive oil. Refrigerate.

Salad:

- Combine cheese, celery, pepper, olives, mushrooms, and scallions in a large bowl. Pour dressing over salad. Refrigerate 2 hours.

- Toss with spinach just before serving.

- Yield: 8-10 portions

NOTE: The dressing may be sufficient for two salads depending on personal taste.

Dilly Beans

2 pounds fresh whole green
   beans, blanched

1 cup water

¾ cup white vinegar

½ cup sugar

2 cloves garlic, sliced

2 teaspoons fresh tarragon,
   chopped

1 bay leaf

1 teaspoon salt

1 Tablespoon mustard seed

2 Tablespoons fresh dill,
   chopped

- Combine water, vinegar and sugar in a saucepan.
- Add garlic, tarragon, bay leaf, salt and mustard seed.
- Bring to a boil, stirring constantly. Remove from the heat. Add dill.
- Place beans in 13x9" dish. Pour liquid over beans, turning to coat them well.
- Cover and refrigerate 24 hours. Serve cold or at room temperature.
- Yield: 8 portions

Roasted Red Pepper Dressing

1 small-medium garlic clove,
   minced

1 11½-ounce jar sweet roasted
   red peppers, drained

1 Tablespoon red wine vinegar

1 Tablespoon balsamic vinegar

¼ cup extra virgin olive oil

salt and freshly ground pepper
   to taste

½-1 teaspoon sugar or to taste

1 teaspoon freshly chopped
   parsley, optional

1 teaspoon freshly chopped
   basil, optional

- Mince garlic in food processor. Add red pepper and chop.
- Add vinegars, then add oil in a slow stream through the feed tube.
- Put into a bowl and add salt, pepper and sugar to taste.
- Add parsley and basil, if desired.
- Serve over mixed salad greens.
- Yield: 4-6 portions

Dutch Salad Dressing

2 Tablespoons mayonnaise

1 Tablespoon oil

1 Tablespoon balsamic vinegar

2 cloves garlic, minced

2 teaspoons Worcestershire
   sauce

2 teaspoons sugar

salt and freshly ground pepper
   to taste

- Blend together all ingredients, whisking thoroughly.
- Serve over crisp greens or mixed salad.
- Yield: 4-6 portions

Brunch

Apple Sour Cream Pancakes with Apricot Butter

1 tart apple, peeled, cored and coarsely grated

1½ Tablespoons sugar

½ teaspoon ground cinnamon

⅛ teaspoon ground cloves

½ teaspoon grated lemon zest

½ cup flour

¼ teaspoon salt

1 teaspoon baking soda

1 cup sour cream

2 large eggs

2 Tablespoons unsalted butter, melted

vegetable oil

▶ Apricot Butter:

8 Tablespoons butter, cut into small pieces

½ cup apricot jam or preserves

½ teaspoon grated lemon zest

- Combine grated apple, sugar, cinnamon, cloves, and lemon zest in a small bowl and mix well. Set aside.

- Sift the flour, salt and baking soda together into a mixing bowl.

- In another bowl whisk together the sour cream and eggs. Fold into the flour mixture and mix lightly to form a batter. Stir the melted butter into the batter.

- Add the apple mixture and juices and stir lightly. Cover and refrigerate 15 minutes.

- Lightly oil a large heavy skillet and place over medium-high heat. When the pan is hot, spoon 2 tablespoons batter onto the hot surface.

- Cook the pancakes until bubbles form, about 3 minutes. Turn carefully and brown on the bottom, 1-2 minutes more.

- Keep warm in a preheated 250° oven, covered with foil. Serve with warm Apricot Butter.

Apricot Butter:

- Melt the butter.

- Stir in the jam and lemon zest and stir until heated through. Remove from heat.

- Yield: 4 portions

NOTE: The Apricot Butter can be made a day in advance; keep covered and refrigerated and reheat when needed.

Brunch Eggs with Chèvre and Artichoke Hearts

2 Tablespoons olive oil

1 cup scallions, finely chopped, including 1" of green stems

½ cup red bell pepper, finely chopped

2 teaspoons garlic, finely chopped

12 ounces or 2 jars marinated artichoke hearts, drained, patted dry, and coarsely chopped

8 ounces good-quality chèvre, goat cheese, at room temperature

5 large whole eggs

3 large egg yolks

1 cup heavy or whipping cream

1 cup milk

¼ cup plus 2 Tablespoons grated Parmesan cheese

salt and white pepper to taste

- Preheat oven to 400°.
- Generously grease a 12x8" baking dish with butter.
- Heat the oil in a heavy skillet. Add the scallions and sauté 2 minutes. Add the red peppers and sauté 3-4 minutes. Then add the garlic and cook a minute more. Remove from heat and stir in the chopped artichoke hearts.
- With an electric mixer, cream the chèvre until smooth. Beat in the eggs and yolks one at a time. Add the cream and milk and mix just until blended. Add ¼ cup Parmesan cheese. Add the reserved vegetable mixture and stir well. Add salt and white pepper to taste.
- Pour into the prepared baking dish, and sprinkle with the remaining Parmesan cheese. Bake until the top is browned and a knife inserted in the center comes out clean. Check after 25 minutes; it browns quickly.
- Serve hot or at room temperature.
- Yield: 6 portions

NOTE: Perfect for a buffet. Can be doubled or tripled easily.

Festive Baked Eggs

8 Tablespoons unsalted butter, divided

5 cups leeks, julienned

8 ounces mushrooms, sliced

½ pound prosciutto thinly sliced and cut in ¼" strips

5 cups whipping cream

12 eggs

1 teaspoon freshly grated nutmeg

½-1 teaspoon salt

freshly ground pepper

½ pound grated Gruyère cheese

fresh parsley, chopped

- Preheat oven to 375°.
- Butter 2 3-quart shallow baking dishes, using 2 tablespoons butter.
- Melt 6 tablespoons butter over medium heat. Sauté leeks until soft.
- Add mushrooms, sautéing for 5 minutes.
- Add strips of prosciutto and sauté 2-3 minutes.
- Spread ½ of mixture in each dish.
- Whisk eggs, cream, nutmeg, salt and pepper together.
- Stir in 2 cups of cheese. Pour over vegetable mixture. Stir vegetables with cream.
- Sprinkle remaining cheese over mixture.
- Bake for 30 minutes until golden. Cool 10 minutes.
- Sprinkle with parsley.
- Yield: 16 portions

Eggs Ranchero

2 Tablespoons oil

2 onions, peeled and diced

2 cloves garlic, diced

1 large green pepper, diced

1 4-ounce can green chili
    peppers, diced

2 15-ounce cans stewed
    tomatoes

1 6-ounce can tomato paste

salt to taste

pepper to taste

parsley to taste

12-14 slices firm white bread,
    crusts removed

2 cups shredded cheddar
    cheese

½ pound bacon cooked, drained
    and crumbled

7 eggs

3½ cups whole milk

2 teaspoons dry mustard

1 teaspoon each salt and pepper

- Simmer the first 7 ingredients plus salt, pepper and parsley to taste, on low heat for an hour.
- Butter a 13x9" baking pan.
- Butter the bread and line the bottom of the baking dish with the bread, buttered side up.
- Spread a thin layer of ranchero sauce on the bread.
- Spread a layer of cheese next, then a layer of bacon.
- Repeat layers: bread, sauce, cheese and bacon.
- Beat eggs and milk together. Add mustard, salt and pepper and whisk gently.
- Pour over the casserole.
- Cover and refrigerate overnight. Bake uncovered at 350°, 1½ hours or until brown and set.
- Yield: 12 portions

Soufflé with Herbs and Mushrooms

▶ Garnish:

3 Tablespoons unsalted butter

¾ pound mushrooms, cleaned

1 Tablespoon chopped parsley

salt and pepper to taste

▶ Omelette:

6 egg yolks

1 clove garlic, cut in half

1 Tablespoon minced chives

3 Tablespoons heavy cream

8 egg whites

3 Tablespoons unsalted butter

salt and pepper to taste

- Heat butter in a skillet, adding thinly sliced mushrooms. Sauté until they are dry. Add salt and pepper and chopped parsley. Set aside.
- Preheat oven to 425°. Rub mixing bowl with garlic half and discard.
- Beat egg yolks until pale and thick. Add chives, salt, pepper and heavy cream.
- In another bowl, beat egg whites until stiff but not dry. Fold whites into yolk mixture. Pour into a generously buttered gratin dish. Bake in preheated oven for 10 minutes or until puffed and golden.
- Remove and serve by spoonfuls with sautéed mushrooms as garnish.
- Yield: 6 portions

Harlequin Omelette

1 pound fresh spinach, washed
   and drained

12 ounces very ripe tomatoes

pinch thyme

3 cloves garlic, peeled

8 Tablespoons olive oil

9 eggs

8 Tablespoons whipping cream

3 ounces shredded Gruyère
   cheese

dash nutmeg

salt and pepper to taste

- Preheat oven to 250°.

- Plunge the tomatoes into boiling water for 10 seconds, refresh under running water and peel. Expel the seeds and juice by cutting tomatoes in half and squeezing.

- Heat 2 tablespoons olive oil until a blue haze rises, then add tomato, thyme and a pinch of salt. Cook until virtually all the moisture has gone.

- Repeat the process for the spinach using 3 tablespoons of oil and add the whole cloves of garlic. Remove when all the moisture has gone. Cool the tomatoes and spinach mixture on two separate plates.

- Get out three bowls and break 3 eggs into each. In one bowl whisk together the eggs and spinach, 3 tablespoons of whipping cream, nutmeg, salt and pepper.

- Similarly, whisk the eggs, tomatoes, 2 tablespoons of whipping cream, and salt and pepper in the second bowl.

- Finally, in the third bowl, whisk together the eggs, Gruyère, 3 tablespoons of cream, salt and pepper.

- Oil the inside of a soufflé dish lavishly. Pour in the tomato mixture and stand the dish in a pan half-filled with heated water and cook in the oven 15 minutes. Very gently pour in the cheese mixture and return to oven for 15-20 minutes. Remove from the oven and very gently pour in the spinach mixture and return to the oven for 20 minutes. By then the omelette should be quite firm and cooked through. Let it stand for 20 minutes before turning it out of the dish. Serve hot or cold with a drizzle of olive oil.

- Yield: 4-6 portions

NOTE: If the tomatoes are not very ripe and red in color, add a teaspoon or two of tomato purée to the mixture before cooking.

Mustard Brie Soufflé

6 Tablespoons butter, softened

1 loaf French bread
    cut into 21 ¼" slices

4½ teaspoons Dijon mustard

1½ cups milk

¾ teaspoon salt

pinch of cayenne pepper

4 extra large or 5 large eggs

½ pound baked ham, cubed

¾ pound Brie, rind removed, and
    coarsely chopped

- Using 2 tablespoons of butter, grease a 2-quart soufflé dish.

- Butter the bread with the remaining butter and spread with Dijon mustard on one side.

- Whisk together milk, salt, cayenne and eggs. Arrange half of the sliced bread in the bottom of the soufflé dish, mustard side up.

- Sprinkle with half the ham and half the Brie.

- Repeat using remaining bread, ham and Brie.

- Pour eggs and milk mixture over. Cover and refrigerate overnight.

- Bake in preheated 350° oven, 25-30 minutes, or until golden and bubbling.

- Yield: 4 portions

Vegetable Strata

1½ cups finely chopped onions

1 cup finely chopped scallions

¾ pound mushrooms, thinly
    sliced

3 Tablespoons olive oil

2 red peppers, thinly sliced

2 green peppers, thinly sliced

9 cups Italian bread cubes, in 1"
    pieces

2½ cups shredded cheddar
    cheese

1 cup freshly grated Parmesan
    cheese

12 eggs

3½ cups milk

3 Tablespoons Dijon mustard

hot pepper sauce to taste

salt and pepper to taste

- In a skillet, sauté onions, scallions and mushrooms in olive oil until soft.

- Add peppers and cook until moisture has evaporated, about 10-15 minutes.

- Divide half the bread cubes between 2 buttered 13x9" baking dishes.

- Arrange half of the vegetables over the bread cubes. Sprinkle with half the cheddar and half the Parmesan cheeses.

- Divide the rest of the bread cubes between the baking dishes. Top with vegetables and cheeses.

- Whisk together the eggs, milk, mustard, hot pepper sauce, salt and pepper.

- Pour over the strata. Cover and chill overnight.

- Bake in a preheated 350° oven for 50-60 minutes.

- Yield: 8-10 portions

Brie and Bacon Brunch

▶ **Toast Shell:**

8 slices good quality white sandwich bread, crusts removed

5 Tablespoons unsalted butter, melted, plus more, if needed

▶ **Filling:**

8 ounces Brie cheese, rind left on

5 slices bacon

1 cup finely chopped leeks, white only

8 large eggs

salt and pepper to taste

2 Tablespoons unsalted butter

¼ cup heavy or whipping cream

2 Tablespoons freshly chopped chives or parsley, as garnish

- Preheat oven to 350°.

- Roll bread until flat and line bottom and halfway up sides of 8 or 9" springform pan. Brush with melted butter. Line with foil. Fill with pie weights and bake 12-15 minutes. Bread should be dry. Remove the foil and bake 5 more minutes. Remove from oven and set aside.

- Cut Brie into ½" pieces.

- Sauté bacon until crisp in a large skillet. Remove bacon, drain and crumble, reserving fat.

- Sauté leeks in 1 tablespoon reserved fat until soft, about 5 minutes.

- Mix Brie, bacon and leeks and spread into toast shell. Cover pan with foil and bake 10 minutes. Remove from oven and set aside.

- Mix eggs, and salt and pepper. Scramble eggs in 2 tablespoons butter until soft. Stir in cream.

- Remove sides of springform pan.

- Add eggs to the toast shell and sprinkle with chopped chives or parsley. Cut into wedges and serve.

- Yield: 6 portions

Tomato and Pesto Quiche

15 cherry tomatoes

1½ cups ricotta cheese

⅓ cup sour cream

⅓ cup cream cheese, softened

½ cup grated Parmesan cheese

⅓ cup fresh basil, minced

1 egg

2 egg yolks

½ teaspoon salt

¼ teaspoon white pepper

9" pastry shell, pre-baked

⅓ cup pesto

- Cut tomatoes in half horizontally. With a melon ball tool, scoop out insides. Place tomatoes, cut side down, on paper towels to drain.

- Mix cheeses in a medium bowl until smooth. Beat in basil, eggs, egg yolks and spices.

- Pour cheese mixture into prebaked pastry shell. Arrange cherry tomatoes cut side up on top of cheese mixture. Bake quiche in a preheated 325° oven 45 minutes.

- Remove quiche from oven. Cool to room temperature, about 30 minutes. Fill center of each tomato shell with pesto. Serve at room temperature.

- Yield: 6-8 portions

NOTE: Recipe can be doubled by lining a 13x9" baking dish with pie crust.

Torta Rustica

▶ **Pastry:**
  1 package active dry yeast
  1 cup unsalted butter, melted
  6 eggs, beaten
  4 cups flour
  ½ teaspoon salt

▶ **Filling:**
  4 eggs
  1 teaspoon dried basil
  1 teaspoon fresh thyme
  2 pounds fresh spinach or
    2 10-ounce packages frozen,
    chopped spinach, thawed
  ½ cup whole milk ricotta
    cheese
  1 pound mozzarella cheese,
    thinly sliced
  1 pound mushrooms, washed,
    sliced and lightly sautéed in
    2 Tablespoons garlic oil
  1 red pepper, roasted and thinly
    sliced
  1 yellow pepper, roasted and
    thinly sliced
  1 zucchini, sliced in julienne
    strips
  1 yellow onion, sliced thinly and
    lightly sautéed
  ½ bunch scallions, chopped
    finely

▶ **Glaze:**
  1 egg
  2 Tablespoons heavy cream

- Dissolve yeast in ¼ cup lukewarm water.

- Beat butter and eggs together. Stir in yeast mixture. salt, and half the flour. Blend well. Let mixture stand for 10 minutes.

- Stir in remaining flour and blend well. Cover and allow to stand in a warm place for 1 hour. Punch down dough and cover and refrigerate overnight or for at least 6 hours.

- Preheat oven to 350°. Beat eggs and herbs well. Pour ½ the eggs into buttered and heated 7" crêpe pan or skillet and cook until eggs are set and slightly undercooked. Cook remaining eggs in the same manner and set all aside.

- On a lightly floured surface, roll out ¾ of the dough to a ½" thick round about 12" diameter. Press dough into 9" springform pan, with about 2" deep sides.

- Layer a third of the mozzarella on bottom of pastry shell. Top with 1 of the omelettes, half the spinach, ricotta, mushrooms, peppers, zucchini, onion and scallion. Repeat this layering one more time. Finish with a final layer of mozzarella.

- Roll out remaining dough (save some for decoration on top of rustica if you like) to ½" thick round, slightly larger than 9" in diameter.

- Lay dough over top of the torta, tucking edges inside to overlap slightly the sides of pastry shell. Cut 2 small vents in top of dough to allow steam to escape.

- Beat egg and cream together and brush generously over the top of the dough and any decoration added to top.

- Bake in center of oven for 50-60 minutes or until it is a rich golden brown. Let cool 15 minutes before removing from pan.

- Serve hot, warm or at room temperature.

- Yield: 8 portions

Three Tomato Tart

1 10" pie crust pre-baked in a tart pan for 10 minutes

3 Tablespoons grated Parmesan cheese

2 egg whites

1 cup low fat ricotta cheese

2 cloves garlic, minced

1 Tablespoon freshly snipped lemon thyme or thyme, or 1 teaspoon dried thyme, crushed

2 large tomatoes, sliced

5 yellow or red cherry tomatoes, sliced

2 red cherry tomatoes, sliced

1 Tablespoon olive oil or cooking oil

2 teaspoons fresh lemon thyme or thyme, or ½ teaspoon dried thyme, crushed

- Preheat oven to 325°.

- Sprinkle pie crust with Parmesan cheese.

- In a mixing bowl, beat egg whites slightly. Stir in ricotta cheese, garlic and 1 tablespoon fresh thyme. Spread over pastry.

- Overlap large tomato slices in a circle around the edge. Arrange yellow cherry tomatoes (or red) within tomato ring. Fill center with red cherry tomatoes.

- Stir together olive or cooking oil and 2 teaspoons fresh thyme. Brush tomatoes with oil mixture.

- Bake tart 25-30 minutes, or until heated through and nearly set.

- Serve warm or at room temperature.

- Yield: 10-12 portions

NOTE: Can also be sliced thinly and served as an appetizer.

Asparagus in Provençal Mayonnaise

1½-2½ pounds fresh asparagus, peeled, steamed and cooled

▸ Mayonnaise:

2 cups tightly packed spinach leaves, cooked, squeezed and chopped

3 Tablespoons scallions, minced

3-4 Tablespoons parsley, minced

2 large cloves garlic, minced

3-4 anchovy fillets, minced

½ cup sour cream

1 cup mayonnaise

juice of a large lemon

salt and freshly ground pepper to taste

▸ Garnish:

16 cooked shrimp, marinated in a garlic vinaigrette

2 Tablespoons chives, minced

2 hard-boiled eggs, sieved

- Combine the spinach, scallions, parsley, garlic and anchovies with half the sour cream in a food processor. Mix until smooth.

- Add the mayonnaise, the rest of the sour cream and the lemon juice. Process until smooth. Season with salt and pepper to taste. Refrigerate 4-6 hours or overnight.

- To serve, place asparagus on a rectangular platter in an even layer. Spoon the sauce over stems and garnish sauce with shrimp, chives and sieved egg yolks. Serve slightly chilled.

- Yield: 6-8 portions

NOTE: Use bottled vinaigrette to marinate the shrimp.

Mushroom Strudel

2 pounds Champignon mushrooms

1 pound Shitake mushrooms

1 pound Trumpet mushrooms

3 Tablespoons olive oil

1 Tablespoon minced garlic

1 teaspoon dried thyme

½ cup white wine

1 quart whipping cream

salt and pepper to taste

¼ cup freshly chopped parsley

3 egg yolks, beaten

3 sheets puff pastry

- Wash, dry and slice all the mushrooms.
- Heat olive oil in a large saucepan.
- Sauté garlic and mushrooms. Sprinkle with thyme. Add wine and reduce liquid.
- Add cream and reduce until mixture reaches a stew-like consistency.
- Season with salt and pepper and add parsley.
- Lower heat and add egg yolks. Remove from heat.
- Cool mixture in the refrigerator until it resembles pudding, 2-3 hours.
- Preheat oven to 350°.
- Lay puff pastry on a work table and spread mushroom mixture over the pastry. Roll up. Pinch ends and brush with egg wash.
- Bake for 18-30 minutes or until golden brown.
- May be served with a simple brown sauce or Madeira sauce.
- Yield: 12 portions

This celebrity recipe was submitted by Sutton Place Cafe Alexandria, VA

Berenice's Torte Verde

12-ounce package bulk sausage

⅔ cup cottage cheese

6 eggs (reserve 1 yolk for glazing crust)

1 pound shredded mozzarella cheese

2 10-ounce packages frozen chopped spinach, chopped and squeezed dry

¼ teaspoon freshly ground pepper

2 cloves garlic, minced

pinch thyme

pinch oregano

¼ cup Parmesan cheese

1 sheet frozen puff pastry, defrosted

- Fry and break up sausage meat. Drain fat and add eggs, cheeses, spinach, and seasonings. Refrigerate.
- Roll out puff pastry to 13x13". Drape over a 9" springform pan. Arrange the crust in the pan and fill with the spinach mixture. Gather up the sides of the pastry and draw together. Twist the top.
- Make several small slashes for ventilation. Mix reserved egg yolk with 1 tablespoon water and brush on crust.
- Bake at 375° for 1 hour. Cool 15 minutes. Wonderful hot or cold.
- Yield: 10-12 portions

Poultry

Cantonese Chicken

1 Tablespoon cornstarch

1 Tablespoon sherry

1 egg white

1 Tablespoon sesame oil

2 teaspoons sugar

1½ pounds boneless chicken, cut into 1" cubes

2 Tablespoons soy sauce

⅓ cup water

1 teaspoon cornstarch

1 Tablespoon oil

½-1 teaspoon red pepper flakes

2 cloves garlic, minced

2 Tablespoons fresh ginger, chopped

1 cup onions, peeled and chopped

½ cup salted peanuts

½ pound snow peas, trimmed

½ red pepper, in julienne strips

- Combine cornstarch, sherry, egg white, sesame oil and sugar. Add chicken to coat.
- Combine soy sauce, water and cornstarch. Set aside.
- Heat wok. Add oil. Stir-fry red pepper flakes, garlic, ginger and onions quickly. Add chicken and stir-fry 1 minute.
- Whisk soy mixture and add to wok. Stir-fry 2 minutes.
- Add vegetables and peanuts and cook until chicken is done and vegetables are heated through. Serve with rice.
- Yield: 4 portions

Javanese Chicken

4 boneless chicken breasts, skin on

2 small Granny Smith apples, peeled, cored and halved

4 slices fresh pineapple

4 ounces water

1 onion, peeled and finely chopped

2 cinnamon sticks

▶ Marinade:

1 cup soy sauce

1 cup vinegar

1 Tablespoon garlic, minced

1 Tablespoon ginger powder

¼ cup firmly packed brown sugar

¼ teaspoon ground cloves

dash sesame oil

- Preheat oven to 425°.
- Wrap each chicken breast tightly around an apple half and a pineapple slice. Place in a 4-quart casserole. Put cinnamon sticks along the sides. Add water and spread onion evenly over breasts.
- Roast approximately 20 minutes, or until the skin turns golden yellow.
- Combine marinade ingredients and set aside.
- Remove from oven, drain half the juices and add the marinade.
- Refrigerate overnight.
- To finish, place in a preheated 375° oven for 20-30 minutes.
- Serve with white rice.
- Yield: 4 portions

This celebrity recipe was submitted by Chef J. David Nadeau The Andover Inn Andover, MA

Chicken with Garlic, Goat Cheese and Sun-Dried Tomato Butter

2 boneless, whole chicken breasts, skin on

1 teaspoon garlic in oil

1 teaspoon oregano

1 teaspoon rosemary

½ teaspoon crushed red pepper

¼ teaspoon thyme

pinch salt and pepper

2 sticks unsalted butter

2 Tablespoons roasted pine nuts

2 Tablespoons sun-dried tomatoes, chopped

3 ounces Montrachet cheese

½ teaspoon salt and pepper

1 Tablespoon freshly chopped parsley

1 ounce white wine or dry vermouth

½ teaspoon Worcestershire sauce

- Combine the oregano, rosemary, red pepper, thyme, salt and pepper.
- Rub the chicken breasts with the garlic oil and sprinkle with the herb mixture.
- Grill chicken breasts, skin side down. After the skin is browned, turn and continue cooking until done.
- Combine remaining ingredients.
- Remove chicken to a warm serving platter and top with butter mixture.
- Yield: 2 portions

Chicken Persillade

4 boneless, skinless chicken breast halves

5 ounces herb cream cheese, softened

1 Tablespoon flour

¼ cup shredded carrots

¼ cup coarsely chopped walnuts

¼ cup chopped parsley

⅓ cup fine dry breadcrumbs (seasoned breadcrumbs can also be used)

2 Tablespoons grated Parmesan cheese

2 Tablespoons margarine or butter, melted

- Place each chicken breast half bone side up between 2 pieces of clear plastic wrap or wax paper. Using the flat side of a meat mallet, pound lightly, working from center to edges to form a 5½" square. Remove plastic wrap.
- In a small mixing bowl, beat together garlic and herb cheese and flour until smooth. Stir in carrots, walnuts and half the parsley. Place ¼ of the cheese mixture on each chicken breast half; fold in 2 sides and roll up jelly-roll style. Press edges to seal.
- In a small bowl, combine remaining parsley, breadcrumbs and Parmesan cheese. Brush chicken rolls with melted butter and roll in coating mixture. Place rolls, seam side down, on a wire rack in an 8x8" baking pan. Sprinkle with any remaining coating mixture.
- Bake in 350° oven for 40-45 minutes or until tender and golden.
- Yield: 4 portions

Brandied-Peach Chicken

6 whole boneless, skinless chicken breasts

1¼ teaspoons salt

5 peaches

½ cup finely chopped onion

½ cup cashews, chopped

½ teaspoon ground ginger

4 Tablespoons butter

¼-½ cup brown sugar

2 teaspoons prepared mustard

1 cup sour cream

1 Tablespoon brandy

- Preheat oven to 350°.
- Sprinkle chicken breasts with salt and set aside.
- Cut 3 peaches into small pieces and combine with onion, cashews and ginger.
- Divide this filling among the 6 breasts. Roll and secure each breast with a toothpick.
- Melt butter in a foil-lined baking dish. Place chicken on top and bake for 25 minutes. Turn chicken and continue baking for 20 minutes.
- While chicken bakes, slice the remaining peaches and combine with brown sugar, mustard, salt, sour cream and brandy. Heat for 5 minutes and serve over chicken breasts.
- Yield: 6 portions

NOTE: Elegant with wild rice and snow pea salad.

Spiced Chicken Curry

2½ pounds boneless, skinless chicken breasts

2" fresh ginger root

2 cloves garlic

½ teaspoon salt

½ teaspoon saffron

1 Tablespoon cream

15 ounces plain yogurt

4 ounces almonds

2 ounces hazelnuts

3 large onions

2 teaspoons chili powder

fresh coriander/cilantro leaves

1 Tablespoon oil

- Cut chicken into ½" strips.
- Mince ginger and garlic very finely, mix with salt and rub onto chicken pieces.
- Crush saffron in a mortar and mix with cream and yogurt. Add to chicken and mix well.
- Toast almonds and hazelnuts until golden and chop finely.
- Chop onions and fry until golden brown in the oil.
- Add chicken mixture. Cook gently until chicken is cooked through, about 10-15 minutes, until some of the liquid has evaporated.
- Add nuts and chili powder and simmer gently until chicken is tender and sauce is thick.
- Put on warmed serving dish and decorate with cilantro leaves.
- Serve with boiled rice, such as spiced basmati.
- Yield: 4-6 portions

Grilled Chicken Breasts Indonesia

2 whole chicken breasts

▶ Indonesian Sauce:
⅓ cup water
¼ cup creamy peanut butter
1 Tablespoon medium-dry sherry
4 teaspoons soy sauce
4 teaspoons fresh lemon juice
2 teaspoons firmly packed
   brown sugar
1½ teaspoons minced garlic
¼ teaspoon hot pepper sauce

▶ Pasta bed:
thin spaghetti or linguine
1 Tablespoon sesame seed oil
4 scallions, slivered lengthwise

- Bone chicken breasts, leaving the skin on, and halve each.
- Make sauce by combining the water, peanut butter, sherry, soy sauce, lemon juice, brown sugar, garlic and hot pepper sauce in a small heavy pan or double boiler. Bring to a boil over moderate heat, stirring until smooth. Keep warm.
- Prepare pasta. Drizzle with sesame oil.
- Broil chicken, skin side down, on a lightly oiled grill, for 8 minutes. Turn each piece over and grill for 7 minutes.
- Arrange chicken on the bed of pasta. Serve with sauce. Garnish with scallions.
- Yield: 4 portions

Tandoori Chicken Barbeque

3 pounds chicken legs
½ teaspoons salt
1 medium onion
1" fresh ginger root
2 cloves garlic
1 teaspoon ground coriander
   seeds
1 teaspoon chili powder
1 teaspoon ground cumin
dash red food coloring
6 ounces plain yogurt
2 Tablespoons lemon juice
1 Tablespoon butter or vegetable
   oil

- Skin chicken legs and cut 2-3 deep slashes in the flesh. Sprinkle with salt.
- Mince and combine onion, ginger and garlic to a paste. Add coriander, chili powder, cumin, food coloring and salt mixture. Add yogurt and lemon juice.
- Rub the mixture into the chicken legs. (You may wish to wear gloves for this task.) Set aside chicken to marinate at least 5 hours or overnight.
- Place chicken in a lightly oiled roasting pan and bake in a preheated 350° oven for 25-30 minutes, basting occasionally.
- Before serving, place under the broiler to brown, about 5-7 minutes.
- Serve with spiced basmati rice and lemon wedges.
- This chicken may be prepared directly on the grill. It requires 20-25 minutes depending on the heat.
- Yield: 4-6 portions

Chicken Prunella

1 2½ pound chicken, quartered

3 cloves garlic, minced

1 Tablespoon oregano

salt and pepper to taste

2 Tablespoons red wine vinegar

2 Tablespoons olive oil

¼ cup pitted prunes

2 Tablespoons capers with juice

6-8 Spanish olives

2 bay leaves

¼ cup light brown sugar

¼ cup cup white wine

2 Tablespoons chopped parsley

- In a large bowl, combine chicken, garlic, oregano, salt and pepper, vinegar, olive oil, prunes, capers, olives and bay leaves. Cover and refrigerate overnight.

- Arrange chicken and marinade in a baking dish. Sprinkle sugar on top and pour wine around chicken.

- Bake in a preheated 350° oven, 45-60 minutes.

- To serve, arrange chicken on a platter, spooning juices over top and sprinkle with parsley.

- If desired, this chicken may be finished on a grill. Depending on size of chicken, remove from oven after 30-45 minutes. Keep sauce warm and cook chicken for last 15 minutes over low coals on a grill. Serve in the same manner.

- Yield: 4 portions

NOTE: This recipe expands easily.

Sautéed Chicken and Artichoke Hearts

2 Tablespoons oil

2 cloves garlic, minced

oregano to taste

12 ounces chicken breast cut into cubes

½ cup white wine

¼ cup heavy cream, optional

6 canned artichoke hearts, quartered

1 cup freshly sliced mushrooms

freshly ground pepper to taste

- In a skillet, sauté garlic in oil. Add chicken cubes, sprinkle with oregano, and add wine.

- Cook approximately 15 minutes by bringing to a boil and simmering.

- Add artichoke hearts and mushrooms and sauté for another 10 minutes, or until the artichokes are hot.

- You may add heavy cream at the same time as the artichokes and mushrooms, if you wish.

- Just before serving, season with freshly ground pepper to taste.

- Serve on a bed of rice pilaf.

- Yield: 2 portions

This celebrity recipe was submitted by
Chef John D. Swenbeck
The Grand Turk Tavern
Salem, MA

Chicken, Broccoli and Ziti

1 large bunch broccoli

4 boneless, skinless chicken breast halves, cut into ½" cubes

3 Tablespoons olive oil

3 Tablespoons soy sauce

3-4 cloves garlic, minced

1 pound medium ziti, cooked al dente

8 Tablespoons butter

freshly grated Parmesan cheese

freshly ground black pepper

- Trim broccoli into florets. Peel stalks and slice ¼" thick. Steam just until crisp, about 5 minutes. Drain and rinse under cold water to stop cooking process.

- Sauté chicken in oil, soy, and garlic over medium heat.

- Melt the butter in a large pot. Add the chicken, broccoli, and ziti. Cover and cook 10 minutes, stirring every 2 minutes.

- Top with cheese and black pepper.

- Yield: 6-8 portions

Stir-Fry Chicken with Lime

3 Tablespoons fresh lime juice

2 Tablespoons soy sauce

1 teaspoon minced garlic

1 teaspoon minced jalapeño chili

½ teaspoon freshly grated lime rind

½ teaspoon freshly grated ginger root

4 boneless, skinless chicken breast halves, cut into 1" pieces

1 teaspoon cornstarch

2 Tablespoons vegetable oil

2 thin zucchini, in julienne strips

½ red pepper, in julienne strips

½ yellow pepper, in julienne strips

¼ teaspoon salt

¼ teaspoon freshly ground black pepper

- In a bowl, combine the lime juice, soy, garlic, chili, rind and ginger. Add the chicken.

- Add the chicken pieces, then the cornstarch. Toss to coat. Cover and refrigerate 1 hour.

- Heat 1 tablespoon oil in a large skillet or wok over medium-high heat. Add the zucchini, peppers, salt and pepper. Cook, stirring, until tender but crisp, about 2 minutes. Remove and set aside.

- Heat the remaining oil in the same skillet. Add the chicken and cook, stirring, until the flesh is opaque and firm, 3-5 minutes. Return vegetables to the skillet. Cook, stirring, until heated through, about 30 seconds.

- Serve with noodles, rice, or in warm corn tortillas.

- Yield: 4 portions

Bisteeya (Moroccan Chicken in Pastry)

4 pounds chicken legs and thighs

1 cup chopped fresh parsley

2-3 sprigs fresh coriander

1 large onion, grated

¼ teaspoon turmeric

pinch of pulverized saffron

1¼ teaspoons freshly ground black pepper

1 teaspoon ground ginger

3 cinnamon sticks

¾ pound unsalted butter

salt

1 pound whole blanched almonds

¼ cup vegetable oil

powdered sugar and cinnamon for dusting top

¼ cup lemon juice

10 eggs, well beaten

½-¾ pound phyllo pastry, thawed

- Place chicken in a large casserole with parsley, coriander, onion, turmeric, saffron, pepper, ginger, cinnamon sticks, ¼ pound butter, and salt to taste. Add 3 cups water. Bring to a boil. Cover pot and simmer 1 hour.

- Meanwhile, brown almonds lightly in large skillet over medium-high heat, stirring frequently. Drain thoroughly on paper towels.

- Crush almonds in food processor quickly, but do not over process. Blend in ½ cup powdered sugar and 2 teaspoons ground cinnamon and process quickly.

- Cut ¼ pound butter into bits and add to ground nuts. Mix until well-blended and remove the mixture to a bowl.

- Remove chicken from casserole and set aside. Remove cinnamon sticks and loose bones and discard. Reduce remaining liquid to 1¾ cups.

- Lower heat to simmer and add lemon juice. Add beaten eggs to simmering sauce and stir constantly until the eggs congeal. (They should be curdy, stiff and dry.) Transfer eggs to a wide shallow dish to cool. Salt to taste.

- Shred the chicken into 1½" pieces and season with ginger, salt and pepper. Discard bones, gristle and skin.

- Clarify the remaining butter. Brush some on the bottom of a round 12-14" cake, pizza pan or cast iron skillet. Drape several pastry sheets into the pan, 1 at a time, brushing each very lightly with the clarified butter. Half of the leaves should extend beyond the pan all the way around.

- Place shredded chicken around the edges of the pastry-lined pan. Cover with egg mixture and sprinkle with crumbled almond-sugar mixture.

- Cover with all but 2 of the remaining pastry leaves, brushing lightly between layers with butter.

- Fold the extended pastry up over the top to cover and enclose it.

- Place the remaining 2 pastry leaves on top, lightly buttering each and tucking them in around the edges. Pour any remaining butter around the edges.

- Bake 10 minutes in preheated 425° oven or until golden brown. Remove from oven and shake the pan to loosen pie. Run a spatula around edge and pour off any excess butter.

- Invert onto a large baking sheet and return to oven for 10-15 minutes.

- Remove from oven and dust with powdered sugar and cinnamon. Best served very hot.

- Yield: 12 portions

NOTE: Bisteeya may be made ahead and reheated. Good with Moroccan spicy carrot salad.

Chicken Chili Rellenos

6 large chicken breast halves

1 small onion, sliced

1 carrot, sliced

2 stalks celery, coarsely chopped

4 sprigs parsley, chopped

4 black peppercorns

1 13¾ ounce can chicken broth

3 Tablespoons butter

2 cloves garlic, minced

5 Tablespoons flour

1 cup milk, heated

1 cup sour cream

1 cup fresh cilantro or 3 Tablespoons dried

2 eggs

1½ teaspoons oregano

1 teaspoon cumin

1 Tablespoon chili powder

salt and pepper to taste

2 tomatoes, sliced

1 4-ounce can green chilies, chopped

6 cups corn tortilla chips

2 cups chopped scallions

12 ounces Monterey Jack cheese, shredded

- Place breasts in a large skillet. Cover with onion, carrot, celery, parsley, peppercorns and chicken broth. Bring to a boil, then simmer 15 minutes to poach chicken. Remove chicken.

- Boil poaching liquid uncovered until reduced to about 1 cup. Strain and discard vegetables. Shred chicken, removing skin and bones.

- Preheat oven to 350°.

- Melt butter in skillet and sauté garlic. Gradually stir in flour. Whisk in heated milk and stock, and stir until thick. Set aside.

- Combine sour cream, cilantro, eggs, oregano, cumin and chili powder. Add cream sauce. Season with salt and pepper.

- In a 13x9" casserole, layer half the chips, chicken, scallions, chilies, sauce and cheese.

- Cover with remaining chips and layer chicken, scallions and chilies. Top with tomatoes, remaining sauce and cheese.

- Bake 50 minutes, or until heated through.

- Yield: 8-10 portions

NOTE: Serve with Mexican beer and salad as great après ski fare.

New England Chicken Pie

▶ Pastry:

2¾ cups flour

pinch of salt

½ cup solid vegetable shortening

½ cup butter, cut into pieces

1 egg, lightly beaten

1 teaspoon distilled white vinegar

½ cup ice water

extra flour for dusting

▶ Filling:

2 whole chicken breasts, cut up

4 cups chicken stock, free of fat

½ cup cold water

2 stalks celery, chopped

3 shallots, chopped

2 carrots, chopped

1 large Idaho or russet potato, peeled and cut into ½" pieces

4 Tablespoons butter

4 Tablespoons flour

salt and pepper to taste

1 egg, lightly beaten (for glazing)

Pastry:

- Sift flour and salt into a large bowl. Add shortening and butter and cut into flour until it resembles coarse crumbs.

- In a measuring cup, whisk together egg, vinegar and water. Add to flour mixture and stir until the mixture becomes a dough.

- Dust counter with flour and turn out dough. Knead lightly. Cut the dough in half. Shape into 2 smooth round cakes. Wrap separately in foil and refrigerate while preparing filling.

Filling:

- In a large soup pot, combine chicken breasts and stock and bring to a boil. Skim the top. Add ½ cup cold water to replace the lost liquid. Lower the heat. Add shallots, celery and carrots and simmer 30 minutes, until the chicken is tender.

- Add the potatoes to the liquid and continue to cook for 10 minutes, until tender. Remove the chicken and vegetables from the pot with a slotted spoon. Set aside until cool enough to handle.

- In a large saucepan, melt the butter and stir in the flour, whisking constantly for 2 minutes until the flour is straw-colored. Whisk in the stock until the mixture comes to a boil. Add salt and pepper.

- Pile chicken into a baking dish and add the vegetables. Pour sauce over the top.

- Roll out the 2 pieces of dough into one crust. Place the pastry on the top of the filled dish. The pastry should sit just inside the rim of the baking dish. Poke 3-4 air holes in the top and glaze with beaten egg.

- Bake for 1 hour at 400°.

- Yield: 4-6 portions

Chicken Galloupe

4 boneless, skinless chicken
   breast halves

½ cup flour

salt and pepper

2 cloves garlic, minced

4 ounces mushrooms, sliced

3 Tablespoons vegetable oil

1 teaspoon tarragon

¼ cup lemon juice

¼ cup brandy

¼ cup white wine

¼ cup freshly chopped parsley

- Place breasts between sheets of waxed paper and pound lightly with a mallet or heavy knife to flatten to ¼-½".

- Season flour with salt and pepper and lightly dredge chicken.

- Heat oil in a frying pan and lightly brown chicken on both sides, about 1-2 minutes per side.

- Remove chicken. Add mushrooms and garlic and sauté 2-3 minutes. Return chicken to pan. Add tarragon, lemon juice, brandy and wine. Simmer 5-10 minutes until chicken is done.

- Garnish with fresh parsley.

- Yield: 4 portions

Chicken della Robbia

2 2½-3 pound broiler chickens,
   cut into serving pieces

6 Tablespoons butter

2 medium onions, sliced

½ pound freshly sliced
   mushrooms

1 cup golden or dark raisins

1¼ cups water

2-3 teaspoons salt

¼ cup lemon juice

½ teaspoon ground cloves

½ teaspoon ground allspice

½ teaspoon ground ginger

4 teaspoons cornstarch

½ cup water

2 cups seedless green grapes

2 cups fresh orange sections

12 cherries, pitted

- The day before serving, in a large skillet, sauté chicken in butter. Add sliced onions, mushrooms and raisins. Transfer to a large Dutch oven.

- Add 1¼ cups water, salt, lemon juice, spices and brown sugar. Simmer, covered, turning occasionally, for 40 minutes, or until tender. Refrigerate overnight, if desired.

- Heat slowly and just before serving, add walnut halves. Remove chicken to a serving platter.

- Blend cornstarch with ½ cup water and stir into chicken liquid with a wooden spoon. Heat slowly until thickened and smooth. Add fruit and heat for only 2 minutes. Arrange fruit and sauce in decorative pattern around the chicken.

- Yield: 8 portions

NOTE: Almonds may be substituted for walnuts. Be creative!

Fire Up the Grill!

▶ **Honey-Ginger Marinade:**
¾ cup oil
¼ cup honey
1 teaspoon ground ginger
2 Tablespoons cider vinegar
2 Tablespoons onion, minced
1 garlic clove, minced
4 boneless, skinless chicken breast halves

▶ **Peanut Marinade:**
½ cup chunky peanut butter
½ cup peanut oil
½ cup white wine vinegar
¼ cup soy sauce
¼ cup lemon juice
4 garlic cloves, minced
8 cilantro stems, minced with leaves on stem
2 teaspoons dried red pepper flakes
2 teaspoons chopped fresh ginger
few drops water
4 boneless, skinless chicken breast halves

▶ **Grilled Chicken in Chive Sauce:**
6 Tablespoons olive oil
4 Tablespoons wine vinegar
½ teaspoon pepper
1 teaspoon salt
¼ teaspoon dry mustard
garlic to taste, minced
peel of one lemon, minced
1 Tablespoon chopped fresh chives
4 chicken breasts with wings

- Marinate the poultry from a couple of hours to overnight.
- Guideline cooking times:
  boneless breast: 5-8 minutes per side
  whole breasts: 12-15 minutes per side
  legs or thighs: 10-12 minutes per side

Honey-Ginger Marinade:
- Combine everything and marinate chicken.

Peanut Marinade:
- Combine everything but the chicken in a food processor. Add a few drops of water if it seems too thick.

Grilled Chicken in Chive Sauce:
- Combine everything and marinate chicken.

Dijon Mustard Marinade:
- Combine all.

Chili Yogurt Marinade:
- Combine ingredients and marinate chicken 12 hours.

▶ **Dijon Mustard Marinade:**
2 Tablespoons Dijon mustard
juice of a lemon
¼ cup white wine
2 or 3 garlic cloves, minced
1 Tablespoon fresh rosemary leaves or 1 teaspoon dried
2 Tablespoons chopped parsley
1 Tablespoon olive oil
freshly ground black pepper
4 boneless, skinless chicken breast halves

▶ **Chili Yogurt Marinade:**
1 small onion, minced
1 clove garlic, minced
2 Tablespoons lemon or lime juice
1 Tablespoon chili powder
1 teaspoon paprika
½ teaspoon cinnamon
½ teaspoon turmeric
⅛ teaspoon cloves
1 Tablespoon vegetable oil
1" piece of ginger root, minced
½ cup yogurt
4 boneless, skinless chicken breast halves

Roast Goose with Fruit and Chestnut Stuffing

1 12 pound fresh (or frozen and thawed) goose

1½ cups boiling water

8 ounces pitted prunes

4 ounces dried apricots

1 goose liver

2 Tablespoons unsalted butter

4 celery stalks, chopped

3 shallots, chopped

2 apples, cored and chopped

8 ounces roasted chestnuts, peeled and coarsely chopped

- Place prunes and apricots in a large bowl and cover with boiling water. Let stand 30 minutes. Drain and chop coarsely. Finely chop goose liver.

- Melt butter in heavy skillet and add celery, shallots and apples. Sauté 3 minutes. Add liver and sauté an additional 2 minutes. Add this to the softened fruits. Mix in chestnuts. (Can be made ahead to this point and refrigerated overnight. Bring to room temperature before stuffing goose.)

- Preheat oven to 400°. Season inside of goose with salt and pepper. Fill with stuffing. Truss goose. Place goose on a rack in a large roasting pan. Rub the skin with salt and pierce just the skin with a fork.

- Roast about 30 minutes until the skin begins to brown. Pour off excess fat and reserve.

- Fill shallow roasting pan with hot water and place in the bottom of the oven. Continue roasting goose for 1 hour.

- Pour off excess fat. Turn goose, breast side down and roast 1 hour. Remove the pan of water. Turn the goose breast side up and roast until a thermometer inserted in the thigh registers 185°, about 45 minutes, covering the breast with foil if it appears too brown.

- Transfer the goose to a platter. Tent with aluminum foil to keep it warm. Pour off all but 3 tablespoons of fat from pan. Add flour to roasting pan and stir until brown. Thin with chicken stock. Bring to a boil, whisking constantly. Reduce heat and simmer until slightly thickened, about 8 minutes.

- Season to taste. Pour gravy into sauceboat.

- Yield: 8 portions

NOTE: The goose is wonderful with small roasted potatoes. Peel and halve them and roast about 30 minutes in the reserved goose fat in the oven.

Roast Duckling with Orange and Cognac Sauce

1 4½-5 pound duckling
2 cloves of garlic, minced
1 sprig thyme
1 sprig rosemary
1 bay leaf
rind of 1 orange, thinly pared

▶ Sauce:
3 oranges
2 Tablespoons cognac
1 Tablespoon blackberry jelly
1 pint brown stock
watercress to garnish

- Preheat oven to 450°.
- Remove excess fat from inside of the duck.
- Prick it all over with a fork.
- Fill cavity with garlic, herbs and orange peel.
- Season well inside and out with salt and pepper.
- Place duck on a rack set in a roasting pan. Put in the oven and cook for 30 minutes. Reduce heat to 275° and cook for an additional 90 minutes.
- Peel the oranges and cut out the segments without pith or membrane.
- When duck is cooked, place it on a platter and keep warm. Pour off excess fat from roasting pan leaving the sediment behind. Add cognac and any orange juices and boil well. Add stock and jelly. Simmer to a syrupy consistency. Adjust seasonings.
- Spoon a little of the sauce over the duck. Garnish it with orange segments and watercress. Serve the rest of the sauce as an accompaniment.
- Yield: 4 portions

Duck Breast with 3-Peppercorn Sauce

▶ Per Person:
1 duck breast, skinned
1 Tablespoon duck fat
1 Tablespoon brandy
1 Tablespoon crushed: pink, green and black peppercorns
3 Tablespoons heavy cream
1 pinch tarragon
½ cup cooked wild rice
salt to taste

- Flatten duck breast with a mallet.
- Heat pan and add duck fat. Sauté duck breast about 1 minute per side. Remove.
- Deglaze pan with brandy. Add peppercorns, cream, tarragon and salt to taste. Reduce sauce until thickened, stirring gently.
- Slice duck into strips.
- Arrange wild rice on a platter. Pour sauce around rice. Arrange sliced duck on top of rice.

Sautéed Duck Breast with Autumn Berries

4 duck breasts
½ cup red wine
1 cup reduced brown stock
salt and pepper to taste
1 Tablespoon butter
2-3 cups assorted fresh berries, such as raspberries, blueberries, blackberries, a few cranberries
2 teaspoons sugar
3 Tablespoons brandy

- Score the skin on each breast, cutting the fat not the flesh. Season well on both sides.

- Place a heavy skillet over a high heat. When hot, fry breast, for 2-3 minutes, or until browned. Turn over and cook the other side for 1-2 minutes more. Remove from pan and keep warm.

- Pour off fat from skillet. Deglaze pan with red wine. Add reduced stock, heat through, strain and keep warm.

- Melt butter in a clean skillet. Sauté berries for a few seconds. Sprinkle with sugar. Add brandy. Toss berries for a few more seconds. Serve immediately over sliced duck breasts accompanied by the wine sauce.

- Yield: 4 portions

Grilled Turkey Breast

1½ teaspoons salt
1½ teaspoons dry mustard
1½ teaspoons chili powder
2½ teaspoons tarragon vinegar
5½-6 pound boned turkey breast
¼ cup chopped onion
3 Tablespoons oil
2 Tablespoons salt
⅛ teaspoon crushed red pepper
2 teaspoons pepper
2 teaspoons dry mustard
2 teaspoons chili powder
4 Tablespoons tarragon vinegar
½ teaspoon hot red pepper sauce
2 Tablespoons Worcestershire sauce
2 cloves garlic, minced
3 Tablespoons butter
½ cup water

- Combine first 4 ingredients and rub on both sides of turkey breast. Let stand 1 hour.

- Sauté onions in oil until tender. Add salt, peppers, dry mustard, chili powder, vinegar, pepper sauce, Worcestershire, garlic, butter and water. Simmer 20 minutes.

- Place breast over charcoal fire and grill for almost an hour, basting generously with sauce. (May take less time depending on the heat of the coals.) Let stand a few minutes before slicing.

- Yield: 8-10 portions

NOTE: Can also use an oven stuffer chicken breast. Delicious hot or cold.

Herbed Roast Turkey

1 10-12 pound turkey

salt and pepper

1 small apple, quartered

1 carrot, in 1" pieces

1 stalk celery, in 1" pieces

4 ounces unsalted butter

4 ounces garlic and herb cream cheese

¼ cup finely chopped fresh thyme, sage, basil, parsley and chives

2 garlic cloves, minced

2 Tablespoons cognac

salt and pepper

1 lemon, in ½" slices

- Wash turkey and pat dry. Season the cavity with salt and pepper, and stuff with apple, carrot and celery.

- Combine butter, cheese, herbs, garlic, cognac and salt and pepper.

- Following the contour of the turkey, work your hand under the breast skin to form a pocket between the skin and meat.

- Spread the herb butter mixture under the skin, concentrating on the breast and thighs. Add lemon slices, as desired, to the same pocket areas.

- Place turkey, breast side up, on a rack in a large roasting pan. Cover and roast at 425° for 25 minutes, then reduce oven to 350°. Roast for approximately 3 hours, or until the leg wiggles easily.

- To crisp the skin, increase oven temperature to 425°, uncover, and cook for 5-10 minutes.

- To make gravy, mix cornstarch dissolved in water with pan juices. Add a splash of Madeira wine.

- Serve with wild rice casserole.

- Yield: 10 portions

Stuffing Befitting a Celebration

chopped giblets from the bird

1 cup chopped celery

¾ cup chopped scallions, including green stem

1 garlic clove, minced

6 Tablespoons butter

2 packages wild rice mix

3 cups peeled and chopped apples, soaked in 1 cup sherry

1 cup pine nuts

2 teaspoons grated orange rind

⅛ cup Grand Marnier

salt and pepper to taste

- Sauté first 4 ingredients in 4 tablespoons butter until tender.

- Add rice, apples, sherry and pine nuts.

- Combine well.

- Sauté 5 minutes on low heat.

- Add orange peel, 2 tablespoons butter and Grand Marnier.

- Stir and cook slowly until butter melts.

- Yield: Enough for a 10-pound bird. Wonderful for duck, chicken, pheasant, goose or turkey.

Turkey Roast

5 pounds turkey breast, boned, skin attached

salt and pepper to taste

1 Tablespoon bay leaf, powdered

½ pound prosciutto

6-8 dried porcini mushrooms, softened in ½ cup hot water

3 Tablespoons olive oil

3 Tablespoons butter

1 cup onions, chopped

2 cloves garlic, minced

1 cup carrots, chopped

bouquet garni (parsley, thyme and bay leaf)

2 cups turkey stock

- Place turkey breast, skin side down, on a work surface. Sprinkle with salt, pepper and powdered bay leaf.
- Line up prosciutto, overlapping pieces on half the turkey breast, lengthwise.
- Drain mushrooms, reserving liquid.
- Place mushrooms along the center lengthwise.
- Roll the turkey into a sausage shape, tucking ends under, and wrapping the roast with skin to seal in filling.
- Tie every few inches to help it keep its shape.
- In a large pan, heat the oil and butter and brown the roast on all sides. Remove breast and place on rack in roasting pan.
- Add onions, garlic and carrots and sauté until the onions begin to brown.
- Add bouquet garni, the mushroom liquid and 1 cup of turkey stock.
- Place pan in 350° oven and roast for about 1½ hours.
- Add more stock as needed and baste frequently.
- Remove when done, strain pan liquids and fat and serve the juices alongside as a gravy.
- Yield: 6-8 portions

Edgurdouce (Rabbit in Wine and Fruit)

1¼ cups sweet wine

3 Tablespoons red wine vinegar

1 cup seedless muscatel raisins

1 cup dried apricots

1 teaspoon ground ginger

1 teaspoon ground cinnamon

small piece of fresh ginger, chopped

4 whole cloves

4 juniper berries, if possible

salt and white pepper to taste

1 young rabbit cut into 4 pieces

all-purpose flour for coating

1½ Tablespoons olive oil

orange segments, peeled and pith removed

finely shredded preserved ginger for garnish

- Warm wine and vinegar to simmering. Pour over raisins and apricots. Add spices and seasonings and stir.
- Cover and leave in a cool place overnight.
- Add rabbit portions to fruit and liquid. Cover and leave in a cool place for 6 hours, turning occasionally.
- Dry rabbit with paper towel and coat lightly with flour.
- Heat oil in heavy flameproof casserole. Add rabbit and lightly fry until golden brown. Drain on paper towels.
- Stir wine and fruit into casserole and bring to a boil.
- Return the rabbit to the casserole. Cover with foil or a lid and cook on low for approximately 40 minutes, or until tender. The liquid should hardly move.
- Transfer rabbit to a serving plate.
- Boil liquid until reduced and thickened. Pour over rabbit. Serve garnished with orange segments and finely chopped preserved ginger.
- Yield: 4 portions

NOTE: You may double quantity of rabbit without adding more fruit.

Aromatic Game Hens

2 Tablespoons freshly grated ginger

1 teaspoon cinnamon

2 teaspoons whole anise seed

2 teaspoons salt

½ teaspoon pepper

2 Cornish game hens (about 3 pounds total), rinsed well and patted dry

2 Tablespoons orange juice

1 Tablespoon oil

- Grind ginger, cinnamon, anise, salt and pepper to a powder in a spice mill, small food processor, or in a mortar with a pestle. Cut hens in half.
- Rub spice mixture all over hens. Let stand. Heat grill.
- Combine orange juice and oil to make a basting sauce.
- Brush hens with sauce and put on the grill, skin side down. Cook until juices run clear when meat is pierced, about 20-30 minutes. Brush hens with sauce and turn 2 or 3 times during cooking.
- Yield: 4 portions

Meats

Beef and Vegetables in Spicy Garlic Sauce

1 flank steak, about 1¼ pounds

5 Tablespoons soy sauce

2 Tablespoons sherry

5 teaspoons cornstarch

2 Tablespoons water

1 Tablespoon red wine vinegar

4 Tablespoons sugar

4 Tablespoons oil

2 green peppers, cut in strips

2 red peppers, cut in strips

¼ pound mushrooms, sliced

¼ pound snow peas, trimmed

1 Tablespoon minced garlic

1 Tablespoon minced fresh ginger

¼-½ teaspoon dried red pepper flakes

- Cut beef into very thin strips.
- Combine 2 tablespoons of soy sauce, 1 tablespoon of sherry and 2 tablespoons cornstarch.
- Add the beef slices and mix well.
- Combine remaining soy sauce, sherry, cornstarch, water, vinegar and sugar. Set aside.
- Heat 1 tablespoon oil in the skillet or wok and add peppers, mushrooms and snow peas. Cook 1-2 minutes. Cover and cook 1 minute. Remove and set aside.
- Place 1 tablespoon oil in the wok and add garlic, ginger and dried red pepper. Stir 1 minute.
- Add 2 tablespoons oil and meat. Stir-fry until brown.
- Add sauce and vegetables to pan. Cook 2 minutes.
- Yield: 4 portions

Sukiyaki

vegetable oil spray or cooking oil

1 pound beef tenderloin, sliced thinly across the grain, or pieces of fish, chicken or tofu

2 medium onions, peeled and sliced

1 bunch scallions, sliced

1 cup fresh mushrooms, sliced

½ cup sliced water chestnuts or bamboo shoots

½ bunch watercress, optional

½ pound fresh spinach, cut into 2" pieces

4 stalks celery, sliced

▶ Seasoning Sauce:

½ cup low salt soy sauce

2 Tablespoons sherry or white wine

½ cup water

4 Tablespoons sugar

- Place oil spray or cooking oil on bottom and sides of a wok or frying pan. Place the pieces of meat in the wok. Brown the meat on both sides.
- Combine ingredients for the sauce and pour over the meat.
- Push the cooked meat to the sides of the wok and add the vegetables. Cook about 5 minutes.
- Stir the vegetables together with the meat.
- Serve on top of steaming hot rice.
- Yield: 4 portions

Spicy Beef Vindaloo

2 teaspoons whole cumin seeds

2-3 hot dried chilies

10 black peppercorns

5 cardamom pods

3" stick cinnamon

2 teaspoons mustard seeds

1 teaspoon fennel seeds

5 Tablespoons white wine
vinegar

2 teaspoons salt

1 teaspoon sugar

2 pounds top round steak, cut
into 1" cubes

8 Tablespoons vegetable oil

1 cup chopped onion

1" ginger root, peeled and finely
chopped

10 cloves garlic, peeled

1 Tablespoon ground coriander
seeds

½ teaspoon turmeric

water

- Grind cumin, chilies, peppercorns, cardamom, cinnamon, mustard seeds and fennel seeds until powdery.

- Put this mixture into a bowl. Add vinegar, salt and sugar. Mix thoroughly and set aside.

- Heat 2 tablespoons of oil in a heavy pot. Add onions and fry until well browned.

- Remove the onions and put them in a food processor with 2 tablespoons of water. Blend. Add this to the ground spices. This is the vindaloo paste and may be made ahead of time.

- Blend the ginger and garlic with 2 tablespoons of water in a food processor.

- Heat the remaining oil and brown the meat on all sides.

- Remove the meat with a slotted spoon and set aside.

- Place the ginger and garlic paste in the pot, stirring for a few minutes.

- Add the coriander and turmeric, stirring well.

- Add the meat and the vindaloo paste, plus 1 cup of water.

- Bring to a boil. Cover and simmer gently for 1 hour or until the meat is tender. Stir occasionally while cooking.

- Serve with plenty of fluffy white rice.

- Yield: 6 portions

Roquefort Sauce for Tenderloin

1½ cups heavy cream

¼ cup cognac

⅓ cup beef stock

¼ pound Roquefort cheese, cut
into small pieces

2 Tablespoons green
peppercorns, drained

salt and pepper to taste

- Reduce heavy cream in a saucepan with the cognac and beef stock until thick.

- Blend in Roquefort and whisk until it is melted smooth.

- Lightly crush the peppercorns and add to sauce. Season.

- Yield: 4 servings

Tenderloin of Beef Provençal

5-7 pound whole tenderloin of beef

2 cups fresh white breadcrumbs

¼ cup dry breadcrumbs

¼ teaspoon white pepper

1 teaspoon minced garlic

½ cup olive oil

¼ cup freshly chopped parsley flowers

⅓ cup Dijon mustard

- Trim all outer fat from the tenderloin, then tie the tenderloin using butcher's twine so it is the same size all over, folding up the tail of meat.
- Heat a sauté pan and when hot, brown the meat evenly on all sides. Cool for 20 minutes.
- Remove string if you wish and cover with Dijon mustard.
- Mix all the other ingredients together to form Provençal crumbs.
- Cover tenderloin with crumbs, and bake in preheated 375° oven for 45 minutes.
- Cool 15 minutes before serving.
- Yield 10-14 portions

This celebrity recipe was submitted by
Chef Denise S. Kiburis
Eastern Yacht Club
Marblehead, MA

Tenderloin Salera

1½ pounds tenderloin fillet

½ teaspoon ground cumin

1 teaspoon salt

freshly ground pepper

1 Tablespoon oil

1 Tablespoon butter

¼ cup olive oil

3 Tablespoons lime juice

1 Tablespoon oregano

2 cloves garlic, minced

3 Tablespoons freshly chopped cilantro

2 tomatoes, sliced

1 avocado, peeled and sliced

1 red pepper, sliced in strips or rings

cilantro sprigs

- Season meat with cumin, salt and pepper. In a skillet over medium high heat, quickly brown meat on both sides in oil and butter. Reduce heat to medium and cook another 2-3 minutes on each side until meat is medium-rare. Do not overcook. Remove to shallow glass bowl and chill.
- Slice chilled meat ⅛" thick across the grain. Combine ¼ cup oil with lime juice, oregano, garlic and chopped cilantro. Spoon over meat. Chill 1 hour, periodically turning meat in the marinade.
- Place marinated meat on a chilled serving platter. Place rows of sliced tomatoes and avocados along each side. Decorate with red pepper and cilantro sprigs.
- Yield: 4 portions

Lobster Stuffed Tenderloin

3-4 lobster tails, frozen

1 4-pound beef tenderloin

1 Tablespoon butter, melted

1½ teaspoons lemon juice

6-8 slices bacon, partially
  cooked

8 Tablespoons butter

½ cup sliced scallions

½ cup dry white wine

½ teaspoon garlic powder, or
  garlic salt to taste

- Place lobster tails in lightly salted boiling water. Return to boiling and reduce heat to simmer for 5 minutes. Remove and drain lobster tails.

- Preheat oven to 425°.

- Trim excess fat from the tenderloin. Butterfly the tenderloin by cutting from the top to within 1" of the opposite edge.

- Cut lobster tails in half lengthwise. Arrange the pieces end to end within the tenderloin.

- Combine 1 tablespoon melted butter with lemon juice and drizzle over the lobster.

- Tie the tenderloin around the lobster with string at several points. Place the roast on a rack in a shallow pan.

- Roast for about 40 minutes, or until a meat thermometer reads 140° for rare to 160° for medium.

- Drape the bacon slices over the top of the tenderloin. Roast 5 more minutes to crisp the bacon. Transfer to a serving dish.

- In a saucepan, melt a stick of butter and cook scallions until tender. Add wine and garlic powder. Heat thoroughly. Untie and slice roast. Spoon sauce over slices.

- Yield: 8-10 portions

Sauce Aurora

2 Tablespoons butter

½ cup chopped shallots

4 Tablespoons cognac or other
  good brandy

½ cup beef bouillon

¾ cup heavy cream

¼ cup tomato paste

freshly ground black pepper to
  taste

- Melt the butter and sauté the shallots until limp. Add cognac and cook, stirring, over high heat until reduced by half.

- Stir in bouillon and cook over medium heat until again reduced by half. (The recipe may be prepared in advance to this point.) If made ahead, reheat and add cream, stirring until mixture is hot. Do not boil after adding cream. Remove from heat and stir in tomato paste.

- Season with pepper. Serve over tenderloin of beef.

Wickford Chili

1½ large onions, peeled and diced

2 Italian green peppers, diced

1 28-ounce can crushed tomatoes, or equivalent freshly chopped tomatoes

1 15-ounce can kidney beans

1½ pounds ground beef, or shredded chuck

3 Tablespoons red wine vinegar

1½ teaspoons chili powder, or more to taste

2 teaspoons cayenne, or more to taste

1 teaspoon cumin

2 teaspoons sugar

1 teaspoon freshly ground black pepper

2-3 dashes hot pepper sauce

3 cloves garlic, minced

Optional: ½ cup medium or hot salsa

Toppings: sour cream or shredded cheddar cheese and tortilla chips

- Prepare fresh vegetables and set aside.

- Brown the meat in a large cooking pot. (Ground beef or chuck may be used interchangeably, but be sure to shred the chuck or cut into small bite-sized pieces.)

- After browning the meat, drain off all fat and add the rest of the ingredients. If using fresh tomatoes, add ⅓ cup of water. If using canned tomatoes, add all the liquid from the can. Simmer for at least 1 hour, stirring occasionally, to keep the ingredients from sticking to the bottom of the pan.

- Top servings with shredded cheese or sour cream. Serve with tortilla chips.

- Yield: 6-8 portions

Mushroom Sauce for Tenderloin

6 Tablespoons butter

½ pound mushrooms, sliced

2 onions, peeled and finely chopped

2 cloves garlic, minced

3 Tablespoons chili sauce

½ teaspoon flour

¼ teaspoon marjoram

¼ teaspoon thyme

6 drops hot pepper sauce

3 dashes Worcestershire sauce

5 ounces dry red wine

1 cube beef bouillon dissolved in ¼ cup water

salt

freshly ground pepper

chopped parsley

- In a skillet, melt the butter and sauté the mushrooms, onions, and garlic.

- Add the remaining ingredients except parsley, and mix well. Simmer 10 minutes. Pour over meat and sprinkle with parsley.

Brisket of Beef with Fruit

1 brisket of beef, first cut, about 6 pounds

1 large onion, thinly sliced

1 12-ounce can of beer

1 cup dried pitted prunes

1 cup dried apricots

3 Tablespoons brown sugar

2 Tablespoons orange marmalade

juice and grated rind of a lemon

1 teaspoon Worcestershire sauce

¾ teaspoon ground ginger

½ teaspoon cinnamon

½ teaspoon freshly ground pepper

- Heat oven to 350°. Remove some of the external fat from the beef.

- Arrange half the onion slices on the bottom of a large, shallow pan large enough to contain the brisket. Set brisket on onion slices and cover with remaining onion slices.

- Bake at 350° for 30 minutes. Remove from the oven and cover pan tightly with foil. Return pan to oven and roast for 3 more hours.

- Put beer, prunes, apricots, brown sugar, marmalade, lemon juice and rind, Worcestershire sauce, ginger, cinnamon and pepper into a large saucepan. Heat to a quick boil and remove from heat.

- Reduce oven to 300° and remove pan from oven. Uncover meat and pour fruit mixture over meat and continue roasting 1 more hour. If sauce appears dry, add more beer.

- Remove pan from the oven and let sit 10-15 minutes. Slice against the grain and serve with fruited sauce.

- Yield: 8-10 portions

From *Saugus Center As I Knew It Fifty Years Ago* by Frank M. Ramsdell c. 1935:
Beef in bulk
and plenty of it
at six and a half cents
a pound.
Only four cents a pound
for cheese
With which the market
did abound.

The Veal Chop Special

2 Tablespoons prepared mustard

½-1 Tablespoon brown sugar

4 thick veal loin chops

2 ounces flour

salt and freshly ground black pepper

2 ounces soybean oil

2 Tablespoons butter

6 large mushrooms, sliced

1 Tablespoon fresh tarragon

¼ cup whipping cream

2 ounces white wine

2 ounces veal or beef stock

- Combine mustard and brown sugar and spread on chops.

- Dredge with flour seasoned with salt and pepper.

- Heat oil in skillet and add chops when the oil is hot.

- Brown on all sides, remove and finish in a 350° oven until done to personal taste.

- Drain oil from skillet and add butter and mushrooms. Sauté until nearly wilted.

- Add tarragon and white wine.

- Reduce wine, then add the stock and reduce again.

- Add cream. Reduce over low heat until thickened.

- To serve, pour sauce over chops.

- Yield: 4 portions

Veal Dijonnaise

1 veal tenderloin, 2 if small,
    sliced in medallions
5 Tablespoons butter
1 Tablespoon chopped shallots
6-10 mushroom tops, quartered
6 ounces white wine
6 ounces heavy cream
2 Tablespoons Dijon mustard
1 ounce demi-glace, optional
salt and pepper to taste
chopped parsley

- Sauté veal medallions 8-10 minutes in 2 tablespoons of butter. Remove from pan and keep warm.

- Melt 3 tablespoons of butter in the pan; sauté shallots and mushrooms until golden, 5-8 minutes.

- Add wine and reduce by ⅓. Add cream, demi-glace, and mustard. Stir well. Add salt and pepper to taste.

- Pour sauce over medallions and serve. Dot with chopped parsley.

- Serve with noodles, new potatoes or rice and spinach, asparagus or other fresh vegetables.

- Yield: 4 portions

Veau avec Gin

2 small veal scallops per person
salt and pepper
flour for dredging
butter
finely chopped bacon
onion, finely chopped
mushrooms, sliced
shot or two of gin
freshly ground pepper
pinch marjoram
pinch thyme
½ cup white wine
⅛-¼ cup orange juice

- Pound veal with a mallet to flatten.

- Season with salt and pepper and dredge in flour.

- Sauté veal scallops quickly in hot butter. Remove from pan and set aside.

- Add bacon and onions and sauté until slightly browned.

- Add mushrooms and sauté.

- Add gin and stir. Add spices and stir.

- Add wine, stirring to make sure the pan drippings are well incorporated.

- Reduce liquid slightly. Add orange juice and stir.

- Return veal to sauce to heat through.

- To serve, sprinkle with parsley to garnish.

- Yield: portions depend on quantity of meat

Glazed Veal Roast

5 pounds boneless loin of veal

2 pounds shallots, peeled and sliced

1 teaspoon fresh ground pepper

1 pound bacon, sliced

1½ cups rosé wine

⅓ cup red wine vinegar

⅓ cup sugar

½ cup port wine

- Preheat oven to 350°. Place veal in a roasting pan. Cover top of roast with ½ of shallots and sprinkle with ground pepper.

- Place bacon strips side by side around the roast.

- Pour ½ cup of the rosé wine over the meat.

- Roast uncovered for 1½ hours.

- Place remaining shallots, 2 cups of wine, vinegar and sugar in a small saucepan. Bring to a boil over high heat. Reduce to low heat and simmer 1 hour, until mixture reaches a syrupy glaze. Remove veal from oven. Remove bacon and shallots.

- Coat meat with glaze and roast, uncovered, 45 minutes; basting frequently. Remove meat when done, internal temperature about 165° on a meat thermometer, and let stand 15 minutes before carving.

- Pour cooking liquid from pan into a small saucepan. Spoon off excess grease. Add port wine to roasting pan and bring to a high boil, scraping bits from pan. Pour mixture into the saucepan and boil 1 minute. Serve as sauce over meat or pass separately.

- Yield: 8-10 portions

NOTE: Discarded shallots and bacon can be chopped and added to eggs for breakfast.

Yogurt Marinade for Lamb

2 cloves garlic, minced

2 Tablespoons lemon juice

1 Tablespoon minced fresh ginger

1 teaspoon ground cumin

1 teaspoon ground cardamom

1 teaspoon ground coriander

generous pinch cayenne pepper

1 Tablespoon finely chopped mint leaves

½ cup plain yogurt

- Combine all the ingredients except the yogurt in a blender or food processor. Add 2 tablespoons of the yogurt and process until fairly smooth.

- Stir this mixture into the rest of the yogurt.

- Brush on lamp chops or lamb burgers and allow to marinate at least 2 hours. Or, coat cubes of lamb with the marinade for shish kebab.

- Yield: ¾ cup

Roast Leg of Lamb with Herb Crust

1 boned and rolled leg of lamb, 3½-4 pounds

2 Tablespoons olive oil

3 cloves garlic, minced

1 teaspoon crushed rosemary

2 ounces breadcrumbs

4 Tablespoons finely chopped parsley

1 teaspoon thyme

salt and pepper to taste

- Mix together olive oil, garlic, rosemary, and thyme. Season generously with salt and pepper. Spread the mixture over the lamb and let it marinate 3 hours.

- Preheat the oven to 300° and roast the lamb for 1½ hours.

- Mix breadcrumbs and parsley. Add sufficient meat juices to make a paste. You may need to add a little butter.

- Spread the paste over the lamb and bake another 30 minutes to finish cooking and to brown the crust.

- Yield: 6-8 portions

Delhi Style Lamb Curry

6 Tablespoons vegetable oil

6 ounces chopped onion

1 finely chopped green chili pepper

4 cloves garlic, minced

2½ pounds boned shoulder of lamb, in cubes, fat removed

1 Tablespoon ground cumin seeds

2 teaspoons ground coriander seeds

½ teaspoon ground turmeric

1 teaspoon cayenne

2 teaspoons salt

1 pound tomatoes, peeled and chopped, or a 16-ounce can of tomatoes

1 pound potatoes, peeled and cut into 1" cubes

2 cups water

- Heat oil in a heavy casserole. When hot, add onions, chili and garlic. Stir-fry until the onions are brown.

- Add meat, stir and cook for 5 minutes.

- Add cumin, coriander, turmeric, cayenne, salt and tomatoes.

- Continue to cook over high heat 10 more minutes.

- Add potatoes and water. Reduce heat to low and partially cover the casserole. Cook gently for 1 hour and 15 minutes, or until the meat is tender and the sauce is thick. Stir occasionally while cooking.

- Yield: 6 portions

Lamb, Corn and Pepper Hash

1 Tablespoon vegetable oil

1 Tablespoon butter

1 medium onion, peeled and finely chopped

1 small red pepper, finely diced

2 cups diced leftover roasted leg of lamb, in ¾" cubes

1½ cups diced leftover roasted potatoes

½ cup cooked corn kernels

¼ cup coarsely chopped parsley

¾ teaspoon salt, optional

¼ teaspoon freshly ground pepper

¼ cup lamb broth, or beef or chicken broth

1 Tablespoon Dijon mustard

- Heat oil and butter in a large heavy skillet over medium heat. Add onion and pepper. Cook, stirring, until onion is lightly browned, about 5 minutes.

- Meanwhile, combine lamb, potatoes, corn and parsley in a large bowl.

- Add lamb mixture to the skillet. Cook, stirring frequently, 2-3 minutes. Sprinkle with salt and pepper. Continue cooking until the mixture starts to turn crusty and golden brown, about 10 minutes.

- Mix broth and mustard and pour over hash. Stir until completely blended, then press hash against bottom of skillet. Cook without stirring until most of the liquid evaporates, about 2 minutes.

- Serve hot.

- Yield: 4-6 portions

NOTE: So tasty a use for leftover lamb, you may want to roast extra potatoes just to make this dish.

Barbecued Boneless Leg of Lamb

1 leg of lamb, boned and butterflied

1 large plastic bag (heavy)

2 cups sour cream

¼ cup lemon juice

2 Tablespoons freshly ground pepper

2 garlic cloves, minced

1 Tablespoon dry mustard

3 Tablespoons crushed dried mint leaves

- Remove thick skin from lamb. Place all the ingredients including the lamb in a bag. Seal bag and massage mixture well into meat. Refrigerate 24 hours.

- Remove lamb from bag. Spread mixture evenly over meat. Place on a hot grill. Cook 15-20 minutes on each side, depending on how thick the lamb is and how well you like your meat cooked. The meat is best if it is a little pink when served.

- Portions depend on meat size.

Southwestern Stir-Fry

1 pound pork tenderloin, cut into strips

2 Tablespoons dry sherry

2 teaspoons cornstarch

1 teaspoon cumin

2 cloves garlic, minced

½ teaspoon salt, or to taste

1 Tablespoon cooking oil, preferably olive oil

1 green pepper, seeded and cut into strips

1 medium onion, thinly sliced

12 cherry tomatoes, halved

- Combine sherry, cornstarch, cumin, garlic and salt in a medium bowl. Add pork slices and stir to coat.

- Heat oil over medium-high heat in a heavy skillet. Add the coated pork and stir-fry about 3-4 minutes.

- Add the remaining ingredients, cover the pan, and simmer 3-4 minutes. Do not overcook.

- Serve hot with chili salsa or plain, over rice. Other vegetables may also be added, if desired.

- Yield: 4 portions

Pork in Squash Boats

½ pound boneless lean pork, cut into cubes

1½ teaspoons cooking oil

1 small tomato, peeled, seeded and cut up

1 small onion, peeled and cut in wedges

¼ cup dry red wine

¼ cup water

2 Tablespoons raisins

2 Tablespoons snipped dried apricots

1 small clove garlic, minced

¼ teaspoon dried thyme

¼ teaspoon dried tarragon

¼ teaspoon salt

dash pepper

½ cup green pepper, sliced

2 Tablespoons sliced ripe olives

1 medium-sized spaghetti squash

- In a medium saucepan, brown the pork in hot oil. Add the tomatoes, onion, wine, water, raisins, apricots, garlic, thyme, tarragon, salt and pepper. Bring to a boil, and then reduce heat. Cover and simmer for 1 hour.

- Add the green pepper and olives. Simmer, covered, for 5 minutes.

- Cut squash in half, lengthwise, and remove the seeds. Place cut side down in a baking dish. Microwave on high for 10-14 minutes. Let it stand 10 minutes.

- Invert on a serving platter and fluff with a fork.

- Spoon hot pork mixture into squash boats and serve.

- Yield: 2 portions

Smoke-Roasted Pork Tenderloin with Bourbon

1 cup olive oil

½ cup bourbon

3 Tablespoons honey

½ cup lemon juice

1½ Tablespoons ginger root, peeled and grated

1 Tablespoon garlic, minced

¼ cup soy sauce

½ cup onion, thinly sliced

2 Tablespoons fresh sage, coarsely chopped

2 teaspoons black pepper

1 teaspoon salt

3 pork tenderloins

charcoal

wood chips

- Combine all the ingredients except the final 3 to make the "soak" and blend well.

- Lay pork tenderloins in a glass dish and pour the marinade over them. Let sit in the refrigerator 24 hours. Remember to turn tenderloins several times.

- When ready to cook, pat the tenderloins dry.

- Preheat charcoal grill and soak wood chips in water for 30 minutes. Add chips to hot coals.

- Roast the pork for about 40 minutes, or 165° on a meat thermometer, basting occasionally with marinade.

- When done, let pork sit on the edge of the grill for about 10 minutes so the juices will be drawn back into the meat.

- Yield: 6 portions

Roast Loin of Pork à la Boulanger

2 pounds potatoes, peeled and thinly sliced

1 large Spanish onion, peeled and thinly sliced

3 Tablespoons finely chopped parsley

2 teaspoons finely chopped thyme

salt and black pepper

½ cup chicken stock

½ cup light cream

2 teaspoons Dijon mustard

4 Tablespoons butter

3 pound piece lean loin of pork or 6 large chops

- Preheat oven to 350°.

- In a bowl toss potatoes with onion, herbs, salt and pepper.

- Mix together the chicken stock, cream and mustard. Pour over the potatoes and mix well.

- Butter a large shallow baking dish. Cover the bottom with raw potato slices, spreading them evenly. Cover potatoes with all the liquid.

- Place pork loin or chops on top and dot with butter. Roast for 2 hours or until pork is thoroughly cooked and potatoes are crisp and tender.

- Serve straight from the dish.

- Yield: 6 portions

Pork Medallions with Hazelnut Hollandaise

½ cup hazelnuts, toasted and skinned

1 Tablespoon unsalted butter at room temperature

3 egg yolks

1½ Tablespoons fresh lemon juice

pinch of cayenne pepper

1 cup plus 3 Tablespoons unsalted butter

salt and pepper to taste

6-ounce pork tenderloin, 1 per person

- Toast hazelnuts at 350° for 10 minutes. Peel off skins.

- Process the hazelnuts and 1 tablespoon butter in a food processor until ground.

- Process egg yolks, lemon juice, cayenne pepper in a blender for 30 seconds.

- Melt 1 cup butter in a small saucepan until bubbly. With blender running, pour in hot butter in a thin steady stream to make a thick creamy sauce. Season to taste with salt and pepper. Add hazelnut butter and process just until combined.

- Remove the sauce to a double boiler and keep warm while sautéing the pork.

- Season the pork with salt and pepper.

- Melt 3 tablespoons butter in a heavy skillet over medium-high heat. Add pork and sauté for 5-6 minutes on each side.

- Place pork on warmed plates and top with a tablespoon or so of the hazelnut hollandaise.

- Yield: 6 portions

Fish and Seafood

Sole Stuffed with Crab

6 large fillets of sole with fresh
 lemon squeezed on top

8 ounces fresh crabmeat, or
 frozen or canned

½ cup cheddar or your favorite
 cheese in chunks or shredded

4 scallions, chopped, greens
 and all

1 Tablespoon fresh lemon juice

3 Tablespoons mayonnaise

8 drops of hot pepper sauce

3 Tablespoons butter, melted

⅛ teaspoon dried chives

⅛ teaspoon dried tarragon

- Keep sole chilled in refrigerator.
- Combine next 6 ingredients.
- Place ⅙ of crabmeat stuffing along the center of each sole fillet.
- Roll up and secure with toothpick, if necessary.
- Preheat oven to 350°.
- Bake 15 minutes and pour butter, chives and tarragon, which have been melted together, over rolls of sole.
- Yield: 4-6 portions

Scrod with Orange Madeira Sauce

1½ teaspoons grated orange
 rind

⅓ cup chicken broth

2 Tablespoons fresh lemon juice

4 Tablespoons unsalted butter

2 Tablespoons Madeira

1¾ pounds scrod fillets with
 skin, 1" thick

¼ cup heavy cream

salt and pepper to taste

- Combine all ingredients except heavy cream and fish in a 12" stainless steel pan.
- Boil and reduce a little.
- Add scrod, skin side up.
- Cover and gently simmer 8 minutes, or until scrod flakes easily.
- Carefully remove scrod from pan and peel off skin.
- Turn up heat under pan juices, boil and reduce to syrup consistency, about 1 minute.
- Add heavy cream and continue boiling until slightly thickened.
- Stir in salt and pepper to taste.
- Spoon on top of scrod and serve immediately.
- Yield: 4 portions

Bahama Fish Supreme

3 Tablespoons butter

2 Tablespoons olive oil

1 medium onion, peeled and chopped

1 clove garlic, chopped

1½ pounds fish (grouper, snapper, haddock, etc.)

¼ cup light rum

2 cups tomatoes, peeled and diced

¼ pound mushrooms, sliced

juice of a lemon

½ cup dry white wine

salt and pepper to taste

1 teaspoon curry powder, optional

- Heat butter and oil in a large, heavy skillet and simmer onions and garlic.
- Add fish, cut in large chunks, and brown lightly on all sides.
- Spoon rum over fish and flame.
- When flames die out, add tomatoes, mushrooms, half the lemon juice, and the wine and season with salt and pepper.
- Cover and simmer gently for 15-20 minutes.
- Dilute curry powder with remaining lemon juice and add to fish.
- Let simmer 1-2 minutes more while stirring gently.
- Serve with steamed rice.
- Yield: 4 portions

NOTE: This is a wonderful, traditional 17th-century island recipe.

Scrod with Tomato Buerre Blanc

▶ Fish:

2 pounds fillet of scrod ¾-1" thick

1 cup garlic breadcrumbs

4 lemon wedges

▶ Sauce:

½ cup chicken broth

¼ cup dry white wine

sprig of fresh tarragon or ½ teaspoon of dried

2 small ripe tomatoes, coarsely chopped

1 teaspoon of your favorite tomato sauce

3 Tablespoons chopped shallots

8 Tablespoons unsalted butter, cut into 6 pats

salt and pepper to taste

Fish:

- Preheat oven to 350°.
- Squeeze lemon on fillets and cover with crumbs.
- Bake 15 minutes.

Sauce:

- Combine all ingredients except butter in a 1-quart stainless steel heavy pan and boil until only 2 tablespoons of liquid remain. Be careful not to scorch the sauce.
- Lower heat to medium low and stir in butter 2 pats at a time.
- When totally melted and well incorporated, stir in next 2 pats and stir until totally blended, and then the final 2 pats.
- Add salt and pepper.
- Keep sauce warm, but do not boil, and serve under fillets on a serving platter.
- Yield: 4 or more portions

NOTE: This dish is also excellent prepared with striped bass.

Bundles of Sole with Sauce Mousseline

▸ **Bundles of Sole:**
24 thin asparagus spears
2 scallions
6 strips of pimento
6 skinless sole fillets
salt
white pepper

▸ **Sauce Mousseline:**
1 cup of unsalted butter, softened
4 egg yolks
1 Tablespoon freshly squeezed lemon juice
½ cup of heavy cream
salt
white pepper

▸ **Garnish:**
6 lemon slices and 6 sprigs of dill

- Trim asparagus into even lengths, peeling the stalks, if desired.

- In a large 2" deep skillet, cook asparagus in boiling water until tender, 3-5 minutes. Using a slotted spoon or tongs, remove the asparagus. Reserve liquid in skillet.

- Quickly plunge the asparagus into ice water. Drain on paper towels.

- Bring reserved liquid to a simmer. Cut long green shoots from onions. Add green shoots to simmering liquid. Simmer 3-4 minutes, or until tender.

- Quickly plunge into ice water. Drain on paper towels.

- Gently rinse sole. Pat dry with paper towels. Season with salt and white pepper.

- Lay fish on a flat surface. Divide asparagus spears crosswise on each fillet. Roll up fillets from narrow end. Place a strip of pimento on top of each roll. Tie rolls with blanched green onion shoots.

- Put fillets in a steamer pan and place over gently boiling water. Steam for 5-8 minutes, or until fish is done. Pour ¼ cup of sauce in the center of each dinner plate, place a bundle of sole in the center of the sauce, garnish with a thin slice of lemon and a sprig of dill.

Sauce Mousseline:

- In the top of a double boiler, whisk egg yolks with lemon juice. Place over barely simmering water, add ½ the butter and stir until butter is melted and sauce begins to thicken a little, stirring constantly.

- Add the remaining butter and continue stirring until sauce is thick.

- Remove from heat and set aside. (If necessary, sauce can be held at this point up to 1 hour by placing pan in a container of lukewarm water.)

- Just before serving, beat the cream until soft peaks form. Fold the whipped cream into the cooled sauce.

- Season to taste with salt and pepper.

- Yield: 6 portions

This celebrity recipe was submitted by Chef Phyllis Halpin Massachusetts Financial Services Co. Boston, MA

Fabulous Sole with Béchamel Raisin Sauce

2 packages fresh spinach

6 scallions, chopped

1 large garlic clove, minced

3 Tablespoons freshly chopped parsley

8 Tablespoons butter

½ teaspoon rosemary

1 cup breadcrumbs

6 large sole fillets

juice of one lemon

salt and pepper

2 cups béchamel raisin sauce

- Boil spinach, covered, in 2" of salted water for 4 minutes.
- Run under cool water and drain well.
- Chop spinach.
- Sauté spinach, scallions, garlic and parsley in butter.
- Add rosemary and breadcrumbs and mix well.
- Sprinkle fillets with salt and pepper.
- Squeeze lemon juice over the fillets.
- Place spinach stuffing (about ¼ cup) on each fillet and roll up. Secure with toothpick, if needed.
- Place in well-buttered dish.
- Cover with béchamel raisin sauce and bake in a preheated 350° oven for 30 minutes.
- Yield: 6 portions

Béchamel Raisin Sauce

2 Tablespoons butter

1½ Tablespoons flour

1 cup hot milk

salt and pepper to taste

½ cup raisins, soaked in 1 cup sherry

dash nutmeg

dash cinnamon

1 Tablespoon lemon juice

- Melt butter in a saucepan over low heat.
- Stir in flour until smooth.
- Add hot milk and stir until smooth and thickened.
- Add all other ingredients and simmer 12 minutes, stirring occasionally.
- Add to fish casserole dish.
- Yield: 2 cups

Cold Poached Salmon

1 whole salmon, 3-4 pounds
3 shallots, peeled and halved
2 celery stalks, halved
3 sprigs parsley
3 sprigs dill
½ lemon, sliced
10 peppercorns
1 teaspoon salt
½ teaspoon star anise

- Put all the ingredients except the fish into a large pot of water and bring to a boil. There must be enough water to completely cover the fish.
- Wrap the fish in cheesecloth for easier handling.
- When the water is boiling, carefully immerse the salmon. Tightly cover the pot. Return water to boil and boil hard for 2 minutes.
- Remove from heat and leave covered for 12 hours or until completely cold.
- Lift the fish carefully from the water, remove the cheesecloth and peel away the skin. Decorate with cucumber slices.
- Yield: 6-8 portions

NOTE: This is a beautifully moist way to cook all cuts of salmon. Serve with dill mayonnaise.

Baked Halibut à la Grecque

1 cup raisins
1 cup white wine
1 large onion, peeled and thinly sliced
1 14-ounce can stewed tomatoes
4 whole cloves
⅔ cup olive oil
2 Tablespoons butter
1½ Tablespoons celery salt
4 halibut fillets or swordfish or scrod, at least 1" thick
juice of a lemon
salt and pepper to taste

- Soak raisins in wine.
- Put sliced onions in a covered saucepan with ½ cup of water. Simmer for 10 minutes.
- Add raisins, wine, tomatoes, cloves, olive oil, butter and celery salt. Heat until butter melts and stir.
- Put a small amount on the bottom of a medium-sized casserole and place fish fillets side by side on top.
- Season them with salt, pepper and juice of a lemon.
- Cover with remaining onion mixture and bake for 30-40 minutes in a preheated 350° oven.
- Remove cloves and serve.
- Yield: 4 portions

NOTE: This recipe is unusual, easy and very delicious. Serve family style so everyone can dunk French bread in broth.

Fourth of July Salmon with Egg Sauce

1 4-6 pound salmon, cleaned and dressed, or 6 salmon steaks

1 teaspoon salt (for whole fish)

1 lemon, thinly sliced

▶ Egg Sauce:

4 Tablespoons butter

4 Tablespoons flour

2 cups hot milk

2 hard-boiled eggs, coarsely chopped

1 Tablespoon capers

salt and pepper to taste

3 Tablespoons chopped parsley

- Preheat oven to 425°.

- For whole fish, clean, pat dry, salt inside cavity, and insert half the lemon slices. For steaks, put slices of lemon on both sides.

- Wrap in 2 or 3 layers of aluminum foil, leaving some room around the fish. The goal is to have the fish cook in its natural juices.

- Bake on a pan with a rim, about 45 minutes for a whole fish, a bit less for individual steaks.

- Put fish carefully onto serving platter.

Egg Sauce:

- Melt butter in a saucepan over low heat blending in flour and stirring until it bubbles. Gradually add milk, stirring until sauce thickens. Simmer 1 minute.

- Add eggs, capers and seasonings, then the parsley. Pour over individual servings.

- For whole fish, before serving and to carve, make an incision down the center and peel back the skin. Cut down from top, slide a knife under flesh and ease each section off the bones. Steaks can be easily skinned and bones removed before serving, if you wish.

- Yield: 6 servings

Poached Salmon Fillet

3 Tablespoons vinegar

1½ teaspoons salt

1 pound salmon fillet with skin, preferably center cut, approximately 1" thick

- In a medium-sized saucepan, place 2" of water, vinegar and salt.

- Bring to a simmer over low heat and add salmon fillet.

- Continue to simmer uncovered 8-10 minutes, depending on thickness of fillet.

- Remove fillet, peel off skin and serve with your favorite sauce, or simply lemon.

- Yield: 3 portions

NOTE: Tasty with Normandy sauce (see page 112).

Tuna with Cranberry Cassis Sauce

▶ **Tuna:**
  4 1" thick tuna steaks
  juice of 3 limes

▶ **Sauce:**
  ¼ cup red wine vinegar
  3 Tablespoons sugar
  3 cups bottled clam broth,
    chicken broth, or apple juice
  3 Tablespoons butter
  1 cup finely chopped onion
  ⅓ cup finely chopped carrot
  3 Tablespoons flour
  1 cup fresh or thawed
    cranberries
  ⅓ cup Crème de Cassis liqueur

Tuna:

- Place tuna in a buttered casserole and squeeze the lime juice over both sides of the fish. Cover casserole and refrigerate at least 1 hour.

- Then bake in a preheated 425° oven for 25 minutes.

Sauce:

- In a small saucepan, combine vinegar and sugar over medium heat. Stir until dissolved. Bring to a boil and reduce by half, about 5 minutes.

- Add clam broth, chicken broth or apple juice. Stir and simmer 10 minutes.

- While simmering, melt butter in a large pan. Add onion and carrot.

- When slightly browned, add flour and stir for 1-2 minutes until smooth. Add broth to onion and carrot roux. Stir until smooth.

- Add cranberries and Crème de Cassis.

- Salt and pepper to taste.

- Simmer 5 minutes. The cranberries should pop.

- Serve with cooked tuna.

- Yield: 4 portions

NOTE: The sauce can be made a day ahead and reheated.

Grilled Bluefish with Mustard Marinade

2 pounds bluefish, skinned and
  cut into 4 pieces
salt and freshly ground pepper
  to taste
4 Tablespoons olive oil
2 Tablespoons lemon juice
1 Tablespoon Dijon mustard
8 Tablespoons dry breadcrumbs

- Sprinkle both sides of fish with salt and pepper.

- Mix together olive oil, lemon juice and mustard.

- Pour over fish in a baking dish, turning to coat evenly.

- Sprinkle breadcrumbs over fish.

- Marinate about 1 hour at room temperature.

- Broil on grill 4-5 minutes on each side until golden.

- Serve with lemon wedges.

- Yield: 4 portions

Halibut Dijon

4 halibut steaks, 1" thick

⅛ teaspoon pepper

2 Tablespoons butter or
margarine, melted

2 egg whites

¼ cup grated Parmesan cheese

2 Tablespoons Dijon mustard

2 Tablespoons chopped
scallions

- Sprinkle fish steaks with pepper. Place fish on a rack in a broiling pan and brush with 1 tablespoon of butter.

- Broil fish 2-3" from heat until light brown, about 5 minutes.

- Turn and brush with remaining butter. Broil until fish flakes easily with a fork, about 5-8 minutes.

- Beat egg whites until stiff, but not dry. Fold in cheese, mustard and scallions.

- Spread mixture over fish. Broil until tops are golden brown, about 1½ minutes.

- Yield: 4 portions

For two centuries Salem was an important American seaport. The waterfront was a mélange of sights, sounds and the odors of the sea. Cod drying in ordered rows on hundreds of racks lined the shore. Sloops returned from the rich fishing banks off Cape Cod, or brought timber from Maine, or exotic goods from the Indian Ocean.

Grilled Tuna Steaks with Avocado Salsa

4 tuna steaks, cut from the
center of the loin, about 1"
thick

½ cup extra virgin olive oil

¼ cup freshly squeezed lemon
juice

1 clove garlic, finely chopped

freshly ground black pepper and
salt to taste

▶ Avocado Salsa:

2 ripe but fairly firm avocados,
diced into ¼" pieces

½ cup olive oil

⅓ cup freshly squeezed lemon
or lime juice

½ cup finely chopped scallions

¼ cup freshly chopped cilantro

2-3 dashes hot pepper sauce

freshly ground pepper and salt
to taste

- In a small bowl combine the olive oil, lemon juice, garlic, salt and pepper.

- Place the tuna steaks in a ceramic baking dish and pour the marinade over the steaks. Turn steaks and let marinate for no more than 1 hour.

- Grill the steaks over a hot charcoal or gas grill for 5 minutes on each side, basting with the marinade. Tuna is often cooked rare, but most people prefer it opaque throughout. Serve hot with avocado salsa.

Avocado Salsa:

- Combine diced avocado, olive oil, lemon or lime juice, scallions and seasoning until well blended. Do not mash avocado. Serve at once or cover with plastic wrap until serving.

- Yield: 4 portions

This celebrity recipe was submitted by Nancy Gilman Fatfingers Marblehead, MA

Grilled Swordfish with Catalan Sauce

▶ **Sauce:**

¾ cup blanched whole almonds,
or roasted salted cashews

1 large sweet red pepper

2 large ripe tomatoes, peeled
and seeded

1 large garlic clove

½ cup olive oil

½ cup loosely packed fresh mint
leaves

salt and pepper to taste

▶ **Fish:**

2 pound swordfish fillet, 1" thick

2 Tablespoons mayonnaise

Sauce:

- Prepare the sauce first.
- If using almonds, spread them on a cooking sheet and toast them for 8-9 minutes, or until golden, at 375°. Remove from oven and cool.
- Roast red pepper by placing 2-3" from broiler and turning every few minutes until all sides are dark brown.
- Plunge into ice water for 5 minutes, then peel, seed and coarsely chop pepper.
- Place nuts, pepper, tomatoes, garlic and oil in a food processor and process until mostly smooth.
- Add mint and process until coarsely chopped
- Pour into saucepan and heat gently; do not boil.
- Add salt and pepper to taste.

Fish:

- Spread both sides of swordfish with mayonnaise and grill 3-5 minutes on each side until still moist, but cooked through. Do not overcook.
- Yield: 4-6 portions

Friday Night Fish

1½ pounds fish fillets, saltwater
fish recommended

3 Tablespoons butter, softened

1 Tablespoon lemon juice

1 teaspoon dried tarragon

½ teaspoon grated lemon peel
or lemon-pepper

⅓ cup dry white wine or
vermouth

3 Tablespoons minced fresh
parsley

1 teaspoon dried chives, or 1
Tablespoon minced fresh

½ cup round, buttery cracker
crumbs, optional

- Preheat oven to 425°.
- Place fish in lightly buttered baking dish.
- Mix together butter, lemon juice, tarragon and lemon peel or lemon-pepper.
- Spread on top of fish fillets.
- Pour wine over fish.
- Sprinkle parsley, chives and crumbs over fish.
- Cover dish with foil and bake for 15-20 minutes until fish flakes with a fork.
- Transfer to a serving platter and pour pan juices over fish.
- Yield: 4 portions

Grilled Swordfish with Red Pepper Purée

▶ Purée:

3 large sweet red peppers

5 ripe plum tomatoes, quartered

6 Tablespoons unsalted butter, melted

3 sprigs fresh oregano, optional

3 sprigs fresh tarragon, optional

▶ Fish:

6-7 ounce swordfish steak per person, or 2 or 3 larger steaks, 1" thick

mayonnaise

The Purée:

- Place peppers on a broiling pan and broil until dark brown on all sides.
- Plunge into very cold water for 5 minutes.
- Then peel, seed and coarsely chop.
- Peeling and seeding tomatoes is optional. The taste will be the same, but peeling and seeding produces a more elegant purée.
- Combine quartered tomatoes, butter and peppers (add ¼ cup of tomato juice if tomatoes are not juicy), plus the herbs.
- Simmer uncovered 10-15 minutes.
- Place in a food processor and purée 3 minutes.
- Heat and serve.

The Fish:

- Spread swordfish with thin layer of mayonnaise, to prevent sticking to the grill.
- Grill 5 minutes on each side 3" from coals. Check to be sure it is cooked through. Do not over grill. Serve immediately with purée on top.
- Yield: 6 portions

At the turn of the 19th century, Salem native Nathaniel Bowditch revolutionized the navigational tables which are still used today.

Seviche (Marinated Scallops)

2 pounds scallops

1 lemon, squeezed

2 limes, squeezed

1 cup fresh cilantro leaves

1 small green chili, seeded and finely chopped

1 clove garlic, minced

¼ cup olive oil

salt and pepper to taste

- Rinse scallops and drain well.
- Place in a bowl. Add lemon and lime juices, olive oil, cilantro, chili and garlic. Season and toss well.
- Cover and refrigerate for 4 hours, until scallops are firm and white.
- To serve, arrange lettuce leaves on a large platter or individual plates. Remove scallops from the marinade with a slotted spoon and serve on lettuce leaves.
- Yield: 6-8 portions

Italian Stuffed Swordfish

2 pounds swordfish steaks, 1" thick (4 ½ pound steaks)

1 medium onion, thinly sliced

8 Tablespoons unsalted butter, melted

¼ cup freshly chopped parsley

2 Tablespoons freshly chopped basil

4 thin slices mozzarella cheese

juice of half a lemon, or to taste

salt and pepper to taste

- Soak onion for 30 minutes in ice water, drain, then pat dry.
- Melt 2 tablespoons butter in a saucepan and lightly sauté onion. Remove from heat and toss with parsley, basil, salt and pepper.
- Slice a pocket in the swordfish steaks along the flesh side. Insert mozzarella in the pocket and also ¼ of stuffing.
- When the steaks are stuffed, brush tops lightly with melted butter and season with salt and pepper. Place on a cool broiler pan 3" from heat source.
- Broil 5 minutes; turn over, brush with butter and season. Broil another 5 minutes. Remove from heat.
- Combine remaining butter with lemon juice. Pour over steaks and serve. Garnish with a basil leaf.
- Yield: 4 portions

Shrimp and Scallop Primavera

2 pounds shrimp

2 pounds scallops

2 pounds fresh cut pasta cooked al dente

2 red peppers cut in julienne strips, blanched 2 minutes

2 cups black olives

1 pound pea pods, cooked 1 minute

1 jar capers, optional

▶ Vinaigrette Dressing:

3 Tablespoons Dijon mustard

2 Tablespoons red wine vinegar

3 teaspoons sugar

1½ teaspoons salt

1½ teaspoons ground pepper

½ teaspoon minced chives

1½ cups olive oil

- Cook shrimp and scallops in separate pots in boiling water for 2 minutes.
- Clean shrimp and cut lengthwise.
- Combine all vinaigrette ingredients and put in blender.
- Just before serving, add dressing to taste to pasta and toss. Serve at room temperature.
- Yield: 12 portions

Stir-Fry Shrimp with Asparagus and Pea Pods

1½ pounds fresh asparagus
1 teaspoon ground ginger
1 Tablespoon sherry
1 Tablespoon soy sauce
1 Tablespoon cornstarch
2 cloves garlic, minced
1 pound raw shrimp, peeled
4 Tablespoons vegetable oil
¼ cup chicken broth
3 scallions, chopped
12 pea pods, trimmed
1 Tablespoon sugar
dash cayenne, optional

- Rinse asparagus and slice off tips.
- Then slice in ⅓" pieces, only the green part of the stalk. Set aside sliced asparagus.
- In a glass bowl, combine ginger, sherry, soy sauce, cornstarch and garlic.
- Add shrimp, toss until they are coated, and let stand at least 15 minutes in the refrigerator.
- Heat 2 tablespoons of the oil in a wok or large pot. Add asparagus and toss for 1 minute.
- Add broth and cover the 30 seconds. Uncover and cook 1 minute more.
- Pour asparagus and liquid into a bowl and set aside.
- In same pan, heat 2 tablespoons oil.
- Drain shrimp, saving marinade, and stir-fry 1 minute in the oil.
- Add the asparagus and the liquid and the reserved marinade.
- Add scallions, pea pods, sugar and cayenne. Heat through and stir well.
- Serve over rice.
- Yield: 3 portions

Grilled Marinated Shrimp

48 medium shrimp, shelled and
   deveined
¼ cup olive oil
¼ cup fresh orange juice
¼ cup fresh lemon juice
3 cloves garlic, finely chopped
1 jalapeño chili pepper, seeded
   and finely chopped
½ cup fresh cilantro leaves,
   chopped
salt and pepper to taste

- In a large bowl, mix the olive oil, orange and lemon juices, garlic, chili, cilantro, and salt and pepper.
- Add the shrimp and toss well.
- Leave to marinate for at least an hour in the refrigerator.
- Heat grill or broiler.
- Cook shrimp for 3-4 minutes on each side.
- Serve with spicy rice and a salad.
- Yield: 4 portions

Stillington Shrimp

2 pounds medium shrimp
2 Tablespoons olive oil
3 cloves garlic, finely chopped
2 Tablespoons chopped parsley
juice of a lemon
1 cup dry white wine
salt and pepper to taste

- Peel shrimp leaving the tails on.

- Heat oil in a large skillet. Add garlic and shrimp, stirring and tossing 5-6 minutes until they appear cooked on all sides.

- Add lemon juice, wine, parsley, and season well with salt and black pepper. Simmer for an additional 5 minutes.

- Serve with a crisp green salad and crusty French bread to dip in the delicious juices.

- Yield: 4 portions

Marinated Shrimp and Scallops with Curry Tomato Coulis

▶ Marinade:
  8 Tablespoons butter, melted
  ⅓ cup sherry
  2 garlic cloves, minced
  freshly ground pepper to taste
  4 sprigs each torn small, or to taste, fresh rosemary, fresh oregano, and fresh tarragon

▶ Shrimp and Scallops:
  12 jumbo deveined and shelled shrimp
  12 sea scallops

▶ Coulis:
  2 large shallots, thinly sliced
  2 Tablespoons olive oil
  1 teaspoon mustard seeds
  1½ teaspoons curry powder
  ½ teaspoon sugar
  4 large ripe tomatoes, chopped, peeled and seeded
  1 Tablespoon lemon juice

Marinade:
- Combine all marinade ingredients well.

- Add shrimp and scallops to the marinade, coat them well and stir every 10 minutes for 1 hour.

Coulis:
- In a saucepan, lightly sauté shallots in olive oil. Stir in rest of ingredients and heat until tomatoes release their juice, about 3 minutes, over medium heat.

- Keep the coulis warm.

- After 1 hour marinating, place shrimp and scallops on a preheated griddle and grill 2 minutes on each side.

- Serve on top of coulis with warm French bread for dunking.

- Yield: 3 portions

The Ultimate Shrimp Curry

2 medium onions, peeled and chopped

4 cloves garlic, minced

5 bell peppers, seeded and chopped, assorted colors are nice, but not necessary

1½ Tablespoons ground ginger

1 Tablespoon ground cumin

2 teaspoons ground turmeric

2 teaspoons salt

1 teaspoon ground coriander

1 teaspoon ground cardamom

½ teaspoon ground cloves

1 large onion, peeled and sliced

6 Tablespoons vegetable oil

2 pounds medium shrimp, shelled and deveined

juice of a lemon

1½ cups chicken broth

- Place the 2 medium onions, garlic, peppers, ginger, cumin, turmeric, salt, coriander, cardamom and cloves in a food processor and briefly process until chopped, but not puréed.

- Heat oil over low heat. Add sliced onion and slowly sauté until dark brown. This is a tasty, crunchy addition to the curry. Do not burn the oil.

- Add ingredients from processor and cook slowly and thoroughly, stirring often.

- Add shrimp and cook until opaque, but not totally white. Add lemon juice and broth.

- Heat through and serve with steamed rice.

- Yield: 8 portions

NOTE: Suggested, but optional condiments: chopped fruit (fresh or spiced), peanuts or pine nuts, sweetened shredded coconut, chutney, and/or chopped scallions.

Seafood Diablo

½ cup chopped onion

¼ cup chopped celery

1 garlic clove, minced

2 Tablespoons olive oil

¾ cup (14½ ounce can) whole peeled tomatoes, with juice, cut up

¼ cup red wine

½ teaspoon dried thyme leaves

¼ teaspoon salt, optional

¼ teaspoon red pepper flakes

1 pound medium shrimp, peeled and deveined

½ pound scallops

½ pound whitefish, haddock or scrod

2 Tablespoons freshly chopped parsley

- In a medium saucepan, sauté onion, celery and garlic in olive oil.

- Stir in tomatoes and juice, wine and seasonings. Heat to boiling. Reduce heat, boil gently 10 minutes, stirring occasionally.

- Add shrimp, scallops and white fish. Cover. Boil gently about 10-15 minutes, just until white fish is flaky.

- Sprinkle with parsley and serve over fresh pasta or rice.

- Yield: 2-4 portions

Spicy Cajun Shrimp

1 pound shrimp, cleaned and deveined

1 teaspoon cayenne pepper

½ teaspoon black pepper

½ teaspoon crushed red pepper

½ teaspoon dried thyme leaves

1 teaspoon dried basil leaves, crushed

½ teaspoon dried oregano leaves, crushed

⅓ cup butter or margarine

1½ teaspoons minced garlic

1 teaspoon Worcestershire sauce

¼ cup beer at room temperature

1 large tomato, coarsely diced

- In a small bowl, combine the seasonings.

- Combine the butter, garlic, Worcestershire and seasonings. Mix in a large skillet over high heat. When the butter is melted, add the tomato, then the shrimp.

- Cook for 2 minutes, stirring evenly. Add the beer and cover. Cook for 1 minute longer. Remove from heat.

- Yield: 4 portions

NOTE: Delicious served over linguine.

North Shore Fish Cakes

6 Tablespoons butter

⅓ cup chopped scallions

2 cups potatoes, finely chopped and cooked

1 Tablespoon sour cream

1 pound flaked white fish (cod, scrod, haddock, etc.), cooked

1 egg

½ teaspoon dry mustard

salt and pepper to taste

3 Tablespoons parsley, minced

¾ cup herbed breadcrumbs

1 Tablespoon olive oil

- In a skillet, heat 2 tablespoons butter and sauté scallions for 5 minutes, but do not let them brown. Set aside.

- Cook potatoes until just done. Stir completely with butter and sour cream.

- Combine potato mixture with fish and set aside.

- Beat the egg, and add mustard, salt and pepper in a medium bowl. Stir scallions and butter into the egg mixture. Gently combine potatoes and fish with the egg mixture.

- Form the mixture into cakes about 3" in diameter and sprinkle with breadcrumbs.

- Heat the remaining butter and oil in a skillet. Sauté fish cakes slowly over medium heat, about 3 minutes on each side, or until nicely browned.

- Yield: 4-6 portions

Brussels Mussels

2 quarts mussels

8 Tablespoons dry white wine

2 shallots, finely chopped

2 sprigs parsley, chopped

2 sprigs thyme

½ bay leaf

8 black peppercorns, crushed

4 cloves garlic, finely chopped

4 Tablespoons finely chopped parsley

6 ounces stale white breadcrumbs

4 Tablespoons butter

- Scrub mussels and remove "beards". Discard any that are not tightly closed.
- Put mussels in a heavy pot with a tight fitting lid. Add wine, shallots, parsley, thyme, bay leaf and pepper. Cover and cook 5-7 minutes over high heat until all mussels have opened. Discard any that have not opened.
- Drain and reserve liquid. Remove top shells.
- Strain liquid and reduce by half.
- Melt butter in a large frying pan and add garlic and parsley. Simmer 2-3 minutes.
- Add breadcrumbs to soak up all the butter. Sprinkle with mussel liquid.
- Add mussels and coat well with the breadcrumbs.
- Turn onto a large pan and brown for 2-3 minutes under a hot broiler.
- Yield: 4 portions

Mussels Provençal

½ cup freshly chopped parsley

6 scallions, chopped

6 shallots, chopped

¼ cup butter

½ cup dry white wine

1 bay leaf

1 14-ounce can stewed tomatoes

3 sprigs fresh or pinch dried thyme

3 sprigs fresh or pinch dried rosemary

3 sprigs fresh or pinch dried tarragon

3 sprigs fresh or pinch dried basil

3 dozen mussels or littleneck clams, well rinsed

- Sauté parsley, scallions and shallots in butter for 5 minutes.
- While sautéing, heat wine with bay leaf.
- Combine and then add tomatoes and herbs.
- Cook for 2 minutes until bubbling.
- In a separate pot, steam mussels or littlenecks 5-10 minutes over 1" water, tightly covered.
- As soon as clams have opened, remove from heat and drain clean.
- Pour sauce over clams and serve with bread for dunking in broth.
- Yield: 4 portions

Soft Shell Crabs with Ginger-Lime Beurre Blanc

▶ **Sauce:**

½ cup chicken broth or fish stock or chicken broth with ⅛ teaspoon of concentrated seafood base in it, available at a fish market

½ cup dry white wine

¼ cup fresh lime juice

1 teaspoon ginger or 1 Tablespoon grated fresh ginger

3 Tablespoons chopped shallots

½ pound unsalted butter, sliced

salt and pepper to taste

▶ **Crabs:**

8 soft shell crabs, just killed and cleaned

3 Tablespoons butter

Sauce:

- Put all ingredients (except butter, salt and pepper) in a 1 quart stainless steel heavy saucepan and boil until just 2 tablespoons of liquid remain. Be careful not to scorch.

- Lower heat to medium-low and add butter 1 tablespoon at a time, continually stirring until all is melted and blended in.

- After one stick of butter is well blended, taste the sauce. You may prefer it this way, although adding the second stick, in the same manner, creates an elegant, excellent sauce as well.

- Add salt and pepper.

- Keep warm, but do not boil, until serving.

- To sauté crabs, melt butter in a large frypan over medium heat.

- Place crabs upside down in pan and sauté until shell pinkens, 4-6 minutes depending on size of crabs.

- Turn over, cover pan, and sauté crabs 3-5 minutes longer.

- Serve with sauce under the crabs.

- Yield: 3-4 portions

NOTE: To clean a soft shell crab, turn on its back and remove triangular apron. Lift flaps on each end and remove spongy lungs so you can see cartilage. With scissors, cut off the head just behind the eyes. Squeeze the body to release the sack. Throw away the sack, head and lungs. It sounds much harder than it is!

Clams au Beurre Blanc

½ cup butter, at room temperature

2 Tablespoons lemon juice

2 Tablespoons freshly chopped parsley

⅓ cup white wine

1-2 cloves garlic, minced

1 quart steamer clams

minced onion

peppercorns

lemon

French bread

- Place butter in a saucepan.

- Add lemon juice and parsley and whisk together to the consistency of a thin mayonnaise.

- Put on heat for a minute and then actively whisk.

- Heat wine and garlic together and then whisk the mixture slowly into the butter.

- Steam the clams in water, minced onion, peppercorns and ½ lemon until opened.

- Place cooked clams in individual dishes and pour sauce over all.

- Yield: 4 portions

NORTH SHORE CLAMS
No visit to Boston's North Shore could be complete without sampling the famed Ipswich and Essex clams—the sweetest in the nation! One of the earliest towns in Massachusetts, Ipswich was settled in 1633, just three years after Boston.

Scallops Verde

3 pounds very fresh bay or sea scallops

2 cups dry white wine

2 teaspoons salt

4 cups mushrooms, cleaned and cut into large chunks

2 cups watercress leaves

4 cups spinach leaves

▶ Sauce:

2 egg yolks

2 cups good oil (preferably virgin olive oil or a mixture of olive and peanut oil)

½ teaspoon freshly ground white peppercorns

small strips of tomato skin for garnish

- Remove the small muscle or nerve on the scallops. If you use sea scallops, slice in half or three slices if they are large.

- Place the scallops, mushrooms, wine and salt in a large non-aluminum saucepan and heat on medium heat until it almost comes to a boil. Stir occasionally. The scallops should just barely cook through and they do not even need to come to a full boil.

- Strain the mixture in a colander and cover to prevent too much drying. Place the juices back into a saucepan and add the watercress and spinach.

- Remove the watercress and spinach with a slotted spoon and place in the container of a food processor. Reduce the juices to 1 cup and add to the greens. Blend for a few seconds until smooth.

Sauce:

- Add the egg yolks and the cream to the greens and blend for a few seconds until smooth. Add the pepper and the oil with blender on as you would make a mayonnaise. It should have the consistency of salad dressing.

- Place some sauce in each individual plate with a few scallops in the center. Decorate with the tomato skin. The sauce should be cool, and the scallops at room temperature.

- Yield: 12 portions

Boiled Lobster

1" water in lobster pot

salt

4 1½ pound live lobsters

8 Tablespoons melted butter

juice of a lemon

NOTE: Two-pound lobsters require 15-20 minutes to cook.

- Place water in a lobster pot with a handful of salt, 3-4 tablespoons.

- Cover and bring to a boil over high heat.

- Drop in lobsters and immediately recover pot tightly. The steam kills the lobsters and they feel no pain.

- Simmer 12-15 minutes.

- Remove lobsters from the pot and allow them to rest. Melt butter and add lemon juice. Serve in small bowls for dipping lobster meat.

- Yield: 4 portions

Nantucket Scallops with Spring Vegetables and Chardonnay Sauce

1 ounce shallots, peeled
1 small bay leaf
½ teaspoon whole peppercorns
1½ cups Chardonnay wine
½ cup heavy cream
½ cup unsalted butter
1 Tablespoon olive oil
12 ounces Nantucket scallops
⅓ cup leeks, cut in julienne strips
⅓ cup carrots, cut in julienne strips
⅓ cup yellow squash, cut in julienne strips

Sauce:

- In a medium saucepan, place the shallots, bay leaf, peppercorns, and Chardonnay. Heat to simmer and reduce by two-thirds.

- Add cream and reduce until slightly thickened.

- Remove from heat and add butter, whisking continuously until incorporated.

Scallops:

- Using a hot saucepan, coat the bottom with olive oil and add scallops.

- Cook for 1-2 minutes. Remove from heat, reserving the liquid in pan.

- Add the julienned vegetables to the pan and quickly blanch all vegetables using the scallop juice as the liquid.

- Place vegetables on a serving plate and arrange in a nest. Put scallops in middle of vegetables and finish by covering scallops with sauce.

- Yield: 2 portions

This celebrity recipe was submitted by Chef Brian Stapleton The Ritz-Carlton Hotel Boston, MA

McClain's Marblehead Seafood Casserole

½ pound butter
small package round, buttery crackers, crushed
1 pound haddock fillet
½ pound (generous) lobster meat
½ pound (generous) scallops
½ pound shrimp
½ pound tomalley, or 1 can of lobster paste, optional
½ bottle clam juice
⅓ cup milk
dash or two hot pepper sauce

- Preheat oven to 325°.

- Mix butter with cracker crumbs.

- Put aside a few crumbs to sprinkle on top.

- Cut fish, lobster, scallops and shrimp into chunks.

- Place in lightly buttered casserole in layers, alternating with crumbs.

- Then add clam juice and milk.

- Mix in a few drops of hot pepper sauce.

- Sprinkle remaining cracker crumbs on top.

- Bake for 30 minutes.

- Yield: 6 portions

This celebrity recipe was submitted on behalf of McClain's Fish Market Marblehead, MA

Celebrations

Cultural Celebration

Throughout this collection there are references to sea captains, merchants and mariners as well as the great overseas trade empire. The Peabody Museum of Salem, begun in 1799, is a repository of artifacts collected by these enterprising skippers throughout the years. The five interrelated collections, totalling more than 300,000 objects, are presented through exhibits in Maritime History, Asian Export Art, Ethnology, Natural History and Archaeology.

The museum's handsome new wing is devoted to Asian Export Art. It is here in the atrium with one of the fascinating Foo Dogs (c.1840) that provides the setting for a refined cocktail party.

- **Lemon Cup Scallops**
- **Spinach Wrapped Chicken with Oriental Dip**
- **Pork Won Tons**
- **Spicy Shrimp with Snow Peas**
- **Indonesian Satay with Peanut Sauce**
  Spiced Almonds
- **California Rolls**

NOTE: ● indicates recipe is included in the collection.

In Celebration of Friends and Neighbors

The parlor of the Gardner-Pingree House of Salem's Essex Institute provides an elegant setting for a coffee hour. The stately brick mansion in the Federalist style was designed by Samuel McIntire in 1804 and reflects the privileged lifestyle enjoyed by Salem merchants during the golden age of the early 19th century. McIntire's sheaf of wheat carved in the mantle post inspired our cookbook page design.

The Essex Institute's museum neighborhood provides a reflection of Essex County's distinguished history. The museum galleries, library collections and preserved historic landmark houses give a close-up look at three centuries of life in the communities located on Boston's North Shore.

- **Lemon Poppy Seed Teacake**
- **Lemon Croissants**
- **Currant Scones**
- **Raspberry Heart Cookies**
- **Marblehead Fudge Ecstacies**
- **Pecan Bars**
- **Apricot Balls**

Celebrating the Winter Solstice

One of Marblehead's earliest patriots and a wealthy merchant was Colonel Jeremiah Lee in whose home we celebrate a hearty repast of roast lamb and roast garlic in front of the huge kitchen fireplace. Colonel Lee built his lovely Georgian mansion in 1768. Today the Lee Mansion is the home of the Marblehead Historical Society and welcomes visitors during the summer months.

A frequent destination for tourists attracted by Marblehead's rich history, galleries and shops is the nearby Abbot Hall, home of the famed 19th century painting "The Spirit of '76" by Archibald Willard.

- **Tasty Lentil Soup**
- **Roast Leg of Lamb with Herb Crust**
- **Garlic Roasted Potatoes and Onions**

   Pan Roasted Vegetables
- **Sesame Semolina Bread**
- **Incomparable Pumpkin Pie**

Harvest Celebration

Topsfield is situated in the very center of Essex County, 25 miles north of Boston on the Ipswich River. The Agawam Indians who relinquished their title to the land in 1639, called it Shenewemedy, "pleasant place by flowing waters." Like all inland towns of the period, Topsfield was a farming community — corn, flax, and sheep were raised from early times.

The Parson Capen House, built in 1683, is maintained by the Topsfield Historical Society. The delightful 17th century herb garden seen through the kitchen window and named for the first mistress of the house is lovingly cultivated by the Priscilla Capen Herb Society.

Mixed Green Salad with Fines Herbes
- **New England Chicken Pie**
- **Squash and Apple Bake**
- **Corn and Red Pepper Muffins**
- **Assorted Relishes**
- **Apple Torte**

Fresh Apple Cider

Celebrating the Catch

The rocky shore along Cape Ann, named in honor of the British Queen, provides the perfect setting for a New England clambake. This wonderful area is filled with colorful fishing harbors, small sandy coves, winding streets and charming old houses. The first year-round settlement of the north coast of Massachusetts was established here in 1623.

The Museum of Cape Ann, managed by the historical society, provides a safe haven for the nation's largest collection of Fitz Hugh Lane (1804-1865) drawings and paintings. Also featured in its permanent collections are an extensive exhibit of the area's fishing industry and displays of American decorative arts and furnishings.

- **Lobster and Corn Chowder**
- **Seafood Kebabs**
- **Mussels Provençal**
- **Boiled Live Lobsters**
- **New Potatoes with Green Beans**
- **Murphy's Crusty White Bread**
- **Garlic Spread for Bread**
- **Dutch Blueberry Pie**

Bridal Celebration

Fearful for his family's safety during the War of 1812, wealthy Salem merchant Joseph Peabody purchased an outlying Danvers farm. The site was close enough to the Salem seaport to be convenient and enough inland to provide a safe haven. During the 1890s Joseph Peabody's descendants reconstructed the house in the Colonial Revival style. Devotion to the family estate continued with succeeding generations and after 1930 Peabody's great-grandson William Crowninshield Endicott, Jr., called the property Glen Magna Farms, believing that to be the name of the Endicott ancestral home in England.

Among the buildings added to the estate was a precious summer house shown in the background which was designed for the Derby family by the noted 18th century architect Samuel McIntire. Tea was often served in the summer house.

- **Cheesecake Elegante**
- **Lattice Peach Tart**
- **Chocolate Roulade**
- **English Trifle**
- **Poached Pears with Cardinale Sauce**
- **Kiwi Tartlets**
- **Carrot Cake**
- **Chocolate Dipped Strawberries**

A Romantic Celebration

Originally called Marble Harbor because the rocky cliffs looked like marble to passing fishing boats, Marblehead incorporated in 1649. The town prospered from a tiny fishing village through the era of the clipper ships when Marblehead vessels sailed the seven seas. During the Revolutionary War, fortunes and lives were freely given in the cause of Independence. General Washington commissioned the "Hannah," manned and owned by Marblehead men, as the first American warship, supporting the town's claim as the "Birthplace of the American Navy." Today Marblehead is regarded as the Yachting Capital of America. The harbor provides a dramatic setting for a romantic candlelight dinner.

- **Chicken and Vegetable Terrine**
- **Poached Halibut with Souffléd Tartar Sauce**
- **Minted Green Beans and Peas**
- **Lemon Rice**
- **Frozen Apricot Soufflé**

Celebrating New England Hospitality

The quiet, pretty inland town of Boxford incorporated in 1685 is the site of the Federal period Holyoke-French House, carefully maintained by the Boxford Historical Society. Each year, the Society holds an Apple Festival to benefit the house.

- **Torta Rustica**
- **Confetti Pasta Salad**
  Basket of Crudités
- **Peasant Bread**
- **New England Baked Beans**
- **Hermits**
- **Beacon Hill Brownies**
- **Apple Crisp Bars**
  Assorted Cheese and Fruit

Scallops Baked in Apples

2 pounds scallops, rinsed and drained
6-8 large baking apples
¼ cup lemon juice
⅓ cup minced shallots
2 Tablespoons butter
2 Tablespoons brandy or cider
1½ cups heavy cream
dried or fresh dill to taste

- Preheat oven to 425°.
- Cut off top quarter of apples and drop tops into water with ¼ cup lemon juice.
- Scoop out apple pulp leaving ¼" thick case.
- Chop pulp.
- Cook shallots until soft. Add apple pulp and scallops. Cook until opaque, about 3-5 minutes. Drain and remove from pan.
- Add brandy and cream to pan, scraping brown bits. Reduce by half.
- Mix with scallop mixture.
- Stuff into apple shells and put lid on; bake for 20 minutes.
- Remove lid and sprinkle with dill. Put lid on and serve.
- Yield: 6-8 portions

Baked Stuffed Lobster

4 live lobsters, 1¼-2 pounds each
½ pound butter
approximately 1½ cups round buttery crackers, crushed
1 teaspoon parsley flakes
¼ teaspoon dried thyme
pinch nutmeg
sherry, to moisten the stuffing
¾ pound mixed chopped cooked lobster, shrimp and scallops, optional extras to add to stuffing

- Put lobsters on their backs and cut them with a knife or scissors from head to tail. Remove stomach sac and discard. Remove coral and liver and reserve.
- Place lobsters in a large baking pan. Flatten tails and crack claws so they will cook through.
- To make stuffing, sauté coral and liver in butter. You may add cooked lobster or shrimp or scallops, if you wish in bite-sized pieces. Coral and liver are done when they turn pink and green respectively.
- Preheat oven to 425°.
- Toss mixture with crackers, parsley, thyme and nutmeg. Moisten stuffing with sherry if too dry.
- Stuff lobsters with the mixture.
- Bake 12 minutes per pound.
- Yield: 4 portions

Maryland Crab Cakes with Lobster and Cognac Sauce

▶ **Crab Cakes:**

1 pound lump crabmeat

2 Tablespoons chopped parsley

1 Tablespoon Old Bay seasoning

1 teaspoon dry mustard

1 teaspoon white
  Worcestershire sauce

2 cups fresh breadcrumbs

1 large egg

1-2 ounces mayonnaise

1 Tablespoon lemon juice

dash of hot pepper sauce

olive oil

▶ **Sauce:**

1 Tablespoon chopped shallots

1 teaspoon chopped garlic

1 ounce brandy

3 cups lobster or seafood stock

1 teaspoon tomato paste

3 Tablespoons flour

3 Tablespoons butter

1 cup heavy cream

1 teaspoon thyme

olive oil

salt and pepper

paprika

Crab Cakes:

- Clean crabmeat and discard any remaining shells.

- Mix together crab, parsley, Old Bay, mustard, Worcestershire, egg, mayonnaise, and half the breadcrumbs. Be careful not to break up the crabmeat.

- Add hot pepper sauce to taste.

- Make into desired size patties (4-6) and coat in the remaining breadcrumbs.

- Fry in olive oil until golden brown.

Sauce:

- Heat stock.

- In 3-quart saucepan, sauté shallots and garlic until translucent.

- Deglaze pan with brandy and reduce liquid.

- Add stock.

- Add paprika, thyme and tomato paste. Simmer.

- In a small pan, melt the butter, Whisk flour into butter to make a roux. Simmer 4-5 minutes.

- Add roux to consommé and whisk.

- Add cream and reduce liquid again to original consistency.

- Season with salt and pepper.

- Strain mixture through cheesecloth.

- Spoon over crab cakes.

- Yield: 4-6 portions

This celebrity recipe was submitted by Sutton Place Gourmet Washington, D.C.

NOTE: Pieces of cooked lobster meat may be added for garnish.

The Absolute Best Lobster Newburgh

▶ Sauce:

4 Tablespoons butter

6 Tablespoons flour

2¼ cups heavy cream

2¼ cups milk

1 12-ounce can evaporated milk

salt and pepper to taste

½ teaspoon nutmeg

½ cup fine sherry

¾ cup fresh mushrooms, halved

3 Tablespoons shallots, chopped

1 Tablespoon of your favorite tomato sauce, for pink color

▶ Lobster:

8 Tablespoons butter

8 cups lobster meat chunks, lightly steamed half the usual time, 6 minutes

8 Tablespoons fine cognac

Sauce:

- Melt butter in a pot. Remove from heat and stir in flour until smooth.

- Add 1 cup cream and stir again until smooth.

- Place on low heat and add remainder of cream, milk and evaporated milk, 1 cup at a time, whisking slowly after each addition until smooth.

- Continue, slowly whisking to keep the bottom from scorching and to keep the sauce smooth.

- Add the rest of the sauce ingredients and continue slowly whisking.

- Keep sauce from simmering, but it will thicken as it grows hotter. When thickened, remove from heat.

Lobster:

- In another heavy pot, melt the butter over low heat and add lightly cooked lobster meat in it. Toss to coat.

- In a heat-proof bowl, put cognac and ignite it.

- Then add this to the lobster meat and stir.

- Pour lobster meat into the sauce.

- Stir and keep warm and covered (do not boil) until served. A 225° oven will maintain the newburgh.

- Yield: 8-10 portions

Béchamel Sauce

2 Tablespoons butter
2 Tablespoons flour
½ teaspoon salt
⅛ teaspoon pepper
⅛ teaspoon paprika
⅛ teaspoon nutmeg
½ cup chicken broth
½ cup milk

- In a heavy 1-quart saucepan over low heat, melt the butter.
- Add the flour, salt, pepper, nutmeg and paprika to the melted butter. Stir together until smooth.
- Gradually add the milk and chicken broth, stirring constantly until thickened or smooth.
- Serve hot on cooked fish, seafood, poultry, or vegetables.
- Yield: 1 cup

Dill or Tarragon Mousseline

1 egg
3 egg yolks
2 Tablespoons white wine vinegar, or tarragon vinegar, or basil vinegar
½ teaspoon salt
¼ teaspoon pepper
8 ounces sour cream
4 Tablespoons unsalted butter, softened but not melted
⅓ cup loosely packed dill sprigs, chopped, or fresh tarragon, chopped

- In the top of a double boiler removed from the heat, combine eggs, vinegar, salt and pepper.
- When well whisked, beat in the sour cream.
- Place over simmering water in the bottom of the double boiler (top pan of boiler should not touch simmering water in the bottom).
- Continue to whisk slowly 7-8 minutes, being sure to scrape the bottom and sides often.
- When sauce is the consistency of pudding, about 7-8 minutes, remove from heat and whisk in remaining ingredients.
- Keep warm until served over grilled salmon.
- Yield: 5 portions

Champagne Sauce for Fish

1 cup chicken stock

½ teaspoon dried thyme or 1½ teaspoons chopped fresh

1 shallot, minced

⅛ teaspoon ground nutmeg

1 cup champagne

1 cup sour cream

2 Tablespoons cold, unsalted butter in ½" pieces

salt and pepper to taste

¼ cup champagne

1½ teaspoons flour, optional

- Combine first 5 ingredients in a saucepan and boil over medium-high heat until reduced to only 2-3 tablespoons.
- Stir in sour cream and simmer over low heat for 3 minutes.
- Remove from heat and whisk in butter.
- Season with salt and pepper.
- Just before serving, stir in ¼ cup champagne. If the sauce seems thin, whisk in the optional flour.
- Yield: 4 portions

Normandy Sauce

1 small onion, thinly sliced

5 Tablespoons butter

2 large apples, cored and sliced thinly

½ cup apple juice

¼ cup orange liqueur

1 cup heavy cream

1 Tablespoon flour, if necessary

6 medium fresh mushrooms, sliced in thirds

salt and pepper to taste

- In a skillet, sauté onion in butter until soft. Add the apples and sauté an additional minute.
- Add cider and reduce by half.
- Stir in liqueur and cream.
- Place in food processor and purée for 1 minute. Return to saucepan.
- If sauce is thin, stir in flour, otherwise omit, then add mushrooms and heat 5-10 minutes.
- Serve with your favorite grilled fish.
- Yield: 2 cups

NOTE: This sauce can be made ahead and heated later. In the summertime, substitute fresh peeled peaches for apples and omit the mushrooms. Serve with grilled swordfish.

Butters for Fish

▶ **Wasabi Butter:**
½ cup unsalted butter, softened

1 teaspoon wasabi (Japanese horseradish powder)

5-6 drops lemon juice

▶ **Dill Lemon Butter:**
½ cup unsalted butter, softened

1 clove garlic, minced

2 teaspoons lemon juice

grated rind of 1 lemon

2 Tablespoons fresh dill, chopped

▶ **Lime Ginger Butter:**
½ cup unsalted butter, softened

2" piece ginger root

1 teaspoon lime juice

▶ **Chive-Cucumber Butter:**
½ cup fish stock or clam juice, or chicken broth

½ cup dry white wine

¼ cup tarragon or basil vinegar

½ cup seeded, peeled and chopped cucumber

3 Tablespoons chopped shallots

½ pound unsalted butter, sliced into 16 Tablespoons

¼ cup finely snipped chives, fresh, if possible

Wasabi Butter:
- Mix all ingredients together.
- Roll into cylinder, wrap and chill until firm.
- Slice and serve with grilled tuna.
- Yield: 4 portions

Dill Lemon Butter:
- Mix all ingredients.
- Roll into cylinder, wrap and chill until firm.
- Slice and serve with shrimp.
- Yield: 4 portions

Lime Ginger Butter:
- Peel and grate ginger root.
- Mix butter, ginger root and lime juice.
- Roll into cylinder, wrap in plastic and chill.
- Slice and serve with salmon.
- Yield: 4 portions

Chive-Cucumber Butter:
- Combine stock, wine, vinegar, cucumber and shallots in a 1 quart saucepan and boil until only 2 tablespoons of liquid remain. Do not scorch.
- Turn heat to low and whisk in butter 1 tablespoon at a time.
- Make sure each tablespoon is melted and incorporated before adding next tablespoon.
- Stir in chives.
- Do not boil; keep warm until serving.
- This sauce is very elegant if you blend it in the food processor as soon as it is ready.
- Reheat quickly and serve with poached salmon.
- Yield: 6 portions

Nancy's Mustard Sauce for Fish

¼ cup olive oil

¼ cup chopped fresh parsley

3 Tablespoons chopped scallions

3 Tablespoon honey mustard

1 Tablespoon butter, melted

1 teaspoon seasoned salt

juice of half a lemon

- Combine all ingredients with a whisk over low heat in a small saucepan.
- When well blended and just warm, serve with your favorite fish.
- Yield: 3 portions

Souffléed Tartar Sauce

½ cup mayonnaise

¼ cup sweet pepper or capers

2 Tablespoons chopped parsley

1½ Tablespoons lemon juice

¼ teaspoon salt

⅛ teaspoon cayenne

2 egg whites, beaten stiffly, but not dry

- Combine all ingredients except egg whites.
- Fold in beaten egg whites.
- Spread evenly on nearly fully cooked fish and broil briefly until sauce puffs and is golden.
- Yield: 6 portions

NOTE: Especially good served with poached halibut.

Pasta and Rice

Stir-Fry Pasta and Vegetables

¼ cup olive oil

several cloves of garlic, thinly sliced

4 medium tomatoes

1 zucchini

1-1½ cups sliced mushrooms

2½ cups fresh broccoli florets

freshly ground pepper

1-1½ teaspoons crushed basil

1 cup fresh shelled peas, optional

1 box linguine

Parmesan and Romano cheese

This is one of those recipes where measurements can be approximate.

- Dice zucchini; cut tops of broccoli into bite-sized florets and slice the mushrooms. Cut tomatoes in half and scoop out pulp. Chop pulp finely. Cut the tomato shell into thin strips.

- Begin cooking linguine according to package directions.

- Heat skillet, preferably nonstick, on high. Add olive oil and sliced garlic. Remove the garlic as it begins to brown.

- Add broccoli to hot, garlic-flavored oil and cook for 1-2 minutes. Add zucchini and cook for 1 minute; add mushrooms and continue sautéing. Add freshly ground pepper.

- Sprinkle with the basil. Add the peas, stirring constantly.

- Add chopped tomato pulp and heat for a moment.

- Finally, add the sliced tomato shell and heat thoroughly. Vegetables should be crisp, and like stir-fry, need to be constantly stirred on medium to high heat.

- Drain linguine, return it to the pot and toss with the sautéed vegetables.

- Serve with grated cheeses.

- Yield: 4 portions

NOTE: Ingredient quantities may be varied to suit personal taste. It is also good cold the next day.

Spinach Pasta with Gorgonzola

¼ pound imported Gorgonzola cheese, crumbled

½ cup milk

3 Tablespoons butter

⅓ cup whipping cream

1 pound spinach pasta, cooked al dente

½ cup grated Parmesan cheese

- Combine Gorgonzola, milk and butter in a saucepan or double boiler over low heat until hot and smooth.

- Add cream and heat until sauce is hot and well blended.

- Add sauce to cooked spinach pasta and toss until evenly coated.

- Add Parmesan cheese and toss again.

- Yield: 4-6 portions

Pasta with Roasted Garlic and Broccoli

1 whole bulb of garlic

¾ cup olive oil

1 bunch broccoli

¾ cup of fresh basil leaves

½ cup heavy cream

salt and freshly ground pepper
   to taste

1½ pounds linguine or other
   pasta

¾ cup freshly grated Parmesan
   cheese, or to taste

- Peel the outside skin (tissue only) from the bulb of garlic and place in a small heatproof dish. Pour 1 tablespoon olive oil over the garlic and bake in 325° oven until the bulb begins to brown, about 1 hour. Cool slightly and remove the inside from each clove. Set aside.

- Cut stems from the broccoli florets. Chop the stems roughly and blanch both stems and florets in boiling water for approximately 6 minutes.

- In a food processor, place blanched broccoli, basil leaves and peeled, baked garlic. Process quickly, on and off, adding the remaining oil through the top opening until a thick consistency is attained. Add the cream and process quickly. Add salt and pepper and set aside. (You may thin the sauce with a bit of the water from the pasta, if desired.)

- Bring 4 quarts water to a rapid boil and cook pasta al dente. Drain and return to pot. Add grated cheese and turn onto serving plate. Top with the green sauce.

- Yield: 12 appetizer or 6 entrée portions

Fettucine alla Joanna

1 pound fettucine noodles

½ package frozen peas,
   defrosted

6-8 slices lean prosciutto

1 cup heavy cream

2 Tablespoons freshly chopped
   parsley

2 Tablespoons minced onion

4 Tablespoons butter

1 large egg yolk, slightly beaten

½ cup grated Romano cheese

½ cup freshly grated Parmesan
   cheese

freshly ground white pepper

- Cook noodles in boiling, salted water for 9-11 minutes. Drain and toss in a tablespoon of butter.

- Melt 3 tablespoons butter in a large saucepan over low heat. Sauté prosciutto and onion for 4-5 minutes.

- Slowly add cream, then the peas, stirring until heated. Remove from heat.

- Add noodles and toss lightly for 1 minute. Add egg yolk and toss for another minute. Add cheese as final step and toss until noodles are well coated.

- Serve hot with more grated cheese and garnish with chopped parsley and pepper.

- Yield: 6 portions

Pasta Provençal

1 7-ounce jar roasted red peppers drained and cut into ½" strips

1 2-ounce can anchovy fillets, drained and finely chopped

⅓ cup extra virgin oil

¼ cup freshly chopped parsley

2 Tablespoons capers, chopped

2 Tablespoons minced garlic

½ teaspoon ground pepper

¼ teaspoon salt

¼ teaspoon red pepper flakes

1 pound of fusilli or pasta of choice

¼ cup freshly shaved Parmesan cheese

¼ cup freshly grated Parmesan cheese

¼ cup roasted pignoli or pine nuts

- Combine all ingredients except pasta, Parmesan cheese and nuts in a large serving bowl.
- Cook pasta according to package directions and drain well.
- Transfer pasta to a serving bowl. Toss well with pepper mixture.
- Add Parmesan and nuts. Toss again. Serve immediately.
- Yield: 4 portions

NOTE: This can be also served as a salad by adding a little balsamic vinegar and black olives.

Linguine with Sun-Dried Tomatoes and Zucchini

3 Tablespoons butter

3 Tablespoons olive oil

¼ cup finely chopped onion

1 Tablespoon finely minced shallots

½ cup diced prosciutto ham

2 pounds zucchini, sliced into rounds and quartered

¼ cup sun-dried tomatoes

1 pound linguine, cooked

freshly ground pepper to taste

freshly grated Parmesan cheese

- Melt butter in a skillet. Add oil and cook onions and shallots until transparent.
- Add zucchini and cook, stirring for 3 minutes.
- Add prosciutto, pepper and sun-dried tomatoes.
- Toss with drained linguine. Pass freshly grated Parmesan cheese.
- Yield: 4 portions

Pasta Primavera with Chicken

1½ pounds boneless, skinless chicken breast halves

1 Tablespoon butter or margarine

1 Tablespoon light olive oil

1 garlic clove, minced

½ cup finely chopped onion

2 medium zucchini, cut diagonally ¼" thick

1 medium carrot, cut diagonally ¼" thick

3 dozen snow peas, trimmed

1½ cups sliced mushrooms

3 or 4 plum tomatoes, diced

3 Tablespoons freshly chopped parsley

2 Tablespoons chopped chives

salt and pepper to taste

1½ cups light cream (or to lighten, use ¾ cup chicken stock and ¾ cup light cream)

2 Tablespoons tomato paste

2 Tablespoons grated Parmesan cheese

1 pound linguine or spaghetti

- Grill or pan fry chicken and cut into ¼" strips. Set aside.

- Melt margarine and oil in a large skillet. Brown onion and garlic. Add vegetables one at a time and stir-fry until cooked al dente. Remove from pan and set aside. Add herbs, cream and tomato paste to pan. Stir frequently until sauce thickens. Add Parmesan cheese and simmer.

- Cook pasta al dente and drain.

- Return vegetables and chicken to sauce. Toss to coat. Heat through. Serve on top of pasta. Garnish with fresh parsley and serve with grated Parmesan cheese.

- Yield: 6 portions

Many Essex County communities were involved in the leather industry including Beverly, Danvers, Peabody, Haverhill, Salem, and Wenham. However, in 1907 the largest shoe factory in the world was in Lynn. Lydia E. Pinkham's Vegetable Compound, famous herbal medicine used primarily by women through the United States, was also gaining popularity at the turn of the century. Proceeds from Lydia E. Pinkham's enterprise provided funds for a free medical clinic.

Linguine with Scallops

¾ pound linguine

1 pound sea scallops, side muscle removed

4 Tablespoons butter

2 medium cloves garlic, chopped

1 rounded Tablespoon of freshly chopped ginger

1 cup chicken stock

4 stalks scallions, green part only, cut thinly on the diagonal

salt and freshly ground pepper to taste

2 Tablespoons freshly chopped parsley

- Put a large pot of lightly salted water on to boil for the linguine. While pasta is cooking, prepare the sauce.

- In a 12" sauté pan, large enough to hold all the scallops without crowding, place scallops, 3 tablespoons of butter, garlic, and ginger. Cook over high heat until the scallops become firm and opaque, about 5 minutes. Stir occasionally to coat all the scallops with the seasonings. Reduce heat and add the chicken stock and scallions. Add salt and pepper to taste.

- Add the drained linguine and toss to coat. Add 1 tablespoon butter and the chopped parsley.

- Stir briefly to melt the butter and serve immediately.

- Yield: 4 portions

This celebrity recipe was submitted by Chef Kate Hammond The Grape Vine Salem, MA

NOTE: Sprinkle with freshly grated Parmesan cheese, if desired.

Seafood Lasagne

Lasagne noodles

▶ **Cheese Filling:**
2 cups ricotta cheese

4 egg yolks

3 Tablespoons freshly grated
   Parmesan cheese

¼ teaspoon nutmeg

1 teaspoon salt or to taste

1 teaspoon freshly ground
   pepper

½ teaspoon sugar

5 Tablespoons minced scallions
   or chives

▶ **Seafood Filling:**
¾ pound sea scallops

¾ pound salmon fillet

¾ pound medium shrimp,
   shelled

court bouillon to cover (see
   page 25)

▶ **Sauce:**
2 Tablespoons butter

2 Tablespoons flour

2 cups heavy cream

2 cups reserved court bouillon

¾ cup freshly grated Parmesan
   cheese

8 ounces mozzarella, thinly
   sliced

• Cook lasagne noodles and immediately transfer to a bowl of cold water with a splash of olive oil in it. When cooled, lay noodles between dampened towels.

Filling:

• Combine ricotta, egg yolks, Parmesan cheese, nutmeg, salt, pepper, sugar and scallions in a bowl and blend. Set aside.

• Cut scallops in half or in quarters, if preferred.

• Poach scallops, salmon and shrimp about 3-5 minutes in court bouillon. Remove seafood and let cool in colander.

• Strain bouillon and reserve 2 cups.

Sauce:

• Melt the butter in a saucepan and whisk in flour to make a roux. Cook for 3-4 minutes.

• Whisk in the cream and bring sauce to a boil to thicken.

• Add the 2 cups of court bouillon and cook the sauce over medium heat until it is reduced to 3 cups.

• To assemble, preheat oven to 350°, and butter a 13x9" lasagne pan.

• Spoon in a layer of the sauce, and cover with a layer of pasta. Do not overlap the noodles.

• Layer as follows:

seafood

cheese filling

sauce

pasta

• Finish with a layer of sauce.

• Sprinkle with Parmesan cheese and lay mozzarella slices over the top.

• Bake for 45 minutes. Let rest for 15 minutes before serving.

• Yield: 8-10 portions

MANCHESTER-BY-THE-SEA
This busy land-locked harbor town sheltered by wooded hills was incorporated in 1645. Legend has it that sea serpents frolicked just off the coast. Could be! In 1980, a 450-pound, 12-foot long squid with 16-foot tentacles washed ashore very near the harbor.

Linguine and Lobster

3 garlic cloves, minced

1 Tablespoon freshly chopped parsley

1 onion, peeled and minced

⅓ cup olive oil

4 medium tomatoes, peeled, seeded, and chopped

4-6 basil leaves, chopped

1 teaspoon red pepper flakes

½ teaspoon salt

1 teaspoon freshly ground black pepper

½ cup white wine

1 pound cooked lobster meat, cut into chunks

1 pound linguine

¼ cup freshly grated Parmesan cheese

- In a skillet, sauté garlic, parsley and onion in olive oil.

- Add the tomatoes, basil, seasonings and wine. Cook 5 minutes.

- Add lobster chunks and simmer until lobster is heated through.

- Cook the linguine al dente. Drain.

- Return pasta to the pot and add some of the sauce. Toss well to coat the linguine.

- Serve the linguine on separate warm plates. Spoon the sauce and lobster over each serving. Sprinkle with Parmesan cheese.

- Yield: 4 portions

Linguine with Chicken Livers in Brandy

1 pound linguine

¾ pound chicken livers

1 cup milk

¼ pound unsmoked bacon, chopped

2 cloves garlic, sliced

1 medium onion, peeled and sliced

¼ cup flour

½ cup chicken broth

1 teaspoon grated nutmeg

1 Tablespoon freshly chopped parsley

½ teaspoon thyme

¼ cup brandy

¼ cup butter

¼ cup olive oil

½ cup sliced mushrooms

grated Parmesan cheese

- Soak chicken livers in milk.

- Melt the butter with the olive oil. Add the onions, mushrooms, and garlic and sauté until golden. Remove from the skillet.

- Place the diced bacon in the skillet and cook until crisp. Remove and drain the bacon; drain the chicken livers and coat them with flour. Cook quickly in the skillet. Return the mushrooms, garlic, onions and bacon to the pan. Add the seasonings. Heat thoroughly and add the brandy. Light the brandy and turn the skillet gently so the flame will cover the contents.

- Add the chicken broth and simmer for 10 minutes. Remove from heat. Cook the noodles al dente and drain. Toss the noodles quickly in the skillet until the pasta is well-coated. Serve with Parmesan cheese.

- Yield 4 portions

Angel Hair Pasta with Shrimp and Feta Cheese

▶ **Sauce:**

¼ cup olive oil

½ cup chopped scallions

4 large tomatoes, peeled, seeded, and diced

⅓ cup dry white wine

2 cloves garlic, minced

½ teaspoon oregano

½ cup chopped fresh parsley

salt

freshly ground black pepper

¼ cup olive oil

3 pounds fresh shrimp, shelled and deveined

2 Tablespoons lemon juice

salt

freshly ground black pepper

4 tomatoes, peeled and sliced

¼ pound feta cheese, crumbled

2 packages fresh angel hair pasta

chopped fresh parsley

chopped pitted black olives

- In a heavy skillet, heat the oil and sauté scallions over medium heat until soft. Add remaining sauce ingredients and simmer, uncovered, until the sauce thickens, about 20 minutes. Stir occasionally.

- Preheat oven to 425°.

- In a large skillet, heat the oil and sauté shrimp until they are just pink, about 1 minute or less. Toss the shrimp with lemon juice. Spread sauce evenly on the bottom of a shallow casserole. Layer shrimp on top of sauce. Season with salt and pepper. Place sliced tomatoes on top of shrimp. Sprinkle feta cheese on top of tomatoes.

- Bake for 10 minutes, or until the cheese is somewhat melted.

- Serve on a bed of angel hair pasta and garnish with a sprinkling of chopped parsley and olives.

- Yield: 4-6 portions

Lemon Rice

½ cup unsalted butter

½ cup chopped onion

2 cloves garlic, minced

2 cups converted rice

3½ cups chicken stock

grated rind of a lemon

2 teaspoons dill weed

- Melt butter in a skillet and sauté onion and garlic until tender.

- Add rice and stir for 2 minutes, until coated with butter.

- Heat chicken stock and add to onion-rice mixture.

- Cook over medium heat until all the liquid has evaporated.

- Remove from heat and stir in lemon rind and dill weed.

- Yield: 6 portions

Parmesan Cheese Risotto

5 cups chicken broth

½ cup dry white wine

2 Tablespoons sweet butter

1 Tablespoon olive oil

2 large chopped onions

1½ cups Arborio, or other hard rice, brown or white

1 Tablespoon sweet butter

¾ cup freshly grated Parmesan cheese

1 Tablespoon freshly chopped parsley

½-1 tube crushed saffron threads

- Bring chicken broth to a steady simmer in a saucepan.

- Using a heavy 4-quart Dutch oven or large saucepan, heat the butter and oil over moderate heat. Add onions and sauté until soft. Add the rice using a wooden spoon and stir for 1 minute or until rice is well coated. Add the wine and stir until completely absorbed.

- Begin adding the simmering broth ½ cup at a time, stirring frequently. Allow each addition to be absorbed before adding the next ½ cup of broth. Reserve ¼ cup to be added at the end.

- When the rice is tender, but still firm, add reserved broth, turn off heat, and add the last teaspoon of butter, Parmesan cheese, saffron and parsley.

- Stir vigorously and serve at once.

- Yield: 4-6 portions

Spiced Basmati Rice

12 ounces basmati rice

3 Tablespoons vegetable oil

2 ounces finely chopped onion

1 garlic clove, minced

½ fresh hot green chili, finely chopped

¼ teaspoon ground cumin seeds

¼ teaspoon ground coriander seeds

1 teaspoon salt

2 cups chicken stock

- Rinse rice several times under cold running water. Leave to drain for 20 minutes.

- Heat oil in a heavy pan. Add onion and fry until brown. Add rice, chili, garlic, spices and salt. Stir gently to coat the rice for 2-3 minutes.

- Add stock and return to a boil.

- Cover with a tightly fitting lid and reduce heat to very low. Cook 25 minutes until all the water is absorbed.

- Yield: 4-6 portions

Moroccan Couscous Pilaf

1 leek, white part only, sliced
4 Tablespoons butter
3 cups chicken stock
salt and pepper to taste
2 carrots, peeled and sliced
1 turnip, peeled and diced
2 sweet red peppers, seeded and diced
1 19-ounce can chick peas, drained
1 14-ounce package couscous

- Sauté the leeks in butter until soft.
- Add chicken stock, salt and pepper and bring to a boil.
- Add carrots and turnip and cook for 8 minutes. Add red pepper, chick peas, and zucchini and cook for 2 minutes longer.
- Add couscous and stir. Cover and cook for 5 minutes. If the mixture seems dry, add more chicken stock. Serve hot.
- Yield: 6-8 portions

Risotto Florentine

2 pounds fresh spinach
2 medium onions, thinly sliced
3 garlic cloves, minced
1 cup uncooked rice
½ cup olive oil
2 Tablespoons tomato sauce
2 bay leaves
2 cups beef broth, heated
salt and pepper to taste

- Wash, stem and dry spinach.
- Sauté onions, garlic and rice in olive oil until golden. Add tomato sauce and stir.
- Add spinach, bay leaves and hot broth. Cover and simmer 15 minutes.
- Season to taste.
- Yield: 8 portions

NOTE: This is delicious hot or cold.

Orange Rice with Currants, Zucchini and Red Onion

1 cup water
1 cup orange juice
1 cup long grain rice
2 teaspoons chicken bouillon granules
4 Tablespoons currants
1 cup chopped zucchini
2 thick slices red onion, chopped
2 Tablespoons butter

- In a saucepan, bring water, juice, bouillon, currants, zucchini, onion, and butter to a boil.
- Add rice and stir. Reduce to simmer. Cover and cook 20 minutes. Let rest 5 minutes away from heat.
- Yield: 6 portions

NOTE: Wonderful served with marinated beef or chicken.

Vegetables

Artichoke Hearts au Gratin

2 packages frozen artichoke
    hearts
¼ cup butter or margarine
½ teaspoon salt
dash of pepper
½ teaspoon onion powder
¼ teaspoon dried mustard
⅓ cup flour
1½ cups milk
1 egg, slightly beaten
½ cup shredded cheddar and/or
    Swiss cheese
1 Tablespoon fine dry
    breadcrumbs
dash of paprika

- Cook and drain artichoke hearts, reserving ¼-½ cup of liquid.
- Melt butter and stir in seasonings and flour. Gradually add artichoke liquid and milk, stirring constantly. Cook over low heat until creamy and thickened.
- Remove from heat and gradually stir in egg and half of the cheese. Blend well.
- Preheat oven to 450°.
- Place artichokes in a shallow pan. Pour on sauce. Sprinkle remaining cheese, crumbs and paprika on top. Bake 15 minutes.
- Yield: 6 servings

New England Baked Beans

1 pound dried beans (kidney,
    yellow eye, navy, pea, etc.)
water to cover
2-3 slices bacon, chopped or 2
    Tablespoons olive oil
1 medium onion, peeled and
    chopped
1 clove garlic, minced
1 teaspoon dry mustard
½ teaspoon ground cloves
½ cup molasses, optional

▶ Optional additions:

pickle relish, salsa, chili sauce
    (for spicier "southern" New
    England beans), chopped
    tomatoes, chopped green
    pepper or chopped apple

- The night before, carefully pick over and rinse the beans, place them in a container, cover with water, and soak overnight.
- The next morning, place 2 tablespoons olive oil in the bottom of a bean pot with the onion, garlic, beans with water, spices and molasses.
- Keep beans covered with additional water throughout the baking process.
- Place bean pot in a 225° oven and bake 6-8 hours.
- Yield: 8-10 portions

New Englanders prize recipes for baked beans. One Fourth of July tradition includes a picnic of ham, baked beans, coleslaw and ice cream followed by a spirited band concert of patriotic music on the town green. Danvers centenarian Aunt Margaret Hutchinson says the success of her recipe depends on cooking the beans "just until their skins wrinkle when you blow on them."

Microwaved Beets with Currant Sauce

1 pound beets, well scrubbed
   and sliced
½ cup water
2 Tablespoons orange juice
⅛ teaspoon ground nutmeg
½ cup currant jelly
yogurt
mint sprigs

- In a 2-quart microwave casserole, combine beets and water. Microwave, covered, on high 6 minutes, stirring once. Drain.

- Add orange juice and nutmeg. Microwave, covered, on high 5-8 minutes, or until tender, stirring once.

- Put jelly in a glass measuring cup. Cook uncovered on high 1-2 minutes, or until it melts. Pour over beets.

- Microwave, uncovered, on high 1-2 minutes, or until heated through. Transfer beets and syrup to a serving dish. Top with dollops of yogurt. Garnish with sprigs of mint.

- Yield: 4 portions

Broccoli with Cashew Nuts

1 large bunch broccoli, broken
   into florets
2 Tablespoons butter
2 Tablespoons onion, minced or
   finely chopped
1½ cups sour cream
2 teaspoons sugar
1 teaspoon vinegar
½ teaspoon poppy seeds
¼ teaspoon salt
½ teaspoon paprika
1 cup cashew nuts, coarsely
   chopped

- Cook broccoli until tender and drain.

- Melt butter and cook onion until soft and pale yellow. Remove from heat, and stir in sour cream, sugar, vinegar and seasonings.

- Arrange broccoli in the bottom of a casserole, not more than a double layer, and pour sauce on top. Sprinkle with cashews.

- Heat casserole thoroughly in preheated 350° oven.

- Yield: 4 portions

Braised Cabbage

5 strips bacon, diced
1 large onion, finely sliced
1 medium head cabbage, chopped
1 clove garlic, minced
1 teaspoon summer savory
3 Tablespoons butter
1 Tablespoon flour
1 cup beef or chicken stock
½ cup white wine
4 fresh tomatoes, quartered
1 teaspoon tomato purée
1 Tablespoon freshly chopped parsley
sour cream
Parmesan cheese

- In a large skillet, sauté bacon and onions until soft.
- Add chopped cabbage, garlic, herbs, butter and flour, stir lightly to blend.
- Add stock and white wine. Cover and simmer until the cabbage is almost tender.
- Add tomatoes and the tomato purée. Simmer until everything is tender.
- Put into a serving dish, garnish with a dollop of sour cream and sprinkle with parsley.
- Serve Parmesan cheese separately.
- Yield: 6-8 portions

Spiced Red Cabbage

1½ pounds red cabbage, thinly sliced
1 large onion, thinly sliced
1 bay leaf
¼ teaspoon dried thyme
½ teaspoon ground allspice
2 garlic cloves, minced
3 Tablespoons olive oil
¾ cup applesauce
1 cup dry red wine
⅓ cup red wine vinegar
2 Tablespoons sugar
1 teaspoon cinnamon
½ cup apple cider
½ cup golden raisins
salt and pepper to taste

- Blanch sliced cabbage in a large kettle of boiling salted water for 2 minutes and drain.
- In the clean kettle, sauté the onion, bay leaf, thyme, allspice and garlic in olive oil over low heat until the onion is softened.
- Add cabbage, applesauce, wine, vinegar, sugar, cinnamon and cider.
- Bring to a boil and simmer, covered, for 30 minutes.
- Add raisins and simmer, uncovered, stirring occasionally for 10 minutes, or until most of the liquid is gone. Discard the bay leaf.
- Season to taste.
- Yield: 4-6 portions

Carrots with Lemon and Honey

6 cups sliced carrots
¼ cup butter, melted
3 teaspoons honey
½ teaspoon salt
½ teaspoon pepper
2 Tablespoons lemon juice
¼ teaspoon grated lemon peel
½ cup chopped walnuts or
  slivered almonds

- Cook carrots until tender. Drain.
- Mix the remainder of the ingredients. Pour over carrots and toss.
- Yield 6-8 portions

In the 1840s more than a million dollars worth of onions were grown in Danvers and shipped each year from Salem seaports to cities all along the east coast. Hence, the town earned the nickname "Oniontown." Equally famous is a type of carrot called "Danvers half-longs," allegedly named because the rocky soil interfered with the full growth of the vegetable!

Roasted Onions with Sage

2 pounds small yellow onions,
  peeled with stems left on
salt and freshly ground pepper
  to taste
2 Tablespoons olive oil
2 Tablespoons balsamic vinegar
1 teaspoon dried sage or a
  handful of fresh sage leaves,
  coarsely chopped

- Preheat oven to 400°.
- Cut onions into quarters but not all the way through the stems, so the onions stay together. Place them in a baking dish. Sprinkle with salt, pepper, oil, vinegar and sage. Toss gently to coat thoroughly.
- Cover baking dish with foil and bake 1½-2 hours, or until tender when pierced. Halfway through the baking, uncover and carefully turn each onion. Recover for last half of the baking time.
- Yield: 4-6 portions

Tomatoes Stuffed with Zucchini Pesto

6 large tomatoes
6 medium zucchini
½ cup pesto
⅓-½ cup freshly grated
  Parmesan cheese

- Preheat oven to 300°.
- Cut tops from tomatoes. Scoop out pulp and let tomatoes drain inverted for 30 minutes.
- Grate zucchini. Par boil zucchini for a few minutes and drain well.
- Mix zucchini with pesto and spoon into the tomatoes. Sprinkle with grated cheese.
- Bake 30 minutes.
- Yield: 6 portions

Green Beans with Basil and Orange

12 ounces whole green beans or Italian green beans, cleaned

salt and pepper to taste

2 Tablespoons water

2 teaspoons fresh basil or ½ teaspoon dried basil, crushed

1 teaspoon water

1 teaspoon finely grated orange peel

2 Tablespoons mayonnaise

2 Tablespoons plain low-fat yogurt

orange slices and basil sprigs for garnish

- Combine beans and 2 tablespoons water in 1½-quart microwave casserole. Cook covered on high for 6 minutes, or until tender, stirring once. Sprinkle with salt and pepper and set aside.

- In a glass measuring cup, combine cut fresh or dried basil, 1 teaspoon water, and orange peel. Cook uncovered on high for 30 seconds.

- Blend with mayonnaise and yogurt and stir until smooth.

- Drain beans. Place on a serving dish. Garnish with orange slices and basil sprigs.

- Serve accompanied by the mayonnaise-yogurt mixture.

- Yield: 4 portions

Minted Green Beans and Peas

1 pound slender green beans, ends snipped

1 pound sugar snap peas or snow peas, trimmed

1 10-ounce package frozen baby peas

1 small lemon, grated

6 Tablespoons butter or margarine

½ teaspoon sugar

2 Tablespoons minced fresh mint

mint sprigs for garnish

- Bring 3 quarts of water to a boil. Add beans to the pan and simmer until bright green and tender, about 3 minutes. Drain beans and rinse under cold running water. Drain again.

- Bring more water to a boil and cook the sugar snap peas until bright green and tender, about 3 minutes (snow peas should be cooked only about 1 minute). Drain and rinse under cold running water. Repeat with the frozen peas, simmering about 1 minute.

- Remove and cut lemon zest into ⅛" julienne strips.

- Heat butter in a skillet and add the vegetables and sugar. Sauté until hot, about 4 minutes.

- Transfer to a warm serving bowl. Toss vegetables with lemon zest and mint. Adjust seasonings to taste and garnish with mint sprigs. Serve immediately.

- Yield: 8-10 portions

Minted Eggplant

3 Tablespoons vegetable oil
2 Tablespoons water
1 large onion, peeled and sliced
2 medium eggplants, peeled
1 cup low-fat plain yogurt
3 Tablespoons chopped fresh
   mint
2 cloves garlic, minced
¼ teaspoon salt
freshly ground pepper to taste
dash of paprika

- Heat 1 teaspoon each of oil and water over medium heat. Cook the sliced onion until softened and remove the onion.

- Cut eggplant into ¼" slices. Brush remaining oil over the eggplant slices. In a pan over medium heat, cook eggplant, a few slices at a time, turning once until tender, about 10 minutes.

- In an ungreased baking dish, arrange slices of eggplant alternating with onion in an overlapping fashion.

- Combine yogurt, fresh mint, garlic, salt and pepper. Pour this mixture over the eggplant slices. Sprinkle with paprika. Bake in a preheated 350° oven until hot and bubbly, about 15 minutes.

- Yield: 6 portions

NOTE: If mint is not available, use parsley.

Grandma Mariano's Escarole and White Cannellini Beans

¼ cup olive oil
3-4 cloves garlic, minced
¼ pound lean salt pork, cubed
   or sliced
1 head green escarole, trimmed
¼ cup chicken stock
16-ounce can cannellini beans
salt and freshly ground black
   pepper to taste
crushed hot red pepper flakes
   to taste

- In a 2-quart saucepan, sauté garlic and salt pork in olive oil until lightly browned.

- Add escarole and chicken stock and cook over medium-high heat until greens soften, about 10 minutes. Do not overcook.

- Add beans and reduce heat to simmer, for 4-5 minutes.

- Add salt and pepper to taste.

- Yield: 4-6 portions

NOTE: Wonderful with rice on a cold winter day.

Warmed Endive Vinaigrette

4 endive
9 Tablespoons olive oil
2 Tablespoons white wine
   vinegar
2 cloves garlic, minced
2 teaspoons Dijon mustard
⅛ teaspoon salt
freshly ground pepper to taste

- Steam endive whole for 10 minutes. While hot, roll them in a marinade made of all the other ingredients. The marinade can be done ahead. Reheat in the microwave before serving.
- Serve warm.
- Yield: 4 portions

Leeks Vinaigrette

8 leeks, about 1-1½" diameter
8 Tablespoons olive or salad oil
4 Tablespoons red wine vinegar
2 teaspoons Dijon mustard
½ teaspoon salt
2 dashes freshly ground pepper
4 Tablespoons chopped fresh
   parsley

- Trim about 3" off the green top of the leeks, making sure they are of equal length. Slit the leeks down one side to within 1" of the base. Carefully wash the leeks.
- Place leeks in a large pan; cover with water and bring to a boil. Cook until tender, about 10-12 minutes.
- Combine oil, vinegar, mustard, salt and pepper. Whisk until combined. While the leeks are still warm, cover with vinaigrette. Recipe may be made ahead to this point. Bring to room temperature before serving.
- Just before serving, sprinkle with parsley.
- Yield: 4 portions

Microwaved Corn on the Cob

fresh corn with husks
salt and pepper to taste
butter

- Rinse corn with husks intact in cold water.
- Put corn in the microwave and cook on high for 10 minutes.
- Remove and serve with butter, salt and pepper to taste.
- The husks and silk will easily peel away.

Mushroom Casserole

1½ pounds fresh mushrooms

1 clove garlic, minced

1 yellow onion, peeled and chopped

chopped parsley

1 teaspoon salt

½ teaspoon pepper

⅓ cup olive oil

2 Tablespoons wine vinegar

3 ounces butter or margarine

½ cup breadcrumbs

1 Tablespoon Parmesan cheese

- Preheat oven to 350°.
- Mix all the ingredients together and place in a casserole dish.
- Bake, uncovered, 25-30 minutes, stirring once or twice during the cooking process.
- Yield: 6-8 portions

Potatoes Baked in Parchment

▶ per person:

4 small red potatoes

4 cloves garlic, unpeeled

sprig of rosemary or ⅛ to ¼ teaspoon dried rosemary

several sprigs of thyme or ⅛ to ¼ teaspoon dried thyme

1 Tablespoon virgin olive oil

salt and pepper to taste

- If the potatoes are very small (1" across) leave whole; if not, cut into inch-size pieces, leaving skins on.
- Preheat oven to 400°. If parchment paper is not available, this recipe works equally well with foil.
- Have a piece large enough to hold a single portion of potatoes.
- Lay on the potatoes, garlic, herbs, salt and pepper and drizzle with olive oil. Seal the parchment or foil to make a large roomy pouch in which to steam the potatoes.
- Bake 40-50 minutes.
- Serve at once in a pre-heated dish or in the parchment at the table.
- Yield: 1 portion

Potatoes with Sesame Seeds

2 pounds potatoes
6 Tablespoons oil
2 teaspoons cumin seeds
2 teaspoons black mustard seeds
2 Tablespoons sesame seeds
½ teaspoon cayenne pepper
1 Tablespoon lemon juice

- Boil potatoes in their skins, about 20 minutes. Drain and set aside to cool for 3-4 hours.
- Dice the potatoes into 1" cubes.
- Heat oil in a large frying pan. When hot, add the seeds. As soon as they pop, add the potatoes. Stir-fry for 5-6 minutes.
- Add salt, lemon juice, and cayenne pepper.
- Stir again for 5 minutes, until golden brown.
- Yield: 6 portions

Garlic Roasted Potatoes

3 pounds medium-sized red potatoes, cut into ½" slices
¼ cup olive oil
6-8 cloves garlic, chopped
freshly ground black pepper
1 Tablespoon freshly chopped parsley
1 teaspoon lemon peel, cut in thin strips, yellow only
½ teaspoon salt

- Preheat oven to 375°.
- In a large shallow glass baking dish, toss together the potatoes with oil, garlic and pepper.
- Bake, turning several times, for 1 hour, or until potatoes are golden and tender.
- Place in a serving dish. Add parsley, lemon peel, salt and more pepper, if desired.
- Toss lightly.
- Serve warm or at room temperature.
- Yield: 8 portions

The Great Potato Cake with Goat Cheese and Leeks

4 large white thin-skinned potatoes

8 ounces goat cheese

2 Tablespoons sour cream

2 Tablespoons chopped fresh basil, or 2 teaspoons dried

1 Tablespoon chopped fresh rosemary or 1 teaspoon dried

3 cloves garlic, slivered

¼ teaspoon kosher salt

⅛ teaspoon freshly ground black pepper

½ cup pure olive oil

¼ cup leeks, whites only, finely chopped

4 Tablespoons unsalted butter

- Rinse and peel the potatoes.

- Using the shredding blade in a food processor, cut potatoes into matchstick-sized pieces.

- In a separate bowl, combine goat cheese, sour cream, basil, rosemary, garlic, salt and pepper.

- In a skillet, heat the olive oil until just smoking and add enough potato sticks to cover the bottom of the pan. Place the goat cheese mixture in the center, spreading out toward the edges. Sprinkle leeks on top of the cheese. Place dabs of butter around the outside of the goat cheese layer.

- Cover with additional potatoes.

- Press another pan of same size or a plate on top.

- Cook for approximately 6 minutes, over medium heat, until the bottom is browned and crusty and the "cake" is stuck together.

- Cut in wedges, flip over, and cook until the other side is crusty and golden.

- Yield: 8 portions

Stir-Fry Snow Peas

2 Tablespoons peanut oil

2 ½" slices ginger root, finely chopped

1 clove garlic, chopped

2 cans sliced water chestnuts

½ pound snow peas, trimmed

½ teaspoon sugar

½ teaspoon salt

1 Tablespoon dry sherry

3 Tablespoons dry roasted unsalted peanuts or cashews

- Heat oil in a wok or frying pan until very hot.

- Add the ginger and garlic and stir-fry for 1 minute.

- Add water chestnuts and stir-fry for 3 minutes. Add snow peas and stir-fry for 3 more minutes. Sprinkle with sugar, salt and sherry and toss thoroughly.

- Garnish with peanuts or cashews and serve.

- Yield: 4 portions

Stir-Fry Ratatouille

4 Tablespoons vegetable oil
1 medium onion, peeled and sliced
2 cloves garlic, minced
8 medium mushrooms, halved
1 small sweet red or yellow pepper, cubed
2 cups unpeeled eggplant
1 small zucchini, sliced
2 tomatoes, cut in wedges
½ teaspoon thyme
½ teaspoon basil
salt and pepper to taste

- In a skillet, heat half the oil over medium-high temperature. Sauté onion, garlic, mushrooms, sweet peppers and stir until tender. Remove to a side dish.
- Heat the remaining oil. Add eggplant and zucchini and sauté until tender.
- Return onion, garlic, mushroom, pepper mixture to the skillet. Add tomatoes, thyme and basil.
- Cover and simmer 5 minutes. Add salt and pepper to taste.
- Yield: 6 portions

NOTE: Excellent hot or cold. Can also be covered with shredded cheese and placed under the broiler until the cheese melts.

Julienne of Curried Sweet Peppers

¼ cup olive oil
2 pounds sweet red and yellow peppers, halved and seeded
2 teaspoons curry
freshly ground pepper to taste

- Slice peppers into julienne strips.
- Heat oil in a large skillet or wok until hot.
- Add curry and stir.
- Add pepper strips and sauté 4-6 minutes, until tender but crisp.
- Season with pepper.
- Yield: 4-6 portions

Turnip and Apple Purée

1 small turnip, peeled and cubed
1 large apple, peeled, cored and cut into chunks
¼ cup low-fat plain yogurt
1 Tablespoon butter or margarine
pinch nutmeg
salt and pepper to taste

- Cook turnip 15-20 minutes, until nearly tender. Add apple and cook 5-10 minutes until both are tender. Drain.
- Place turnip and apple mixture in a food processor and blend until smooth. Add yogurt, butter, nutmeg, salt and pepper. Blend until combined.
- Yield: 2 portions

NOTE: Can be made ahead. Reheat in a saucepan over low heat or in a microwave oven. Recipe can be prepared a day in advance without yogurt. Add when reheating. Pear can be used instead of apple.

Stuffed Sweet Peppers Apulia

6 sweet yellow peppers

½ cup soft breadcrumbs

6-8 anchovy fillets, chopped

1-2 Tablespoons capers, chopped

2-3 Tablespoons pine nuts

2-3 Tablespoons seedless golden raisins

salt and pepper to taste

3 sprigs parsley, finely chopped

olive oil

- Wash peppers and char under a hot broiler until the skins blacken and blister. Rub off the thin outer skin and cut each pepper in half lengthwise, discarding seeds, cores, and stems.

- Preheat oven to 375°.

- Mix together breadcrumbs, anchovies, capers, pine nuts, raisins, salt, pepper and parsley. Add just enough oil to make a paste.

- Stuff a little of this mixture into each half pepper and arrange in a baking dish.

- Sprinkle with olive oil and bake 30 minutes.

- Yield: 4 portions

Butternut Squash with Cranberries and Apples

1½ pounds butternut squash, peeled

¼ cup brown sugar

¼ cup unsalted butter, softened

¼ cup sugar

1 cup cranberries

2 tart green apples, peeled, cored and sliced

¼ teaspoon cinnamon

freshly grated nutmeg

1 teaspoon sugar

- Bake or steam squash until tender. When cool, put pulp into a food processor. Process with brown sugar and butter.

- Cook apples in a saucepan with ⅛ cup sugar over moderate heat, stirring constantly until tender, 8-10 minutes.

- Cook cranberries in a saucepan with ⅛ cup sugar over low heat 3-5 minutes, or until the berries pop.

- Gently combine squash mixture, apples and cranberries. Spoon mixture into a buttered baking dish.

- Preheat oven to 350°.

- Combine cinnamon, nutmeg and sugar and sprinkle over mixture. Bake for 15-20 minutes, or until bubbly.

- Yield: 4 portions

Spaghetti Squash with Cheese

1 spaghetti squash,
about 4 pounds

2 Tablespoons butter or
margarine

¼ cup minced onion

¼ cup diced green pepper

¼ cup diced red pepper

½ teaspoon oregano

¼ teaspoon marjoram

¼ teaspoon basil

¼ teaspoon garlic, minced

2 cups shredded Monterey Jack
cheese

1 2¼-ounce can sliced black
olives

salt and pepper to taste

- Preheat oven to 350°.

- Pierce squash with fork in several places. Place on a baking sheet and bake 45 minutes. Turn and bake 45 minutes longer, or until soft when pierced with with a fork. (Squash may also be cooked in a microwave.)

- When the squash is cool enough to handle, cut in half and scoop out the seeds.

- Remove spaghetti-like strings found inside with a fork and reserve.

- Melt butter in a skillet. Sauté onion and peppers until tender.

- Add squash strands, oregano, marjoram, basil, garlic, cheese and olives. Season to taste with salt and pepper. Toss until cheese is evenly distributed.

- Place in 1½-quart casserole and return to oven until cheese is melted, about 10-15 minutes.

- Yield: 6 portions

Zucchini Potato Pie

1 pound potatoes, about 3
medium potatoes

2 Tablespoons butter

2 eggs

8 ounces mozzarella cheese,
finely diced

½ cup grated Parmesan cheese

1 large zucchini, grated

¼ cup minced onion

¼ teaspoon salt

¼ teaspoon pepper

2 Tablespoons fine dry
breadcrumbs

- Peel and cook potatoes in boiling salted water until tender, about 25 minutes. Drain and mash.

- Stir in the remaining ingredients, except breadcrumbs and 1 tablespoon butter.

- Generously butter a 9" pie plate and sprinkle with half the breadcrumbs.

- Fill with potato mixture. Smooth top and sprinkle with rest of crumbs and dot with remaining 1 tablespoon butter.

- Bake 30 minutes in a preheated 400° oven until pie is puffed and golden.

- Yield: 4 portions

NOTE: Pie may be prepared ahead and refrigerated up to 8 hours before baking. Increase baking time by 15 minutes.

Spinach Roulade

▶ **Filling:**

1½ pounds fresh mushrooms, finely chopped, reserving 3-4 large caps for garnish

1 large clove garlic, minced

4 Tablespoons butter or margarine

¼ cup dry sherry

4 Tablespoons fresh parsley, chopped

4 Tablespoons freshly chopped chives

½ teaspoon salt

sour cream to bind, about 1 Tablespoon

▶ **Roulade:**

2 packages fresh spinach, wilted in hot water and chopped, or 3 packages chopped frozen spinach, defrosted

4 eggs, separated

6 Tablespoons melted butter or margarine

½ teaspoon salt

pinch of nutmeg

⅓ cup grated Parmesan cheese

Filling:

- Sauté mushrooms and garlic in butter 3-4 minutes. Add sherry and continue cooking over medium heat, stirring constantly until all the liquid is evaporated.

- Add parsley, chives and salt. Remove from heat. Just before spreading on spinach roulade, bind with enough sour cream to hold the mixture together.

Roulade:

- Butter a 15x10" jelly roll pan generously and line with wax paper. Butter paper heavily.

- Cook or defrost spinach, and squeeze liquid out, by hand.

- In a bowl, combine spinach, butter, salt and nutmeg.

- Beat in egg yolks, one at a time.

- In a separate bowl, beat egg whites to the soft peak stage and fold into spinach. Spread mixture into prepared pan, smoothing out evenly to edges. Sprinkle with half the Parmesan cheese.

- Bake in a preheated 350° oven for 12 minutes, or until barely firm to the touch.

- To assemble, with a spatula, loosen all the edges of the roll from the pan.

- Place a sheet of waxed paper, buttered, with the butter side down on the roll.

- Invert on the counter and carefully remove the bottom paper, using a spatula if necessary to scrape loose any clinging areas.

- Spread mushroom mixture evenly over hot spinach roll.

- Roll up beginning at the short end, using paper to aid the rolling, if necessary.

- Ease the filled roulade onto a warm platter, seam side down.

- Sprinkle with remaining cheese. Garnish with reserved mushroom caps, lightly sautéed. Keep warm on a hot tray or in a low oven. Can be made ahead. Reheat on a serving dish in 200° oven for 20-30 minutes.

- Yield: 6-8 portions

NOTE: Serve with sautéed cherry tomatoes and a green salad for a luncheon dish. Also good for a buffet.

Vegetable Curry

12 ounces potatoes

1 large eggplant

4 ounces peeled tomatoes

1 ounce fresh garlic, peeled

2 ounces fresh ginger, peeled

¼ cup cooking oil

½ teaspoon cumin seeds

½ teaspoon black or white mustard seeds

½ teaspoon ground turmeric

1 teaspoon ground cardamom

½ teaspoon ground coriander

1½ teaspoons salt

8 jalapeño chilies

6 ounces frozen peas or broad beans, thawed

1½ cups water

1 Tablespoon chopped fresh coriander leaves (cilantro)

- Peel potatoes and cut into 1" cubes. Cut unpeeled eggplant into 1" cubes.

- Place tomatoes, garlic and ginger into a blender and blend to a thickish paste.

- Heat oil to high temperature in a large saucepan. Add cumin and mustard seeds and cook a few seconds.

- Add tomato, ginger and garlic paste and all other ingredients except fresh coriander leaves. Stir continuously and cook about 5 minutes.

- Add the water, bring to a boil and simmer gently for about 30 minutes.

- Place in a serving dish and garnish with fresh coriander.

- Yield: 4 portions

NOTE: This recipe makes a hot curry. You can reduce the number of chilies, as you prefer.

Summer Vegetable Platter

1 large green pepper, thinly sliced

1 sweet red pepper, thinly sliced

1 sweet yellow pepper, thinly sliced

3 medium zucchini, and/or summer squash, sliced

1 medium eggplant, quartered and sliced

3 large white and Bermuda onions, sliced

⅔ cup olive oil

salt and pepper

1-2 cloves garlic, minced

⅓ cup Greek style black olives, halved

- Lightly oil a shallow baking dish and arrange vegetables in neat rows.

- Pour on remaining olive oil and sprinkle with salt, pepper and garlic.

- Push the olive halves between the rows of vegetables.

- Bake in a preheated 400° oven for 30 minutes.

- If serving cold, you may want to sprinkle with vinegar.

- Yield: 6 portions

Breads

Bolton Apple Muffins

1¾ cups flour
1¼ cups sugar
1 teaspoon baking soda
1 teaspoon cinnamon
½ teaspoon salt
½ teaspoon cloves
⅛ teaspoon nutmeg
1 cup chopped apple
⅔ cup raisins
½ cup vegetable oil
2 eggs
½ cup chopped walnuts

- Preheat oven to 325°.
- Grease and flour muffin tins.
- Sift together dry ingredients. Mix in apples, raisins, oil and eggs. Blend in nuts.
- Place 2 tablespoons of batter in each muffin cup.
- Bake 30 minutes. Remove from cups. Store in an airtight container.
- Yield: 24 muffins

Apricot Cream Cheese Bread

1 cup dried apricots, chopped
½ cup golden raisins
4 Tablespoons butter, softened
½ cup firmly packed brown sugar
½ cup sugar
1 large egg
2 cups flour
2 teaspoons baking powder
½ teaspoon baking soda
¾ cup orange juice
½ cup chopped walnuts
6 ounces cream cheese
⅓ cup sugar
1 egg
1 Tablespoon grated orange rind

- Preheat oven to 350°. Grease and flour a 9x5" loaf pan.
- Soak apricots and raisins for 30 minutes in boiling water to cover.
- Cream butter with sugars. Add egg.
- Sift flour, baking powder and soda. Add alternately to butter mixture with orange juice. Stir in fruits and nuts.
- In a separate bowl, beat cream cheese, sugar, egg and orange rind.
- Pour half of the batter into a loaf pan. Spread cream cheese mixture on top. Pour remaining batter on top.
- Bake 60 minutes. Cool 10 minutes in pan. Must be refrigerated to preserve.
- Yield: 1 loaf

Banana Bran Muffins

¾ cup unbleached white flour
½ cup whole-wheat flour
¼ cup sugar
1 Tablespoon baking powder
1½ cups whole bran cereal
¾ cup skim milk
1 cup mashed ripe banana
1 egg
¼ cup vegetable oil
½ cup chopped nuts, optional

- Preheat oven to 400°.
- In a small bowl, combine the flours, sugar, and baking powder. Set aside.
- In a large bowl, mix together the cereal, milk and banana. Let stand for 1-2 minutes until the cereal softens.
- Add the egg and the oil to the cereal mixture. Beat well with a spoon.
- Stir in the flour mixture and nuts until just combined.
- Divide the batter among 12 greased muffin cups.
- Bake the muffins for about 25 minutes, or until golden brown.
- Cool on rack.
- Yield: 12 muffins

Glorious Muffins

1¼ cups sugar
2¼ cups flour
1 Tablespoon cinnamon
2 teaspoons baking soda
½ teaspoon salt
½ cup coconut
½ cup raisins
2 cups grated carrots
1 apple, grated
8 ounces crushed pineapple, drained
½ cup pecans, chopped
3 eggs
1 cup vegetable oil
1 teaspoon vanilla

- Preheat oven to 350°.
- Sift flour, sugar, cinnamon, soda, and salt.
- Add coconut, raisins, carrots, apple, pineapple, and nuts.
- Beat eggs with oil. Add vanilla. Blend with fruit mixture.
- Spoon into muffin tins lined with paper. Fill generously.
- Bake 35 minutes.
- Yield: 24 muffins or 2 loaves

NOTE: Mixture may also be divided and baked in 2 loaf pans. Bake 50-60 minutes. Test with skewer before removing from oven.

Blueberry Brunch Cake

3 cups flour
2 teaspoons baking powder
1 teaspoon salt
1 cup vegetable oil
2 cups sugar
⅔ cup milk
4 eggs
2 teaspoons vanilla
4 cups blueberries

- Preheat oven to 350°.
- Combine flour, salt and baking powder in a large bowl. Add oil and sugar.
- Combine milk and eggs and add to ingredients. Add vanilla. Beat 3 minutes at medium speed.
- By hand, gently fold in berries. Pour into a greased bundt pan. Sprinkle sugar on top.
- Bake 55 minutes. May be frozen.
- Yield: 12 portions

Hawaiian Banana Bread

2 cups white sugar
1 cup butter at room
  temperature
6 ripe bananas, approximately 3
  generous cups
4 eggs, well-beaten
2½ cups flour
2 teaspoons baking soda
1 teaspoon salt

- Preheat oven to 350°.
- Cream together sugar and butter until light and fluffy. Add bananas and eggs. Beat well until well mixed.
- Sift dry ingredients 3 times. Blend with banana mixture. Do not overmix.
- Pour into 2 lightly greased loaf pans. Bake 45-60 minutes, until firm in center and the edges separate from pans.
- Cool on racks for 10 minutes before removing from pans. May be frozen.
- Yield: 2 loaves

Point Camp Cornbread

1 cup cornmeal
1 cup flour
½ cup sugar
1 Tablespoon baking powder
½ teaspoon nutmeg
1 teaspoon salt
1 large or 2 small eggs
1 cup fresh or evaporated milk
4 Tablespoons butter, melted
2 tart apples, unpeeled and
  diced

- Preheat oven to 450°.
- Mix dry ingredients. Set aside.
- Mix eggs with milk and melted butter.
- Add to dry ingredients.
- Add apples and stir gently.
- Pour mixture into greased 9" square pan. Lower oven to 425° and bake 25-30 minutes.
- Yield: 8-12 pieces

New England Blueberry Muffins

1¼ cups sugar, scant, plus a bit for muffin tops

½ cup butter

2 eggs, well beaten

2 cups flour

2 teaspoons baking powder

½ teaspoon salt

2½-3 cups fresh blueberries, or frozen, thawed and drained

½ cup milk

- Preheat oven to 375°.
- Cream butter and sugar until fluffy. Add eggs and blend well.
- Sift dry ingredients and add alternately with milk.
- Gently stir in blueberries by hand.
- Grease muffin tins thoroughly, including the top surface.
- Fill tins high. Sprinkle tops with sugar (can also use cinnamon-sugar).
- Bake 25-30 minutes until golden around the edges.
- Cool 30 minutes before removing from pan.
- Yield: 12 large muffins

Orange Date Muffins

1 orange

½ cup orange juice

½ cup chopped dates

4 ounces butter, softened

1 egg

1½ cups sifted flour

¾ cup sugar

1 teaspoon baking powder

pinch of salt

½ cup chopped walnuts, optional

- Preheat oven to 400°.
- Grate the rind of an orange. Then peel, seed and chop the flesh.
- Put in food processor, add ½ cup orange juice and dates. Pulse on and off a few times.
- Add butter and egg.
- Add flour, baking soda, salt and sugar. Mix well. Add nuts, if desired.
- Spoon into greased muffin tins.
- Bake 15-20 minutes.
- Yield: 14-16 muffins

Corn and Red Pepper Muffins

1 cup chopped red pepper

2 Tablespoons butter

1 cup flour

½ teaspoon salt

1½ teaspoons baking soda

½ teaspoon baking powder

1¼ cups cornmeal

¼ cup firmly packed brown
    sugar

1 egg

1 cup buttermilk

- Preheat oven to 400°. Line 12 muffin cups with muffin papers.
- Sauté red peppers in butter until soft. Set aside.
- Sift flour, salt, soda and baking powder. Stir in cornmeal and brown sugar.
- Beat together egg and buttermilk. Stir into flour mixture. Add red pepper.
- Spoon batter into muffin cups. Bake 15-20 minutes, or until tops begin to brown. Cool 10 minutes in the pan before removing.
- Yield: 12 muffins

Trade Winds Bread

3½ cups all-purpose flour

½ teaspoon baking soda

4 teaspoons baking powder

1 teaspoon kosher or coarse salt

⅛ teaspoon freshly grated
    nutmeg

½ teaspoon cinnamon

⅔ cup butter, at room
    temperature

1⅓ cups sugar

4 large eggs, at room
    temperature

2 cups mashed bananas, about 4
    fully ripened bananas

¾ cup chopped walnuts

1 cup diced apricots, tossed
    with a little flour to separate

⅓ cup minced crystallized
    ginger

- Preheat the oven to 350°.
- Sift together the first 6 ingredients, and set aside.
- In a large bowl, cream the butter and sugar.
- Add eggs 1 at a time, mixing until smooth.
- Beat in mashed bananas.
- At low speed, mix sifted ingredients gradually into banana mixture. Beat well.
- Fold in walnuts, apricots and ginger. Blend well.
- Divide batter between 2 greased loaf pans. Bake 45 minutes, or until a skewer tests clean.
- Cool 10 minutes before removing from pans. May be frozen.
- Yield: 2 loaves

Cranberry-Orange Bread

juice and grated rind of an
    orange
2 Tablespoons oil
1 egg
1 cup sugar
1½ cups whole raw cranberries
½ cup walnuts
2 cups flour
½ teaspoon salt
½ teaspoon baking soda
1½ teaspoons baking powder

- Preheat oven to 325°.
- Put the juice of an orange and the grated rind into a measuring cup. Add the oil. Fill the cup to ¾ with boiling water.
- Beat together the egg and sugar in a large bowl.
- Add cranberries and nuts.
- Add the orange mixture.
- Sift flour, salt, baking soda and baking powder. Add this to the bowl and stir well.
- Pour into 1 large or 2 small greased and floured loaf pans.
- Bake for about 60 minutes, or until the bread tests done. May be frozen.
- Yield: 1 large or 2 small loaves

Lemon Poppy Seed Teacake

½ cup butter
1 cup sugar
2 eggs
rind of a lemon
2 Tablespoons poppy seeds
1½ cups flour
½ teaspoon baking powder
½ teaspoon salt
½ cup milk
⅓ cup sugar
juice of a lemon
½ cup chopped walnuts,
    optional

- Preheat oven to 350°. Grease a loaf pan.
- Cream butter and 1 cup of sugar. Beat in eggs. Stir in lemon rind and poppy seeds.
- Combine dry ingredients and add alternately with milk to the butter mixture.
- Pour into a loaf pan and bake 45-50 minutes. Cool 15 minutes in the pan before removing. Finish cooling on a rack.
- Combine ⅓ cup sugar and lemon juice and spoon over warm loaf.
- Yield: 1 loaf

Autumn Pumpkin Bread

1½ cups sugar
1 teaspoon baking soda
¼ teaspoon baking powder
¾ teaspoon salt
½ teaspoon ground cloves
½ teaspoon cinnamon
½ teaspoon nutmeg
1⅔ cups flour
½ cup vegetable oil
½ cup water
1 cup canned pumpkin
2 eggs
½ cup chopped nuts
½ cup chopped dates or raisins

- Preheat oven to 325°.
- Sift together all the dry ingredients and place in a large bowl.
- Add the remaining ingredients in the order listed, mixing well.
- Grease a 9x5x3" loaf pan and spoon batter into the pan.
- Bake 75-90 minutes until bread pulls away from the sides of the pan and a toothpick inserted in the center pulls out clean.
- Cool on a wire rack and remove from pan. May be frozen.
- Yield: 1 loaf

NOTE: At Christmas, sliced candied cherries are a festive addition.

Harvest Squash Rolls

1 cup warm water, 110°
¾ cup sugar
2 packages active dry yeast
3 Tablespoons oil
2 teaspoons salt
1 cup cooked and puréed squash, acorn or butternut
½ cup non-fat dry milk
5 cups flour

- Combine warm water and sugar in a large bowl. Add yeast and let stand for 5 minutes.
- Add next 4 ingredients and beat at low speed.
- Gradually beat in 2 cups flour.
- Add remaining flour, and knead gently.
- Cover and let rise in a warm place until doubled in bulk.
- Punch down. Roll dough to 1" thickness and then with oiled hands shape into small balls about 1½" in diameter.
- Place rolls in 8x10" baking pan, just touching one another.
- Cover and let rise until doubled.
- Bake in a preheated 400° oven for 20 minutes. May be frozen.
- Yield: 18 rolls

Cinnamon Rolls

2 Tablespoons active dry yeast

½ cup warm water, 105°-115°

⅓ cup plus ½ teaspoon sugar

4-5 cups flour

1 teaspoon salt

1 cup milk, scalded and cooled

⅓ cup vegetable oil

2 eggs, at room temperature

▶ Filling:

8 Tablespoons butter, softened

1 cup firmly packed brown
    sugar

½ cup white sugar

2 Tablespoons cinnamon

▶ Icing:

1 cup sifted powdered sugar

2-3 Tablespoons warm milk

1 teaspoon vanilla extract

- Dissolve yeast in water with ½ teaspoon sugar. Let stand 5 minutes.

- In a mixing bowl, combine 3 cups flour, the remaining sugar and salt. At slow speed, beat in milk, oil, eggs, and yeast mixture. Beat until well blended. Beat in additional flour until dough pulls away from the sides of the bowl.

- On a floured surface, knead dough until it is smooth and elastic. Place in a greased bowl. Let rise until doubled in bulk, about 1 hour.

Filling:

- Beat all the ingredients until smooth. Set aside.

- Grease 2 9" round cake pans.

- On a floured surface, roll out dough into an 18x10" rectangle. Spread with filling. Roll tightly from the long side. Cut into 14 1¼" slices.

- Place 1 roll cut side up in the center of each pan. Arrange remaining slices around center piece. Let it rise until double again, 30-40 minutes.

- Bake in a preheated 350° oven 25-30 minutes.

Icing:

- Beat ingredients together until smooth. Ice each roll. May be frozen.

- Yield: 14 rolls

Currant Scones

4½ **cups flour**

3 **Tablespoons sugar**

2 **teaspoons baking powder**

1 **teaspoon baking soda**

1 **cup unsalted butter, cut into small pieces**

1¼ **cups heavy cream**

1 **cup currants**

¼ **cup Marsala**

caraway seeds, optional

1 **egg**

1 **Tablespoon water**

- Mix together dry ingredients. Cut butter into flour mixture until crumbly. Add cream.

- Heat currants and Marsala to boiling. Simmer 2 minutes. Cool 10 minutes and add to dough. Wrap and refrigerate dough.

- Preheat oven to 350°.

- Roll dough into ¾" thickness and cut out scones with a heart-shaped cookie cutter. Place on parchment-lined cookie sheets and brush with egg and water wash.

- Bake for 15 minutes, or until golden. May be frozen.

- Yield: 36 scones

Murphy's Crusty White Bread

2 **envelopes active yeast**

2 **cups warm water, at least 110°**

2 **Tablespoons sugar**

1 **Tablespoon salt**

¼ **cup oil**

2 **cups all-purpose flour, then**

2-2¼ **cups flour, plus additional flour**

- Place water, sugar, and yeast in a bowl and set aside to rest, 10 minutes or so.

- Add salt, oil, and first 2 cups of flour to the yeast mixture. Beat for 3 minutes until thoroughly combined.

- Stir in flour, ¼ cup at a time, up to 2¼ cups more flour until you make a moderately stiff dough.

- Knead 8-10 minutes. Shape into a ball and place in a greased bowl. Cover with plastic wrap. Let rise 1-1½ hours or until double in size.

- Punch down and divide dough in half. Divide each half into thirds. Shape into balls (6 total). Place balls on cookie sheet. Let rest 10 minutes.

- Roll each ball into a 16" rope. Line up 3 ropes side by side, 1" apart on a greased cookie sheet. Braid loosely beginning in the middle and working to the ends. Tuck the ends under. Repeat for second loaf.

- Cover and let rise 40 minutes.

- Bake in a preheated 375° oven 30 minutes, or until brown. May not be frozen.

- Yield: 2 loaves

Dilly Bread

¼ cup warm water for proofing yeast

1 package active dry yeast

pinch of white sugar

1 cup large curd cottage cheese

1 Tablespoon butter

1 egg

1 Tablespoon minced onion

2 teaspoons dill seed or weed

1 teaspoon salt, plus some additional for top of bread

¼ teaspoon baking soda

2¼-2½ cups all-purpose flour

1 teaspoon melted butter for top of baked bread

- Proof yeast by combining it with warm water and a pinch of sugar. Set aside.

- Put cottage cheese and butter in a small saucepan. Heat, stirring occasionally, until butter is melted. Remove from heat and set aside until just warm.

- Beat egg in a large bowl. Stir in sugar, onion, dill, salt, baking soda, and warm cheese-butter mixture.

- Add yeast.

- Add 1 cup flour and beat with electric mixer for 1 minute.

- Gradually beat in enough flour to form a medium-stiff dough. Beat well.

- Grease a large bowl. Put dough in bowl and cover with a damp cloth. Set in a draft-free place until dough rises to double, about 1 hour.

- Grease a 2-quart casserole or loaf pan. Stir the dough well and put it in the casserole.

- Cover with a damp cloth again and set in a draft-free place so that the dough can rise until almost double in size, about 45 minutes.

- Place casserole in preheated 350° oven and bake until light golden brown, about 40-45 minutes. Bread will shrink slightly from the sides.

- Remove casserole from oven. Turn bread out onto rack and brush top with melted butter and sprinkle with salt. Cool.

- Yield: 1 loaf

Anadama Bread

1 package active dry yeast

½ cup warm water

2 Tablespoons butter

½ cup molasses

2 cups hot water

5 cups unbleached flour
(approximately)

½ cup cornmeal

2 teaspoons salt

- Dissolve yeast in warm water.
- Melt butter and molasses in hot water and cool to lukewarm. Stir in yeast mixture.
- Mix 4 cups flour with cornmeal and salt. Blend with yeast-molasses mixture 1 cup at a time. Continue to add flour until the dough is stiff.
- Turn out onto floured board and knead for 10 minutes, adding flour as necessary. When dough is smooth and elastic, place in well-buttered bowl, turning to coat all over with butter.
- Cover with cloth and set in warm place until doubled in bulk. Punch down and knead again for a minute or so, then form into 2 loaves.
- Put into 2 8" greased loaf pans. Cover and let rise again until dough has risen over tops of pans about ½".
- Bake loaves about 15 minutes in a preheated 400° oven, then reduce heat to 350° and bake for 25-30 minutes longer or until the loaves sound hollow when tapped. Let cool on racks. May be frozen.
- Yield: 2 loaves

Pumpernickel Bread

1 Tablespoon active dry yeast

1½ cups warm water, 105°-115°

½ cup molasses

2½ teaspoons caraway seeds

2 Tablespoons vegetable oil

2 cups rye flour

4 cups white or whole-wheat
flour

cornmeal

- Dissolve yeast in 1½ cups of warm water.
- Mix in the salt, molasses, caraway seeds, oil, and rye flour. Mix well.
- Add 2 cups white or whole-wheat flour.
- Knead in last 2 cups of flour by hand.
- Let rise in a greased bowl for 3 hours.
- Knead again and shape into 2 balls.
- Let rise again for 45 minutes on a baking sheet dusted with cornmeal.
- Bake in a preheated 450° oven 10 minutes, then lower to 350° and bake for 30-35 minutes, or until the bread sounds hollow when tapped. May be frozen.
- Yield: 2 loaves

Rockport, the eastern-most town of the Cape Ann communities, is known today for its charming and scenic views which attract artists and tourists from all points of the compass. From the records of the Sandy Bay Historical Society in Rockport comes this "true" story of the origin of Anadama Bread, that comforting cornmeal and molasses treat. It's unclear just when a local fisherman's wife named Anna daily prepared a breakfast of cornmeal mush and molasses for him. So sick was he of this boring concoction that he decided to add bread flour and yeast to the gruel and bake it, all the time muttering, "Anna, damn her"! Through the 1950s until his death in 1970, William and Melissa Smith trademarked, produced and sold Anadama Bread from Rockport.

Sesame Semolina Bread

1 package active dry yeast

2 cups lukewarm water

3 cups semolina flour

1 Tablespoon salt

2-3 cups unbleached, all-purpose flour

3-4 Tablespoons cornmeal

1 egg

2 Tablespoons sesame seeds

- Proof yeast in a mixing bowl and set aside. Stir to be certain the yeast is thoroughly dissolved.

- Add semolina flour and salt and mix thoroughly.

- Add 2 cups of the all-purpose flour and mix to form a sticky dough. Turn out onto a work surface and let rest. Wash and dry the mixing bowl.

- Knead the dough using the remaining all-purpose flour to keep it from sticking to your hands. Knead for approximately 10 minutes.

- Shape the dough into a ball and place in the clean bowl. Drizzle with vegetable or olive oil and turn it to coat well. Cover the bowl with a towel and set aside until it has tripled in bulk, 2 or more hours. Do not rush the dough by using heat, etc.

- Punch down the dough and turn out onto a lightly floured surface. Knead briefly, for about 5 minutes, and return it to the bowl. Cover and let rise until doubled.

- Punch down the dough and cut into thirds. Shape each third into a thin loaf. Sprinkle on a baking sheet the cornmeal and arrange the loaves, leaving as much room as possible. Cover and let rise again, about 30 minutes, until not quite doubled.

- Preheat the oven to 425°.

- Beat together the egg and 1 tablespoon of water. Brush the risen loaves well with the egg mixture, sprinkle with sesame seeds and make decorative cuts on the diagonal on top.

- Place baking sheet in the oven and reduce the heat to 375°. Bake for 30-40 minutes, or until the loaves are browned and sound hollow when thumped on the bottom.

- Yield: 3 loaves

Portuguese Bermuda Bread

1½ envelopes active dry yeast
¼ cup lukewarm water
6 cups bread flour
1¼ teaspoons salt
1¼ cups sugar
6 eggs, well beaten
2 Tablespoons gin
⅛ teaspoon lemon extract
½ teaspoon vanilla
8 Tablespoons butter

- Dissolve the yeast in the lukewarm water and set aside.
- Sift the flour and salt into a mixing bowl.
- Beat together the eggs, sugar, milk, gin, lemon, and vanilla. Add to the flour mixture, all at once.
- Add the yeast mixture to the batter and beat with a wooden spoon or use the dough hook of an electric mixer until the batter is smooth and elastic.
- Beat in the butter. Add a little flour, if necessary. The dough will be sticky soft.
- Place the dough in a greased bowl. Cover with a damp cloth and set in a warm place to rise, until it is double in size.
- Stir down the dough. Divide into 2 greased 1½-quart ovenproof bowls or 2 9x5x3" loaf pans.
- Bake in a preheated 350° oven 45-60 minutes. Turn out onto a rack and cool.
- When cool, may be frozen.
- Yield: 2 loaves

Lemon Croissants

8 Tablespoons butter, softened
1 cup cottage cheese
1 cup flour
¼ cup sugar
4 ounces cream cheese
1 Tablespoon grated lemon peel
powdered sugar

- Beat cottage cheese and butter together. Add flour. Shape into a circle and refrigerate 1 hour.
- Preheat oven to 350°.
- Beat together sugar, cream cheese, and lemon peel.
- Divide dough into thirds. Roll each piece into a 9" circle. Spread ⅓ of filling on each circle and cut into 8 triangles.
- Roll up beginning from the wide end. Sprinkle with powdered sugar. Bake for 20-25 minutes on a lightly greased cookie sheet. Cool on a rack. May be frozen.
- Yield: 24 croissants

Desserts

Exquisite Bread Pudding

1 loaf Italian bread, sliced into 1" thick pieces

⅓ cup raisins

⅓ cup Cointreau or Grand Marnier

½ cup butter, melted

¾ cup white sugar

½ cup light brown sugar

1½ Tablespoons cinnamon

½ teaspoon nutmeg

4 eggs

2 cups heavy cream

2 cups milk

1 teaspoon vanilla

3 Granny Smith apples, cored and sliced

whipped cream for garnish

- Soak raisins in liqueur.
- Butter a 13x9" baking dish. Arrange bread over the bottom of the dish. Sprinkle with raisins and pour liqueur evenly over the bread. Drizzle butter overall.
- Combine sugars, cinnamon, and nutmeg. Sprinkle ⅔ of the mixture over the bread.
- Lightly beat the eggs and add cream, milk and vanilla. Pour carefully into the baking pan.
- Let the mixture sit 15-20 minutes to allow the bread to absorb the liquid. Arrange apple slices on top and sprinkle with remaining sugars.
- Preheat oven to 350°.
- Place baking dish in a larger pan and fill halfway up the sides with water.
- Bake until well browned and risen. Serve warm with whipped cream.
- Yield: 8-10 portions

NOTE: This reheats well wrapped in foil.

Orange Pudding with Meringues

▶ **Meringues:**

4 egg whites

1 teaspoon vanilla

1 cup sugar

▶ **Pudding:**

1 quart milk

4 eggs, separated

1 large Tablespoon cornstarch

3 large Tablespoons sugar

1 teaspoon vanilla

5 oranges, peeled and segmented

- Preheat oven to 250°.
- To make meringues, beat egg whites stiff. Gradually add ⅔ of the sugar. Fold in the remainder of the sugar.
- Divide into 10 spoonfuls and bake 50 minutes on white paper on cookie sheets. Cool and set aside.
- To make the pudding, combine in a 2-quart double boiler, the milk, egg yolks, cornstarch and sugar. Cook over low heat until thickened. Remove from heat.
- Add vanilla and orange segments. Chill.
- Top with meringues and serve.
- Yield: 8-10 portions

Lemon Snow with Grand Marnier Sauce

▶ **Lemon snow:**
  ⅔ cup sugar
  1 envelope gelatin
  1½ cups boiling water
  ⅓ cup fresh lemon juice
  ½ Tablespoon finely grated lemon peel
  3 egg whites

▶ **Sauce:**
  3 egg yolks
  ¼ cup sugar
  ⅓ cup butter, melted
  3 Tablespoon fresh lemon juice
  3 Tablespoons Grand Marnier
  ½ cup heavy cream
  ½-1 teaspoon finely grated lemon zest

Snow:

- Combine sugar and gelatin in a large bowl. Add boiling water, stirring until gelatin dissolves. Stir in lemon juice and lemon peel.

- Chill mixture until syrupy. (Set bowl in a larger bowl partly filled with ice.)

- Beat egg whites until stiff. Add the syrup mixture, beating until it thickens slightly, approximately 5 minutes. Pour into a serving dish and chill at least 2 hours.

Sauce:

- Beat egg yolks until thick and light colored. Gradually beat in sugar, butter, lemon juice and Grand Marnier. Beat cream until thick and glossy, but not stiff. Fold into egg mixture along with lemon peel.

- Chill 3 hours.

- To serve, decorate lemon snow with mint leaves and pass Grand Marnier sauce in a separate bowl.

- Yield: 6 portions

Zabaglione Marnier Mary Ellen

10 egg yolks at room temperature
½ cup sugar
½ cup Marsala wine
2 Tablespoons Grand Marnier
½ cup dry white wine
1 pint fresh fruit (peaches, blueberries, raspberries)

- Beat egg yolks and sugar in a bowl with a whisk or electric mixer set at high speed, for 3-5 minutes, or until thick and light lemon-colored.

- Add Marsala, Grand Marnier and white wine, a tablespoon at a time.

- Beat well after each addition.

- Place bowl over a pan of simmering water and beat until the mixture has doubled in volume and has the consistency of custard.

- Serve the custard warm or cold over fresh fruit in a goblet.

- Yield: 8 portions

Chocolate Velvet

▶ **Topping:**
½ cup butter
¼ cup brown sugar
1 cup flour
½ cup pecans, chopped

▶ **Velvet:**
1 8-ounce package cream cheese
½ cup sugar, divided
1½ teaspoons vanilla
2 egg yolks, beaten
6 ounces semi-sweet chocolate, melted
2 egg whites
1 cup whipped cream
¾ cup pecans, chopped

- Preheat oven to 400°.
- Combine topping ingredients and spread in 13x9" dish. Bake for 15 minutes.
- Stir to break up the crumbs. Reserve ¾ cup for the topping. Press remaining crumbs into 9" round pan. Cool.
- Cream cream cheese, ¼ cup sugar, and vanilla. Add yolks and melted chocolate. Beat whites, adding the remaining sugar gradually.
- Fold into the chocolate mixture. Fold in the whipped cream and pecans. Pour into crust.
- Sprinkle with topping and freeze until firm.
- Yield: 8-12 portions

Old English Christmas Pudding

8 ounces granulated white sugar
8 ounces ground beef suet
8 ounces golden raisins
8 ounces muscat raisins
8 ounces currants
4 ounces mixed candied peel, finely chopped
8 ounces flour
8 ounces breadcrumbs
2 ounces almonds, finely chopped
grated rind of a lemon
4 eggs
½ teaspoon nutmeg
½ teaspoon salt
4 ounces milk
4-6 ounces brandy

- Mix all the dry ingredients together.
- Stir in well beaten eggs, milk and brandy.
- Turn mixture into 2 very well buttered medium-sized glass ovenproof bowls and steam for 6 hours.
- Puddings can be made ahead and frozen. If so, steam for 5 hours, freeze, steam 1 hour more before serving.
- Serve hot with hard sauce, brandy sauce, or whipped cream.
- Yield: 10-12 portions

Tiramisù

6 ounces semi-sweet chocolate

1 cup sugar

4 egg yolks

1½ teaspoons vanilla

8 ounces cream cheese, cut up

2 cups cold whipping cream

1 Tablespoon instant espresso powder diluted in 1¼ cups hot water, cooled

1 frozen pound cake, cut into 3½x1x½" strips, or lady fingers

- Finely chop chocolate. Set aside.
- Mix sugar and egg yolks in a processor for 30 seconds. Add vanilla. Process cream cheese until smooth. Chill 1 hour.
- Beat cream until stiff. Fold into cream cheese mixture. Cover and chill.
- Pour espresso into a shallow dish. Dip pound cake into espresso then place strips in a shallow 10-cup dish.
- Sprinkle with half the grated chocolate. Spread with cream cheese mixture and sprinkle the remaining chocolate. Cover and chill.
- Yield: 8 portions

English Trifle

▶ Pastry cream:

2 cups milk

4 Tablespoons cornstarch

4 egg yolks

⅔ cup sugar

1 teaspoon butter

1 teaspoon vanilla

pinch of salt

2 Tablespoon Kirschwasser

sponge cake, sliced

strawberries

blueberries

raspberries

Cointreau

whipped cream

- Bring 1½ cups milk to a boil and set aside.
- In remaining ½ cup of milk, dissolve the cornstarch.
- Add egg yolks and sugar and beat.
- Add to boiling milk, stirring constantly.
- Bring to a boil again and add butter, vanilla, salt and Kirschwasser. Cool.
- Place sliced cake in a glass bowl.
- Sprinkle with Cointreau.
- Spread pastry cream over cake and add fruit.
- Add a layer of whipped cream on top of fruit.
- Repeat layers ending with whipped cream. Decorate. Chill until ready to serve.
- Yield: 8-10 portions

Orange Cream

½ cup sugar

2 generous teaspoons grated
   orange rind

½ cup orange juice

1 cup heavy cream

- Combine sugar, orange rind and orange juice in a saucepan.
- Bring to a boil, stirring only until the sugar dissolves. Simmer 10 minutes without stirring. Cool completely.
- Whip cream until soft peaks form. Gently fold into the orange syrup.
- Serve over fresh berries or fruit.
- Yield: 1½ cups

Baked Pears

8 Bosc pears with stems intact,
   peeled

juice of a lemon

1½ cups dry white wine

2 cups water

1¼ cups sugar

zest of 2 oranges, peel removed
   with vegetable peeler

2 cinnamon sticks

⅓ cup Grand Marnier

- Preheat oven to 375°.
- Place peeled pears in cold water mixed with lemon juice.
- In a saucepan, combine the wine, 2 cups water, sugar, orange zest, cinnamon sticks and liqueur. Simmer 5 minutes.
- Drain pears and arrange on their sides in a baking dish. Pour syrup over them.
- Cover tightly with foil and bake 30 minutes.
- Turn pears over and bake covered for 20-30 minutes until they are tender.
- Cool and carefully arrange in a deep serving dish. Ladle syrup over pears.
- Cover and chill overnight.
- Yield: 8 portions

Cardinale Sauce for Poached Pears

10 ounce package frozen
   raspberries, drained

2 Tablespoons superfine sugar

1 Tablespoon Kirschwasser

- Purée raspberries in processor.
- Strain and press through sieve to remove seeds.
- Stir in sugar and Kirschwasser.
- Yield: 6-8 portions

Velvet Cream with Sherried Oranges

2 cups heavy cream
4 Tablespoons sugar
1 teaspoon vanilla
1 package gelatin
½ cup water
6-8 oranges peeled and
    sectioned
1½ cups sugar
1 cup water
juice of ½ lemon
¼ cup good quality sweet sherry

- Mix cream, sugar and vanilla together and stir over low heat until sugar dissolves.
- Soften gelatin over hot water. Add to cream. Stir well. Put in an oiled ring mold. Refrigerate until set.
- Boil sugar and water 5 minutes. Cool.
- Add to syrup. Pour over oranges and chill.
- Put oranges in center of ring mold and serve.
- Yield: 6-8 portions

NOTE: Fresh berries with a bit of sugar and a favorite liqueur may be substituted for the oranges.

Peach Sauce

4 large ripe peaches, peeled and
    pitted
juice of ½ lemon
juice of ½ lime
¼ cup light brown sugar
¼ cup dark rum

- Using an electric blender, add ingredients in the order listed.
- Store in refrigerator.
- Best made day before or early that morning.
- Yield: 2 cups

NOTE: Wonderful as a sauce over ice cream or pound cake.

Raspberry Sauce

2 pints fresh raspberries or
    10-ounce package frozen
    raspberries, thawed
¾ cup currant jelly
1 Tablespoon cornstarch
1 Tablespoon cold water
1 Tablespoon Grand Marnier

- Strain berries to obtain ¾ cup juice. Discard seeds and pulp.
- Combine juice and jelly in a small saucepan. Bring to a boil.
- Combine cornstarch and water and add to syrup. Stir constantly until sauce is clear and thick.
- Remove sauce from heat. Stir in Grand Marnier and cool.
- Serve over ice cream or coeur à la crème. Garnish with a few fresh berries.
- Yield: 6-8 portions

Brandied Peaches

2½ cups water

1½ cups sugar

2 vanilla beans

6 large ripe peaches, unpeeled

½ cup brandy

sprigs of mint

▶ Vanilla Sauce (optional):

⅔ cup powdered sugar

½ cup butter

1 cup heavy cream

1 Tablespoon vanilla

- In a large stainless pan, combine water, sugar and vanilla beans.
- Dissolve sugar over medium heat, brushing pan to involve crystals in syrup. (Use brush dipped in cold water.)
- Bring syrup to a boil. Lower heat and simmer for 10 minutes. Do not stir.
- Add whole peaches to the syrup and simmer gently, uncovered, for 10-12 minutes, or until just tender.
- Cool peaches in syrup then remove with a slotted spoon.
- Add brandy to syrup and cook for 4-5 minutes.
- Pour syrup into a bowl. Peel the peaches and add them to the syrup. Chill.
- Serve peaches in suitably elegant glasses. Pour just a splash of syrup over the peaches and garnish with mint.

Vanilla Sauce:

- In a saucepan, combine sugar and butter and cook over low heat until thickened and smooth. Remove from heat.
- Whip cream into soft peaks.
- Using a whisk, combine with butter and sugar mixture. Add vanilla.
- Yield: 6 portions

Marinated Orange Slices

6 navel oranges, peeled and sliced

¾ cup red wine

⅓ cup sugar

3 whole cloves

1 cinnamon stick

1 Tablespoon lemon juice

- Place oranges in a serving bowl.
- In a medium saucepan, combine remaining ingredients. Bring to a boil. Simmer 5 minutes. Pour syrup over orange slices. Cover.
- Refrigerate 2-3 hours. Remove spices before serving.
- Serve oranges over sponge cake slices and ice cream. Drizzle with syrup.
- Yield: 6-8 portions

Truffle Sauce

3½ Tablespoons unsalted butter

⅔ cup crème fraîche

½ pound Harbor Sweets chocolate cut into small chunks (or another premium rich dark continental chocolate)

⅛ teaspoon of salt

1 Tablespoon cranberry liqueur

2 teaspoons red raspberry seedless jam

2 teaspoons cranberry relish

- Mix butter and crème fraîche in a saucepan at medium heat. When butter is melted, increase to medium-high heat, stirring constantly, until it comes to a boil.

- Remove from heat quickly and stir in the chocolate until it is melted. Continue stirring until it cools on a candy temperature to 99°. Add all the other ingredients, stirring constantly. Let it cool in the refrigerator for 2 hours.

- When ready to serve, heat slightly until sauce is warm to the touch and spoon over premium ice cream.

- Yield: 8 portions

This celebrity recipe was submitted by Ben Strohecker Harbor Sweets Salem, MA

Chocolate Dipped Strawberries

1 pint large strawberries with stems attached

8 ounces dipping chocolate, white, milk or dark

- Line a baking sheet that will fit into the refrigerator with waxed paper.

- Do not wash the strawberries. Pat them clean with damp paper towels.

- Melt chocolate in the top of a double boiler over hot water. Cool slightly.

- Holding each berry by the stem, dip the strawberry into the melted chocolate, allowing excess chocolate to drip off.

- Place the strawberries on the prepared baking sheet.

- Refrigerate until firm.

- May be refrigerated, uncovered, overnight.

- Yield: 1 pint strawberries

Crème Brûlée Fruit Tart

▶ **Crust:**
  1½ **cups flour**
  ⅔ **cup unsalted butter or margarine, softened**
  ⅓ **cup powdered sugar**
  ¼ **cup crushed pecans**

▶ **Filling:**
  ½ **cup brown sugar**
  3 **Tablespoons butter or margarine**
  ½ **cup crushed pecans**
  2 **cups whipping cream**
  1 **package unflavored gelatin**
  1 **Tablespoon flour**
  2 **Tablespoons granulated sugar**
  3 **egg yolks**
  ¼ **cup orange marmalade**
  1 **Tablespoon orange flavored liqueur or water**
  strawberries and sliced kiwi or other fresh fruit

- Line a 10" tart pan with a removable bottom with parchment paper.

- Combine crust ingredients in a food processor and process until crumbly. Press into bottom and up sides of the tart pan. Refrigerate for 1 hour before baking in a preheated 350° oven until light brown, about 12-15 minutes. Cool completely.

- Heat brown sugar and butter in a small saucepan. Cool slightly and spread over crust. Sprinkle with pecans. Bake for approximately 5 minutes.

- Meanwhile, heat a small amount of cream in a heavy saucepan and dissolve gelatin, then add remaining cream and heat to scalding.

- Mix sugar and flour and whisk in egg yolks. Remove a few tablespoons of cream and stir into the egg mixture. Return this to the cream in the saucepan, heating and stirring until thickened. Cool and pour into crust.

- Cover and refrigerate until chilled.

- Heat marmalade and liqueur or water until melted. Cool slightly.

- Remove stems from strawberries of uniform size. Place stem side down evenly around the edge of the tart. Cut kiwi slices in half and arrange a design in the center of the tart. Spoon marmalade mixture over fruit. Keep refrigerated until ready to serve.

- Yield: 8 portions

Microwave Bananas

3-4 **medium bananas, sliced diagonally**
4 **Tablespoons orange juice**
2 **Tablespoons brandy**
¼ **cup crushed ginger cookies**
1½ **Tablespoons brown sugar**
½ **cup heavy cream or yogurt**

- Place bananas in the bottom of a glass dish.

- Mix orange juice and brandy.

- Pour over bananas.

- Sprinkle mixed sugar and cookie crumbs over the top.

- Cover and cook on full power for 4 minutes.

- Pour on cream or yogurt and serve.

- Yield: 4 portions

Hot Fruit Compote

8 ounces macaroons or amaretti cookies

1 pound chopped fruit such as pears, peaches, oranges, bananas, cherries, etc., or you can use drained canned fruit

3 ounces almonds

3 ounces brown sugar

3 ounces sherry or brandy

1-2 ounces butter

- Butter an ovenproof dish.
- Line base with half the cookies.
- Cover with chopped fruit.
- Top with remaining cookies.
- Sprinkle with the almonds.
- Sprinkle with sugar.
- Dot with butter.
- Pour over the sherry.
- Bake for 30 minutes in a preheated 350° oven.
- Yield: 4-6 portions

Ricotta Fritters

8 ounces ricotta cheese

2 eggs

½ cup fast mixing flour

1½ Tablespoons butter, at room temperature

grated peel of a lemon

pinch of salt

1 bar chocolate, broken into small pieces, or 3-4 ounces chocolate bits

vegetable oil

½ cup honey, warmed

- Beat ricotta with a whisk until smooth and creamy.
- In a separate bowl, beat eggs lightly with a fork and add to the ricotta.
- Slowly beat in flour using a whisk.
- Add butter, lemon peel and salt, beating until well mixed.
- Let batter stay at room temperature between 2 and 3 hours.
- Add chocolate.
- Heat oil on medium high. Oil should be halfway up the sides of a large pan.
- Drop batter by tablespoonsful. When the fritter is golden on one side, turn over and cook the other side.
- Remove with a slotted spoon when done.
- Drain on paper.
- To serve, pour warmed honey over fritters.
- Yield: 6 portions

Sweet Short or Basic Pastry for Pies or Tarts

1½ cups flour
1½ Tablespoons sugar, optional
pinch of salt
6 Tablespoons cold butter
2¼ Tablespoons shortening
4-4½ Tablespoons ice water

- Mix flour, sugar and salt. Cut in shortening with pastry blender.
- Gradually add water and form dough into a ball. Chill dough.
- To prebake, shape crust into pie plate. Prick bottom. Line with foil and add pie weights or beans.
- Bake at 400° for 8-9 minutes. Remove foil and weights/beans and bake 2-3 additional minutes.
- Yield: single 8-9" crust

Tangy Lemon Tart

1 9" tart shell or pie shell
1 lemon, very thinly sliced
½ cup sugar for cooking lemon
8 Tablespoons butter
¾ cup sugar for the filling
3 eggs
⅔ cup lemon juice, strained

- Preheat oven to 400°. Bake the pie shell 10-15 minutes. Remove pie shell and set aside to cool. Lower oven to 350°.
- Put the sliced lemon in a non-aluminum saucepan with ½ cup sugar and enough water to barely cover. Bring to a boil. Lower the heat and let the lemon slices boil gently for 30 minutes, watching carefully. If the water completely evaporates, add more water to keep the slices from burning. Drain slices and dry them on a wire rack. Arrange the slices in the bottom of the shell.
- Melt the butter and set aside to cool a little.
- In a mixing bowl, beat together sugar and eggs until they are smooth and pale. Stir in melted butter.
- Gradually whisk in lemon juice
- Pour the mixture into the shell. Bake for 20-25 minutes, or until the filling is set and a knife inserted comes out clean.
- Preheat the broiler. Broil the tart for just a few seconds until it turns a gold spotty brown.
- Serve warm or at room temperature.
- Yield: 6-8 portions

Fruit Tart Toppings

▶ **Intense Berry Topping (for 10" tart):**

½ cup sliced strawberries

2 cups blueberries

1 cup raspberries

½ cup pitted cherries

¾ cup sugar

juice of a lemon

2 Tablespoons cornstarch mixed with 2 Tablespoons water

▶ **Mixed Fruit Topping:**

bananas, kiwis, strawberries, blueberries, etc.

red currant jelly, melted

apricot preserves, melted and strained

▶ **Pear Topping:**

pears, peeled, halved and cored

red currant jelly, melted

- Dissolve sugar and lemon juice in a heavy saucepan. Add fruit and cook 1-2 minutes. Remove fruit with a slotted spoon.

- Depending on the amount of juice, add some or all of the cornstarch and cook 1-2 minutes to thicken. Pour over fruit. Chill.

- Drain fruit and put it into the tart shell. Drizzle some juice over fruit.

Mixed Fruit Topping:

- Combine in an attractive arrangement on top of tart filling. Brush with melted red currant jelly or strained apricot preserves.

Pear Topping:

- Poach in a simple syrup until tender. Glaze with melted currant jelly.

Lattice Peach Tart

▶ **Pastry:**

2 cups flour

1 Tablespoon superfine sugar

pinch of salt

4 Tablespoons butter

4 Tablespoons vegetable shortening

½ teaspoon lemon juice

ice water

▶ **Filling:**

1½ cups pastry cream

1½ pounds ripe peaches, skinned, pitted and sliced

1 beaten egg

2 teaspoons superfine sugar

- Mix flour, sugar, salt, butter and shortening until the mixture resembles fine breadcrumbs.

- Add lemon juice and approximately 2 tablespoons of ice water. Mix until the pastry forms a ball.

- Chill for 30 minutes.

- Roll out and line a greased 8 or 9" pie pan.

- Spread the base with pastry cream.

- Top with peach slices.

- Roll out the remaining pastry and cut into strips. Use these to decorate top of the pie in a lattice pattern.

- Brush the strips with the beaten egg and sprinkle with sugar.

- Bake in a preheated 375° oven for 45 minutes. Cool and serve.

- Yield: 6 portions

Pastry Cream for Tarts

2½ egg yolks (to get one half
- beat yolk and divide)

⅓ cup flour

1 cup hot milk

1½ teaspoons butter

1½ teaspoons vanilla

- Beat yolks and gradually add sugar until thick and lemon-colored.
- Beat in flour. Slowly add milk.
- Pour mixture into saucepan and cook on medium heat, whisking steadily. Cook for 2-3 minutes on low heat until smooth.
- Remove from heat and add butter and vanilla. Cool.

Deep Dish Apple Pie

▶ Crust:

1½ cups flour

1 Tablespoon sugar

2¼ Tablespoons solid vegetable shortening

6 Tablespoons butter, chilled

4½ Tablespoons ice water

▶ Filling:

3 pounds Granny Smith apples, peeled, cored and thinly sliced

1 Tablespoon grated orange peel

2 Tablespoons flour

¼ cup dark brown sugar

¼ cup chopped walnuts

¼ cup raisins

¾ cup honey

1 Tablespoon butter

Crust:

- Mix together the flour and sugar.
- Cut in the shortening and butter with a pastry blender until it resembles coarse meal. Add water and blend together with fingers until a ball forms.
- Wrap and chill while preparing the filling.

Filling:

- Mix apple slices with orange peel and flour.
- Beginning with ⅓ of the apples, layer an 8" soufflé dish with sugar, walnuts, raisins and honey. Dot the top with butter. Repeat layers.
- Preheat oven to 375°.
- Roll out the crust and with a 2" cutter cut circles of dough. Starting around the edge, cover apples with overlapping circles, ending with one in the center.
- Bake 45-60 minutes, or until nicely browned and bubbly. Cool on a wire rack.
- Serve warm with vanilla ice cream or hard sauce.
- Yield: 8-10 portions

Incomparable Pumpkin Pie

2 large eggs plus 1 yolk
½ cup sugar
2 Tablespoons molasses
1 Tablespoon ground cardamom
1 teaspoon cinnamon
¼ teaspoon cloves
¼ teaspoon allspice
½ teaspoon nutmeg
2 cups cooked pumpkin
1 cup heavy cream
¼ cup brandy
¼ cup dark rum
¼ cup curaçao
1 unbaked 9" pie shell, brushed with whipped egg white

▶ **Topping:**
1 cup heavy cream
sugar to taste
1 teaspoon vanilla
dash each of brandy, dark rum, curaçao, optional
grated nutmeg, optional

- Preheat oven to 450°.
- Blend thoroughly the eggs, sugar, molasses and spices.
- Add pumpkin, cream and liqueurs.
- Adjust the seasonings to taste.
- Turn mixture into the pie shell and bake on lower shelf of a 450° oven for 10 minutes.
- Lower oven to 400° and continue to bake until a table knife inserted comes out clean. Remove and cool.

Topping:
- Partially whip the cream. Add sugar, vanilla, and liqueurs and continue to beat until the cream stands in peaks. Smooth on top of cooled pie. Dust with grated nutmeg, if desired.
- Yield: 8 portions

Dutch Blueberry Pie

1½ cups sugar
⅓ cup flour
½ teaspoon cinnamon
4 cups fresh washed berries
1½ Tablespoons butter
½ cup whipping cream
pastry for 2 crust pie

- Preheat oven to 425°.
- Mix together the sugar, flour and cinnamon. Toss lightly with berries, taking care not to crush the fruit.
- Pour into a pastry-lined pan. Dot with butter.
- Cover with top crust which has slits cut in the top. Seal and flute.
- Pour whipping cream through slits in the crust before baking. Bake 35-45 minutes.

Elaine's Sinfully Rich Blacksmith Pie

▶ **Crust:**

10 ounces chocolate wafer cookies

10 ounces graham crackers

16 Tablespoons butter, at room temperature

▶ **Filling:**

¼ cup cornstarch

1 cup plus 3 Tablespoons sugar

½ teaspoon vanilla extract

1½ cups half and half

2 egg yolks

1 whole egg

12 ounces semi-sweet chocolate

3½ cups heavy cream

4 egg whites

- In a food processor, process the chocolate cookies and the graham crackers until fine. Place the crumbs in a bowl and add the butter. Blend thoroughly.

- Line the bottom and sides of a 10" springform pan that is 3" deep with the crust. Chill crust for 1 hour.

- Whisk the cornstarch, 3 Tablespoons sugar, vanilla extract and the half and half in a saucepan until smooth. Bring to a boil over low heat, stirring constantly. When thickened, remove from heat.

- Beat together the egg yolks and the egg. Whisk into the sauce. Return to the heat and stir until the custard simmers. Pour 1 cup of the custard into a mixing bowl and the remainder into a second bowl.

- Break up the chocolate pieces and place in a bowl. Set this bowl into a small basin of boiling water and let stand, stirring occasionally until melted. Add the chocolate to the 1 cup of custard. Cover the crust (bottom and sides) with the chocolate custard mixture. Chill.

- Beat the heavy cream until partly stiff. Gradually add ½ cup sugar and continue beating until stiff. Beat the egg whites until almost stiff and while beating gradually add ½ cup sugar. Beat until stiff.

- Fold the whipped cream and the egg whites into the second bowl of custard.

- Pour the whipped cream mixture into the pan. Smooth the top. Cover with plastic wrap. Chill for several hours. Unmold and serve in wedges.

- Yield: 10 or more portions

NOTE: This is very rich, but worth the calories.

Amaretto Rum Cream Pie

▶ **Crust:**

1⅓ cups amaretto cookie crumbs

6 Tablespoons unsalted butter, melted

▶ **Filling:**

1 Tablespoon or 1 envelope unflavored gelatin

¼ cup cold water

5 egg yolks

¾ cup sugar

½ cup rum

¼ cup strong coffee

1 cup heavy cream

- To prepare pie plate, turn it upside down. Cover it with a sheet of aluminum foil. Press to form. Remove foil. Turn plate over and place foil inside the plate. Press smoothly into place.

- Mix cookie crumbs and butter. Place in the pie plate. Press firmly up the sides and over the bottom of the plate. Place in freezer for 1 hour or more.

- Take out of freezer. Lift out crust and carefully remove the foil. Return crust to plate and refrigerate.

- Sprinkle gelatin over cold water.

- On medium speed, beat egg yolks. Gradually add sugar and beat 3 minutes.

- Add ¼ cup of rum to gelatin and place cup in a pan of warm water over low heat until gelatin dissolves.

- On low speed, beat gelatin into yolk mixture. Add remaining rum and coffee.

- Place bowl in a larger bowl of ice and cold water. Stir occasionally until the mixture is the consistency of thick cream.

- Beat heavy cream until it holds a soft shape. Fold into yolk mixture.

- Pour into pie shell (not all of it will fit). Place pie in freezer for 5 minutes. Gently pour on remaining filling. Refrigerate 6 hours or more.

- Decorate with whipped cream and sweet chocolate shavings.

- Yield: 8 portions

Pear Maple Pie

1 unbaked 9" pie crust

1 large pear, peeled and sliced

4 large eggs

¾ cup maple syrup

1 cup vanilla yogurt

½ teaspoon cinnamon

¼ teaspoon salt

- Spread pear slices evenly over the pie shell.
- Combine remaining ingredients in the blender, and run at high speed for several seconds.
- Pour custard over pears. Bake 45 minutes, or until firm.
- Cool at least to room temperature before cutting.
- Yield: 6 portions

This celebrity recipe was submitted by Chef Scott H. Seaver Claudia's Marblehead, MA

Apple Torte

▶ Crust:

½ cup butter

⅓ cup sugar

¼ teaspoon vanilla

1 cup flour

▶ Filling:

12 ounces cream cheese

¼ cup sugar

1 egg, beaten

1 teaspoon vanilla

⅓ cup sugar

½ teaspoon cinnamon

4 cups peeled and sliced tart apples

¼ cup sliced almonds

1 cup heavy cream, whipped

Crust:

- Cream butter and sugar. Add vanilla and flour.
- Press into bottom and 1" up sides of a greased 9" springform pan. Set aside.

Filling:

- Combine cream cheese and sugar. Add egg and vanilla. Pour into shell.
- Combine remaining sugar and cinnamon. Toss with apples. Arrange slices in concentric circles over cream cheese mixture. Sprinkle with almonds.
- Bake in a preheated 450° oven 10 minutes. Reduce heat to 400° and bake 25 minutes longer. Cool before removing rim of pan.
- Garnish with whipped cream.
- Yield: 8 portions

Chocolate Roulade with Raspberries

6 ounces unsweetened
   chocolate

5 eggs

6 ounces fine sugar

3 Tablespoons hot water

powdered sugar

1 cup heavy cream

½ pint fresh raspberries

- Preheat oven to 350°.

- Break chocolate into a small bowl and place over hot water to melt. Stir occasionally until melted.

- Separate eggs, placing yolks into a large bowl, and the whites into a smaller bowl.

- Add sugar to yolks and beat until pale in color.

- Add the hot water to the melted chocolate.

- Stir thoroughly and add to egg yolk mixture.

- Whisk egg whites until stiff and fold gently through the chocolate mixture. Pour into a greased and lined jelly roll pan. Bake for 15 minutes.

- Cover with a sheet of parchment paper and a damp cloth. Leave overnight.

- Turn roulade onto a sheet of paper dusted well with powdered sugar. Peel away parchment paper.

- Spread with whipped cream and raspberries. Roll up like a jelly roll using sugared paper to help. Chill for several hours.

- To serve, dust with more powdered sugar and slice on the diagonal with a sharp knife.

- Yield: 8 portions

Peach or Strawberry Shortcake

2 cups sifted flour

4 teaspoons baking powder

½ teaspoon salt

2 Tablespoons sugar

½ cup butter, cold

½ cup milk

sliced strawberries or peaches,
   lightly sugared, at room
   temperature

- Preheat oven to 400°.

- Mix flour, baking powder, salt and sugar.

- Using a pastry blender, cut in the butter until it resembles coarse meal. Add milk and mix to form a soft dough. Form into individual cakes or 1 large cake.

- Bake for 25 minutes. Remove from oven, split and butter.

- Place bottom in dish, cover with fruit, put top on. Cover with more fruit.

- Serve with a large pitcher of very cold cream.

- Yield: 6 portions

Frozen Daiquiri Soufflé

10 eggs, separated
2 cups sugar
½ cup lime juice
½ cup lemon juice
finely grated rind of 2 lemons
    and 2 limes
2 packages unflavored gelatin
½ cup rum
2 cups heavy cream
Garnish: Additional whipped
    cream, lemon and lime peel,
    crushed pistachio nuts

- In a small bowl, beat egg yolks until thick and lemon-colored. Add 1 cup sugar, the juices and the rind. Over low heat, stirring constantly, heat until thickened. Cool slightly.

- In a large bowl at high speed, beat egg whites until soft peaks form. Gradually beat in remaining cup of sugar.

- Beat cream until peaks form.

- Fold cream into egg whites and fold this into the egg mixture.

- Turn into a 6-cup soufflé dish. Freeze and then garnish with additional whipped cream, lemon and lime peel, and crushed pistachio nuts.

- Yield: 12 portions

Hot Chocolate Soufflé

6 Tablespoons butter
6 Tablespoons flour
2 cups milk
2 ounces unsweetened
    chocolate
⅔ cup sugar
6 egg yolks
6 egg whites, beaten stiff
1 Tablespoon butter rubbed on
    surface of soufflé dish to
    prevent sticking

- Preheat oven to 375°.

- In a saucepan, melt the butter and add the flour. Stir with a wire whisk.

- Add milk, melted chocolate, and sugar. Continue to stir with whisk.

- Stir in egg yolks using the whisk.

- Fold in stiff egg whites.

- Pour into a hot, buttered soufflé dish.

- Set dish in pan of hot water and bake for 20 minutes. Then reduce heat to 300° and bake 20 minutes or until served.

- Yield: 8-10 portions

PEABODY
A little known fact in the chronicles of Peabody's history is that chocolate was milled near the Square in the 1700s. Gideon Foster, Peabody's Revolutionary War hero, took over the chocolate manufacturing business from his father.

NOTE: Do not open oven until done.

Walnut Meringue Gâteau

5 egg whites

pinch of salt

9 ounces superfine sugar

4 ounces flour

grated rind of 1 lemon

3 ounces walnuts, finely
  chopped

▶ Raspberry Filling:

12 ounces raspberries

7 ounces heavy cream

1 Tablespoon sugar

2 Tablespoons medium sherry

▶ Peach Filling:

3 ripe peaches, peeled and
  sliced

3 Tablespoons brandy

3 ounces sugar

7 ounces heavy cream

- Preheat oven to 350°.
- Line a 9" springform pan with non-stick paper.
- Whisk egg whites and salt to form stiff peaks. Gradually incorporate the sugar, whisking lightly.
- Sprinkle flour, walnuts and lemon peel over mixture and fold in with a fork.
- Pour mixture into cake pan, banging it to settle the ingredients. Bake for 15 minutes then raise temperature to 400° for 20 more minutes. Cool for 15 minutes.
- Turn onto wire rack to cool completely. Chill in refrigerator for 20 minutes.
- Then slice in half horizontally.

Raspberry Filling:

- Sprinkle sherry over both halves of gâteau.
- Whip cream until stiff.
- Mix in half the raspberries and half the sugar.
- Sandwich gâteau with this and top with remaining raspberries and sugar.

Peach Filling:

- Sprinkle both halves of gâteau with brandy.
- Whip cream until stiff.
- Add half the sugar and half the peaches. Use as the filling for gâteau.
- Decorate top with remaining peaches and sugar.
- Yield: 8 portions

Carrot Cake

Cake:
- 2 cups sugar
- 1½ cups vegetable oil
- 4 eggs
- 2¼ cups flour
- 2 teaspoons salt
- 2 teaspoons baking soda
- 2 teaspoons cinnamon
- ½ cup nuts, broken into small pieces
- 3 cups carrots, coarsely grated

Frosting:
- 8 ounces cream cheese, softened
- ½ cup butter or margarine, softened
- 2 teaspoons vanilla
- 1 pound box powdered sugar

Cake:
- Preheat oven to 300°.
- Combine sugar, oil and eggs. Beat for 2 minutes and set aside.
- Sift together flour, salt, baking soda and cinnamon.
- Add sifted ingredients to sugar, oil and eggs, mixing thoroughly.
- Add nuts and grated carrots and stir until blended.
- Pour batter into a lightly greased 13x9" pan and bake for 70 minutes.

Frosting:
- Cream cheese and butter together until well blended.
- Add the sugar gradually, mixing after each addition.
- Add vanilla and mix thoroughly.
- Frost cooled cake.
- Yield: 10-12 portions

This celebrity recipe was submitted by Cile Bellefleur-Burbridge

NOTE: The cake may also be made in 2 8" layer pans and baked for 50 minutes.

Blackberry Cake

- ½ cup butter
- ½ cup white sugar
- 1 egg
- 1 cup flour
- 2 teaspoons baking powder
- ¼ teaspoon salt
- ½ cup milk

Topping:
- 1 cup ripe blackberries
- 4 Tablespoons butter
- ½ cup white sugar
- ¼ cup flour
- ½ teaspoon cinnamon

- Cream butter and sugar and beat in the egg. Gradually add flour, sifted together with baking powder and salt. Beat to a smooth batter, adding the milk. Pour into a greased rectangular 11x7" pan. Sprinkle thickly with well washed and drained blackberries.
- Preheat oven to 350°.
- Cream butter and sugar together until smooth and pale as above.
- Mix in flour and cinnamon to the consistency of breadcrumbs.
- Sprinkle onto blackberries.
- Bake at 350° for 45 minutes-1 hour.
- Cool in pan completely before serving.
- Yield: 6-8 portions

Boxford Apple Cake

2 cups sugar
2½ cups flour
2 teaspoons baking powder
1 teaspoon baking soda
1 teaspoon salt
1 teaspoon cinnamon
1 cup oil
2 eggs
1 teaspoon vanilla
4 cups apples, peeled, cored and diced
1 cup chopped nuts
6 ounces butterscotch bits

- Preheat oven to 350°.
- Stir together the sugar, flour, baking powder, soda, salt and cinnamon.
- Add oil, eggs and vanilla.
- Add apples and nuts and mix well. Mixture will be stiff.
- Pour into a greased 13x9" baking pan. Sprinkle with butterscotch chips.
- Bake for 50-60 minutes.
- Yield: 12-15 portions

NOTE: As a variation, omit the butterscotch chips. Bake in a greased bundt or tube pan. Cool. Glaze with the following:
4 ounces softened cream cheese
2 Tablespoons softened butter
2 cups powdered sugar
½ teaspoon mint flavoring
Beat together cream cheese, butter, and mint flavoring. Gradually beat in sugar. Icing should be thin enough to drizzle down sides of cake.

Blueberry Dessert Cake

▶ Crust:
1½ cups flour
½ cup sugar
1½ teaspoons baking powder
½ cup butter or margarine
1 egg
1 teaspoon vanilla

▶ Filling:
3 cups fresh or frozen blueberries
2 egg yolks
2 cups sour cream
⅓ cup sugar
1 teaspoon vanilla
whipping cream for top, if desired

- Preheat oven to 375°.
- Blend flour, sugar, baking powder and butter in a food processor.
- Blend in egg and vanilla.
- Pat over bottom of a 9" springform pan.
- Top with blueberries, reserving a few for garnish.
- Mix together the sour cream, sugar, egg yolks, and vanilla and pour over blueberries.
- Bake until edges of cream mixture are lightly browned, about 60-70 minutes. Cool. Chill.
- Top with whipped cream, if desired and reserved berries.
- Yield: 8-10 portions

German Chocolate Cake

Cake:
- ¼ pound German sweet chocolate
- ½ cup water
- 2½ cups cake flour
- 1 teaspoon baking soda
- ½ teaspoon salt
- 1 cup butter
- 2 cups sugar
- 1 teaspoon vanilla
- 4 eggs, separated
- 1 cup buttermilk

Frosting:
- 3 cups heavy cream
- ¼ cup plus 2 Tablespoons powdered sugar
- 6 teaspoons instant coffee
- 1½ teaspoons vanilla

- Preheat oven to 350°.
- Melt chocolate in ½ cup water. Let cool.
- Sift flour, baking powder, and salt together.
- Cream butter and sugar until very light and fluffy. Beat in egg yolks one at a time. Mix in chocolate on low speed.
- Alternately add the flour in 3 additions, and in 2 additions, the buttermilk. Add vanilla.
- Beat egg whites until stiff but not dry and fold into batter.
- Put in 3 greased and floured 9" cake pans and bake for 30 minutes.
- Cool 10 minutes and turn out onto rack to cool completely.

Frosting:
- Mix all ingredients at high speed in the mixer until stiff. Frost the cooled cake.
- Yield: 12 portions

Incorporated in 1646, Andover is 23 miles north of Boston and covers 32 square miles in Essex County. Through the years it has been variously identified as the Hill (Phillips Academy), the Mill (textile mills aside the Shawsheen River), and the Till (there were 75 large farms at the peak). From the archives of the Andover Historical Society comes this early 1800s Election Day Cake traditionally served to voters with root beer. It was made by Pomp Lovejoy and his wife Rose. Both former slaves, they died in 1826, he at age 102 and she at 99. (We wonder if it was the richness of the cake or the addition of the plums that added longevity and joy to their lives.)

Anise Cake

- 3 eggs, jumbo size
- 1½ cups sugar
- 1 cup oil
- 1 ounce bottle anise extract
- 3 teaspoons baking powder
- 3 cups flour
- ¾ cup milk
- nonpareils for decoration
- powdered sugar
- milk

- Preheat oven to 375°.
- Beat all ingredients together with an electric mixer.
- Pour into a greased and floured tube pan.
- Bake 40-50 minutes. Check cake at 40 minutes. Do not overbake.
- Mix together powdered sugar and a few drops of milk to a smooth consistency.
- When cool, drizzle top with frosting. Sprinkle with colored nonpareils.
- Yield: 12-20 portions

Macadamia Fudge Cake

▶ **Cake:**
1 cup flour
¾ cup white sugar
¾ cup sour cream
½ cup softened butter
¼ cup unsweetened cocoa powder
1½ teaspoons instant coffee granules
½ teaspoon baking powder
½ teaspoon baking soda
¼ teaspoon salt
½ teaspoon vanilla

▶ **Topping:**
½ cup sugar
4 ounces (4 squares) semi-sweet chocolate
1 cup heavy cream
2 Tablespoons butter
1 Tablespoon corn syrup
1 teaspoon vanilla
1 7-ounce jar macadamia nuts, halved

▶ **Crust:**
1¼ cups graham cracker crumbs
¼ cup melted butter
¼ cup sugar

▶ **Filling:**
2¼ pounds cream cheese, at room temperature
1⅔ cups sugar
5 eggs, at room temperature
1 cup Irish cream liqueur
1 Tablespoon vanilla
1 cup mini-chocolate bits, optional

- Preheat oven to 350°. Grease a 9" round cake pan. Line bottom with wax paper and grease again.
- Combine all ingredients on low speed until blended.
- Pour into prepared pan. Bake 30-35 minutes, or until a toothpick inserted comes out clean.
- Cool on cake rack for 10 minutes. Remove from pan, peel off wax paper and cool completely.

Topping:
- Combine sugar, chocolate, cream, butter and corn syrup in a saucepan. Cook over medium heat, stirring constantly until the mixture boils. Reduce heat to medium low and cook 5 minutes, stirring. Remove from heat and stir in vanilla.
- Cool 10 minutes.
- Stir in nuts. Pour topping evenly over cake.
- Refrigerate until firm.
- Yield: 12 portions

Irish Cream Cheesecake

- Preheat oven to 325°.
- Mix together crumbs, butter and sugar and pat into a large springform pan that has been sprayed with no-stick spray.
- Bake for 8 minutes.
- Using an electric mixer, beat cream cheese until smooth. Slowly mix in sugar.
- Beat in eggs one at a time. Blend in liqueur and vanilla.
- If you wish, sprinkle ½ cup chocolate chips on crust. Next pour in filling and add remaining chocolate bits on top.
- Bake until puffed, springy in the center and light golden brown, about 1 hour 10 minutes.
- Cool completely and refrigerate.
- Yield: 16-18 portions

Election Day Cake
1 lb. of sugar
1 lb. of butter
4 lbs. of flour
½ pint of sweet lively yeast, mixed with warm milk
One half the quantity of butter and sugar to be put in before raising the dough; the other half afterwards, and the dough raised again in pans or molded into cakes. This quantity is sufficient for 3 or 4 common-sized loaves. It requires considerable kneading. To be spiced with cinnamon and nutmeg. The quantity of flour may be increased to 4½ to 5 lbs. if plums are used.

Cheesecake Elegante

½ cup graham cracker crumbs

2 pounds cream cheese, at room temperature

4 eggs

1¾ cups sugar

juice of one lemon

grated rind of one lemon

1 teaspoon vanilla

strawberries, blueberries, or other fruit or berries as available for garnish

▶ Apricot Sauce:

1 10-ounce jar apricot jam

¼ cup sugar

¼ cup water

1 Tablespoon rum or cognac

- Preheat oven to 325°.
- Butter the inside of a soufflé dish, 8" wide and 3" deep. (Do not use a springform pan.)
- Sprinkle with graham cracker crumbs and shake until bottom and sides are coated. Shake out the excess and set aside.
- Place cream cheese, eggs, sugar, lemon juice, lemon rind, and vanilla in a bowl. Start beating at low speed and as ingredients blend, increase speed to high and continue beating until smooth.
- Pour batter into prepared pan and shake to level.
- Set the pan inside another pan and pour in boiling water to a depth of ½". Put in oven and bake for 2 hours.
- Turn off oven and let cake sit in oven for 20 minutes. Remove from oven and from water and set on a rack to cool to room temperature.
- Invert a plate over cake and carefully turn upside down to unmold.
- Garnish with berries and spoon the sauce over all.
- Combine jam, sugar and water in a small saucepan and stir over low heat until blended.
- Strain through a small sieve and then add liquor.
- Yield: 12 portions

Heavenly Fruit Cake

3 cups sifted flour

1½ teaspoons baking powder

½ teaspoon salt

1 cup candied cherries, halved

1 cup candied pineapple, cut in almond-sized pieces

2 cups drained sweet watermelon pickle, cut in almond-sized pieces

1½ cups pecans, broken into pieces

1½ cups filberts

¾ cup blanched almonds, sliced

2 cups golden raisins

1 cup butter, or ½ butter and ½ margarine

2 cups sugar

5 eggs

½ cup cream sherry

- Sift flour, baking powder and salt together.
- Mix all chopped fruits, nuts, raisins with several tablespoons of flour mixture.
- Preheat oven to 325°.
- Grease 2 loaf pans 9x5" in size and line each with greased wax paper.
- Work butter until soft. Add sugar gradually until smooth. Add eggs 1 at a time and beat well after each addition.
- Stir in flour mixture and sherry alternately. Add lastly all the fruit-nut mixture and mix thoroughly.
- Transfer equal portions in pans and press batter down evenly. Bake 1-1½ hours until done when tested.
- Yield: 2 large loaves or 4 small loaves

Holiday Bourbon Cake

1 pound butter or margarine

3 cups sugar

8 eggs, separated

3 cups sifted all-purpose flour

2 teaspoons vanilla

2 teaspoons almond extract

⅓ cup bourbon

½ cup chopped pecans

- Cream butter and 2 cups sugar until light and fluffy. Add egg yolks, 1 at a time, beating well after each addition.
- Add flour alternately with flavorings and bourbon in thirds, beating until smooth after each addition.
- Beat egg whites until stiff but not dry. Gradually beat remaining 1 cup sugar into whites. Fold this mixture gently into the batter.
- Preheat oven to 350°.
- Sprinkle pecans in bottom of well-buttered 10" tube pan. Carefully turn batter into pan. Bake 1½ hours or until done. Do not overbake.
- Yield: 1 large cake

NOTE: This cake freezes very well or keeps well wrapped in plastic wrap and then tinfoil in the refrigerator for 2-4 weeks.

Almond Cookies

8 Tablespoons butter or
   margarine
½ cup sugar
1 egg yolk
½ teaspoon almond extract
6 ounces flour (¾ cup)
1 teaspoon baking powder
pinch of salt
18-20 almonds

- Preheat oven to 350°.
- Cream butter and sugar. Add egg yolk and almond extract and beat thoroughly.
- Add flour, baking powder and salt. Mix well.
- Roll mixture into small balls.
- Place on greased cookie sheets. Firmly press an almond half into each ball of dough.
- Bake for 20-25 minutes until a pale golden color.
- Cool on wire rack.
- Yield: 18-20 cookies

Granny Bissell's Old Fashioned Butter Cookies

4 large eggs
1 pound butter
4 cups sugar
5 cups flour
2 teaspoons salt
2 teaspoons nutmeg, optional

- Preheat oven to 350°.
- Beat eggs and set aside.
- Cream butter and sugar. Add beaten eggs, flour, salt and nutmeg.
- Divide dough into 6 rolls. Wrap in wax paper and chill.
- Roll out dough fairly thinly. Cut with cookie cutters and decorate, if desired.
- Bake 8 minutes or until golden brown around the edges.
- Cool on wire racks.
- Wonderful as a holiday cut-out cookie.
- Yield: 7 dozen

Optional method: Slice rolls into rounds and decorate before baking.

Cream Cheese Fancies

1 cup butter (do not substitute)

3 ounces cream cheese

1 cup sugar

1 egg yolk

½ teaspoon vanilla

2½ cups sifted flour

1 6-ounce package semi-sweet
chocolate bits, melted

- Preheat oven to 375°.
- Cream the butter, cream cheese and sugar together.
- Stir in sugar gradually and beat until fluffy. Add egg yolk and vanilla.
- Stir in the flour, a little at a time, and mix well.
- Put dough through a pastry tube using the large rosette tip. Form cookies into an "S" shape directly onto an ungreased cookie sheet.
- Bake 12-15 minutes, or until lightly browned.
- Remove to a rack to cool thoroughly.
- Dip one end of the cookie into the melted chocolate. Place on waxed paper until the chocolate hardens.
- Yield: 4 dozen

Filled Spritz Cookies

½ cup butter, at room
temperature

½ cup sugar

1 large egg

1 teaspoon vanilla

1½ cups flour

10-ounce jar currant jelly

6 ounces semi-sweet chocolate
bits

chocolate sprinkles

- Preheat oven to 400°.
- Cream together butter and sugar.
- Add egg and vanilla to creamed mixture and beat until combined.
- Slowly add flour to mixture using beater on low speed.
- Put dough into a cookie press. Press onto a greased cookie sheet in long strips.
- Bake for 6-8 minutes.
- Cut the long strips into 2" bars. Cool on cookie racks.
- Spread flat side of cookie with currant jelly. Top with another cookie.
- Melt chocolate chips on top of double boiler or in microwave oven.
- Dip each end of cookie into melted chocolate. Then in chocolate sprinkles.
- Yield: 2 dozen

Diamond Cookies by Delphin

2½ sticks butter
½ cup sugar
2 cups flour
grated zest of an orange
2 teaspoons Grand Marnier

- Preheat oven to 350°.
- In a large bowl, mix butter and sugar. Then add flour, orange zest, and Grand Marnier.
- Gather dough into a ball and shape into a 2" wide tube.
- Refrigerate for 2 hours.
- Cut into ½" slices and place on cookie sheets covered with foil.
- Bake 8-10 minutes, or until golden in color.
- Let cool before serving.
- Yield: 4 dozen

This celebrity recipe was submitted by Delphin's Gourmandise Marblehead, MA

Raspberry Heart Cookies

¾ pound unsalted butter, softened
1¾ cups powdered sugar
1 egg
2 cups flour, sifted
1 cup cornstarch
2 cups finely chopped walnuts
½ cup red raspberry jam

- Cream butter and 1 cup sugar. Add egg.
- Sift flour and cornstarch and blend into creamed mixture. Blend in walnuts.
- Wrap dough and chill 4 hours.
- Roll dough to ¼" thick. Cut with 2" heart cookie cutter. (Half of cookies must have a heart center cut out.) Put on an ungreased cookie sheet. Chill for 45 minutes.
- Preheat oven to 325°.
- Bake for 12 minutes, or until lightly golden. Remove from oven. Spread bottoms with jam and place cut out cookie on top. Sprinkle with powdered sugar.
- Yield: 4 dozen

White Chocolate Macadamia Nut Cookies

1 cup butter or margarine

1½ cups sugar

½ cup brown sugar

2 eggs

1½ teaspoons vanilla

3 cups flour

½ teaspoon baking soda

1 teaspoon salt

1 12-ounce package white chocolate bits

1½ cups chopped macadamia nuts or walnuts

- Preheat oven to 350°.
- Cream butter and sugars until fluffy.
- Add eggs and vanilla.
- Blend in flour, baking soda and salt.
- Stir in white chocolate bits and nuts.
- Drop the batter by teaspoonfuls onto ungreased cookie sheets.
- Bake 10-12 minutes.
- Yield: 6 dozen

Awesome Oatmeal Chocolate Chip Cookies

1½ cups rolled oats

8 Tablespoons butter, at room temperature

½ cup sugar

½ cup firmly packed brown sugar

1 egg

1 teaspoon vanilla

1 cup flour

½ teaspoon baking powder

½ teaspoon baking soda

¼ teaspoon salt

3 ounces semi-sweet chocolate bits (about ½ cup)

3 ounces white chocolate, chopped (about ½ cup)

4 ounces milk chocolate, chopped (about ⅔ cup)

½ cup chopped blanched almonds

- Preheat oven to 375°.
- Place 1¼ cups of oats in a food processor and process until fine, about 1 minute.
- Cream the butter with the sugars in a large bowl until smooth. Add the egg and vanilla.
- Combine the processed oats with the dry ingredients. Slowly add to the butter mixture. Stir in the remaining ¼ cup oats, the chocolates, and the nuts.
- Drop the batter by teaspoonfuls onto ungreased cookie sheets.
- Bake 8-10 minutes until golden brown. Cool slightly before removing.
- Yield: 3 dozen

Marblehead Fudge Ecstasies

12 ounces semi-sweet chocolate bits

2 ounces unsweetened chocolate

2 Tablespoons butter or margarine

¼ cup flour

¼ teaspoon baking powder

pinch of salt

2 eggs

⅔ cup sugar

1 teaspoon vanilla

1 cup chopped nuts

- Preheat oven to 350°.
- In a medium saucepan, heat 1 cup of chocolate bits, the unsweetened chocolate and butter until melted, stirring constantly. Pour into a large mixing bowl and set aside to cool slightly.
- Mix together flour, baking powder and salt.
- Add eggs, sugar and vanilla to chocolate mixture and beat well. Add flour mixture to chocolate mixture and beat thoroughly.
- Stir in remaining chocolate bits and nuts.
- Drop batter by teaspoonfuls onto lightly greased cookie sheets.
- Bake 8-10 minutes or until the edges are firm and surface is dull and cracked.
- Cool on cookie sheets 1 minute before removing. Place on wire racks and cool thoroughly.
- Yield: 3 dozen

West Indies Cookies

1 cup butter or margarine

¾ cup sugar

¾ cup firmly packed brown sugar

2 eggs

1 teaspoon vanilla

2 cups flour

½ teaspoon salt

1 teaspoon baking soda

1 teaspoon baking powder

2 cups rolled oats

2 cups rice cereal

1 cup shredded coconut

chopped nuts, raisins or chocolate bits, optional

- Preheat oven to 350°.
- Cream butter and sugars. Beat in eggs and add vanilla.
- Sift together flour, salt, baking soda and baking powder, and add to creamed mixture.
- Blend in oats, rice cereal and coconut. If desired, add optional ingredients here.
- Shape into balls and flatten on ungreased cookie sheets. (These cookies do not spread while baking.)
- Bake 12-15 minutes. Cool thoroughly on wire racks.
- Yield: 5-6 dozen

NOTE: These taste much like Chinese almond cookies.

Joe Froggers

1 cup butter or margarine
2 cups sugar
2 cups dark molasses
7 cups flour
1 Tablespoon salt
1 teaspoon ground cloves
1 teaspoon allspice
1 teaspoon nutmeg
1 Tablespoon ginger
2 teaspoons baking soda
¾ cup water
¼ cup rum

- Cream shortening and sugar together. Add molasses.
- Sift dry ingredients together.
- Mix water with the rum.
- Add flour mixture alternately with the liquid mixture to the creamed mixture. Stir well between additions. Dough should be sticky.
- Chill dough overnight in the refrigerator.
- Preheat oven to 375°.
- On a well-floured surface, roll dough to ¼-½" thick. Cut with a 4" round cutter, or use the bottom of a 1 pound coffee can.
- Bake 10-12 minutes on greased cookie sheets.
- Yield: 5 dozen

According to information from the Marblehead Historical Society, legend says that Uncle Joe, an old man who lived on the edge of a frog pond in Marblehead, made the very best molasses cookies in town. They were called "Joe Froggers" because they were as large as lily pads and as dark as the frogs in the pond. Fishermen found the cookies would keep well on long sea voyages and began trading them for rum. Today the big molasses cookies will keep as well in the cookie jar as they did in the fishermen's sea chests—if they last that long!

Molasses Drop Cookies

12 Tablespoons butter
1 cup sugar
¼ cup molasses
1 egg
1¾ cups flour
½ teaspoon ground ginger
½ teaspoon ground cloves
1 teaspoon cinnamon
½ teaspoon baking soda

- Preheat oven to 350°.
- Melt butter and add sugar and molasses, mixing well.
- Lightly beat egg and add to butter mixture, blending well.
- In a large bowl, sift flour with spices and baking soda. Add mixture and blend well. (Batter will be wet.)
- Line a cookie sheet with aluminium foil and drop batter by teaspoonfuls on foil, leaving 3" between cookies.
- Bake 8-10 minutes, or until cookies begin to darken. Remove sheets of foil with cookies while still warm. Allow cookies to cool on foil.
- Yield: 2 dozen

NOTE: These soft and chewy cookies will stay moist in an airtight container for at least a week. May also be filled with chopped dates or raisins.

Apple Crisp Bars

Crust:

▶ **Crust:**

⅔ cup butter, softened

1 3-ounce package cream
   cheese, softened

¼ cup firmly packed dark brown
   sugar

1 large egg

1 teaspoon vanilla extract

2 cups all-purpose flour

¼ teaspoon salt

▶ **Filling:**

⅓ cup sugar

2 Tablespoons all-purpose flour

1 teaspoon ground cinnamon

¼ teaspoon grated nutmeg

8 cups thinly sliced tart baking
   apples

1 Tablespoon lemon juice

▶ **Topping:**

1 cup all-purpose flour

¾ cup firmly packed dark brown
   sugar

1 Tablespoon ground cinnamon

½ cup cold butter

Crust:

- Preheat oven to 375°. Lightly grease a 15½x10" jelly roll pan.

- Cream the butter, cream cheese and brown sugar together in a mixing bowl. Add the egg and vanilla.

- Stir in the flour and salt until just blended.

- Using your fingers, press the dough into the pan in an even layer.

Filling:

- Mix the sugar, flour, and spices in a small bowl.

- Sprinkle lemon juice over apples, and toss the apples with the sugar mixture.

- Arrange the apples in an even layer over the crust.

Topping:

- Combine flour, brown sugar, and cinnamon in a small mixing bowl. Cut in the butter until the dough forms coarse crumbs. Sprinkle evenly over the apples.

- Bake for 35-40 minutes, or until the apples are tender and the topping is nicely browned.

- Cool in the pan on a wire rack and cut into 2" squares.

- Serve warm or cold.

- Yield: 3 dozen bars

The Best Hermits

¾ cup vegetable shortening

1 cup sugar

1 egg

¼ cup molasses

2 teaspoons baking soda

2¼ cups flour

1 teaspoon cinnamon

¾ teaspoon ginger

¾ teaspoon cloves

½ cup raisins

½ cup chopped walnuts

- Preheat oven to 375°.

- Mix shortening, sugar, egg, and molasses. Stir in remaining ingredients.

- Shape dough into rolls ¾ length of jelly roll pan. Place 2 rolls on an ungreased pan and press down.

- Bake for 9-10 minutes. Cracks may appear uncooked, but remove and cool. Cut into bars.

- Yield: 4 dozen bars

Lemon Fingers

▶ **Crust:**

16 Tablespoons butter or margarine, at room temperature

¼ cup sugar

3 cups flour

▶ **Filling:**

6 large eggs, at room temperature

1½ cups sugar

1½ Tablespoons grated lemon peel

12 Tablespoons butter, melted

1 cup lemon juice

powdered sugar for topping

- Preheat oven to 400°.

- In a large bowl, combine the butter, sugar and flour with your fingers until crumbly.

- Grease a 15½x10" jelly roll pan. Press dough gently into pan to form a crust.

- Bake 20 minutes, or until sides are brown.

- Remove pastry from oven and reduce oven temperature to 350°.

- Cool pastry to room temperature.

- Whisk eggs and sugar until blended.

- Add lemon peel and slowly stir in melted butter and lemon juice. Mix thoroughly.

- Pour mixture into prepared crust.

- Bake 20 minutes at 350° or until filling is set and bubbling.

- Cool to room temperature. Cut into 1x2" fingers. Refrigerate until ready to serve. Sprinkle with powdered sugar.

- Yield: 70 bars

Pecan Bars

▶ **Crust:**

½ cup powdered sugar

2 cups flour

1 cup butter, softened

▶ **Topping:**

¾ cup butter

¼ cup heavy cream

½ cup honey

1 cup firmly packed light brown sugar

4 cups chopped pecans

- Preheat oven to 350°.

Crust:

- Mix sugar and flour together with a pastry cutter. Blend in butter. Firmly pat mixture into a greased 13x9" baking pan.

- Bake 20 minutes and remove from the oven.

Topping:

- Melt butter in a saucepan. Add cream, honey and brown sugar and stir until well blended. Remove from heat and stir in pecans. Spread over the crust. Bake 30 additional minutes.

- Cut into bars when cool.

- Yield: 2 dozen bars

Orange Date Bars

½ cup butter or margarine

½ cup sugar

1 Tablespoon grated orange peel

2 Tablespoons orange juice

1 cup sifted flour

½ teaspoon baking soda

1 egg

½ cup chopped walnuts

½ cup chopped dates

▶ Frosting:

1 Tablespoon softened butter or margarine

1 cup powdered sugar

4 teaspoons orange juice

- Preheat oven to 350°.
- Grease the bottom of a 9" square pan.
- Melt butter in a saucepan. Remove from heat and set aside to cool. Add sugar, orange peel, and orange juice and blend well.
- Stir in flour and baking soda. Add egg and beat thoroughly.
- Add nuts and dates, stirring lightly just to combine.
- Pour into baking pan and bake 25 minutes. Do not over bake.
- To make the frosting, blend all ingredients until smooth.
- Frost cooled bars.
- Yield: 18 bars

Apricot Almond Shortbreads

1½ cups butter

2 cups sugar

2 egg yolks

½ teaspoon vanilla

¼ teaspoon almond extract

4 cups flour

1⅓ cups blanched almonds, toasted and chopped

1 10-ounce jar apricot preserves

- Preheat oven to 350°.
- To toast almonds, bake in a preheated oven for 10 minutes. Cool.
- Cream butter and sugar until fluffy.
- Add egg yolks, vanilla and almond extracts.
- Add flour and toasted almonds until the mixture forms a soft dough.
- Divide dough in half. Press one half into a 15½x10" jelly roll pan.
- Spread evenly with preserves.
- Cover completely with remaining dough. Flatten mixture with hands, taking care to cover preserves completely.
- Bake 45 minutes, or until golden brown.
- Cut into 3x1" bars.
- Yield: 50 bars

Raspberry Walnut Bars

2 cups unsifted flour

1 teaspoon baking powder

¼ teaspoon baking soda

¼ teaspoon salt

12 Tablespoons softened unsalted butter

¼ cup sugar

½ cup firmly packed light brown sugar

2 egg yolks

1 teaspoon vanilla

1 cup chopped walnuts (reserve 3 Tablespoons)

⅔ cup raspberry preserves with seeds

2 Tablespoons lemon juice

- Preheat oven to 325°. Move oven rack to center of oven. Grease an 11x7" baking pan.
- Mix together flour, baking powder, baking soda and salt.
- In a large bowl, beat butter until creamy. Gradually add sugars. Continue to beat until light and fluffy, 1-2 minutes.
- Beat in egg yolks and vanilla with a spoon. Stir in dry ingredients and all but 3 tablespoons of walnuts.
- Mix jam and lemon juice in a small bowl.
- Press half the dough evenly into the bottom of the prepared pan.
- Spread with jam mixture.
- Crumble remaining dough evenly over top of jam. Sprinkle with reserved nuts.
- Bake 50-60 minutes, or until golden brown. Cool in pan on wire rack.
- Cut into bars.
- Yield: 2 dozen bars

Fancy Nut Bars

▶ Crust:

1½ cups flour

¾ cup firmly packed brown sugar

½ cup butter or margarine

▶ Center:

12-ounce can mixed cocktail nuts

▶ Topping:

½ cup light corn syrup

2 Tablespoons butter

6 ounces butterscotch bits

- Preheat oven to 350°.

Crust:

- Mix together flour, brown sugar and butter. Pat into a 13x9" baking pan.
- Bake 10 minutes. Set aside to cool 10-15 minutes.

Center:

- Sprinkle nuts over cooled crust.

Topping:

- Combine ingredients in a saucepan and bring to a boil until the bits are melted.
- Pour over bars and bake 10 minutes.
- Cool and cut into bars.
- Yield: 2 dozen bars

Beacon Hill Brownies

8 ounces unsweetened chocolate

1 cup butter or margarine

5 eggs

3 cups sugar

1 Tablespoon vanilla

1½ cups flour

2 cups chopped nuts

8 ounces chopped dates, optional

- Preheat oven to 375°.
- Melt chocolate and butter in a saucepan over low heat, stirring constantly. Set aside to cool.
- Beat eggs, sugar and vanilla in a large mixing bowl on high speed for 10 minutes.
- Blend in chocolate mixture on low speed.
- Add flour, just to blend.
- Add nuts and dates.
- Spread in a greased 13x9" baking pan and bake 35-40 minutes, taking care not to overcook.
- Cool in pan. Cut into squares.
- Yield: 24-32 squares

North End Cappuccino Bars

1 cup butter or margarine

8 1-ounce squares unsweetened chocolate

3½ cups sugar

6 large eggs

2 cups coarsely chopped walnuts

1¾ cups flour

¼ cup instant espresso coffee powder

2 teaspoons vanilla

½ teaspoon cinnamon

½ teaspoon salt

powdered sugar for topping

- Preheat oven to 350°.
- Grease and flour a 13x9" baking pan.
- In a heavy 4-quart saucepan over low heat, melt butter or margarine and chocolate. Stir frequently, until smooth.
- Remove from heat and with a wire whisk or spoon, beat in sugar and eggs until well blended. Stir in walnuts, flour, espresso powder, vanilla, cinnamon and salt.
- Spread evenly in pan.
- Bake 40-45 minutes.
- Cool completely in pan. When cool, cut crosswise into 6 strips, then cut each strip into 4 pieces. Sprinkle with powdered sugar.
- Yield: 2 dozen bars

Stephanie's Almond Rocca

1 10-ounce bag sliced natural
  almonds
1 pound unsalted butter
3 cups granulated sugar
6 Tablespoons water
2 Tablespoons corn syrup
12 ounces semi-sweet
  chocolate
4 ounces unsweetened
  chocolate
1 cup finely chopped almonds

- Butter two large baking pans, 13x9" suggested, and set aside.
- Melt butter in a large saucepan. Add the sugar, water and corn syrup. Place 2 candy thermometers in the pan.
- Cook over medium heat at a low, rolling boil, stirring occasionally. When the mixture reaches 300° on the thermometer, quickly add the sliced almonds. Stir well and pour into the buttered pans.
- Spread the candy as evenly as possible. Allow to harden until firm.
- Remove candy from pans and wipe any excess butter from the smooth bottom side.
- Melt the chocolates over hot water. Pour and brush the chocolate thickly over the bottom of the candy and press in the chopped almonds. Allow to harden.
- Break the candy into desired sized pieces and store, covered, in the refrigerator.
- Yield: 4 pounds

Black and White Pecan Turtles

▶ Crust:
  2 cups flour
  1 cup firmly packed brown
    sugar
  ½ cup butter, softened
  1½ cups pecan halves

▶ Caramel layer:
  ⅔ cup butter
  ¾ cup brown sugar
  1 cup semi-sweet chocolate bits
  1 cup white chocolate bits

- Preheat oven to 350°.
- Combine the first 3 ingredients in a food processor and process until fine. Pat firmly and evenly into 13x9" pan.
- Arrange pecans evenly over crust.
- In a small saucepan, combine butter and brown sugar and cook until boiling. Pour over pecans and crust.
- Bake 20 minutes.
- Remove from oven and sprinkle with dark chocolate bits on one half and white chocolate bits on the other. Return to oven just until the bits are slightly melted.
- Spread each side of melting chips separately with a knife in a swirling pattern.
- Cool completely before cutting into squares.
- Yield: 4 dozen squares

Currant Tarts

▶ **Pastry:**
  ½ **pound solid vegetable**
    shortening
  ½ **cup water**
  1 **teaspoon salt**
  3 **cups flour**

▶ **Filling:**
  1 **cup currants or raisins**
  1 **egg, unbeaten**
  1 **cup sugar**
  ½ **cup butter or margarine**
  1 **teaspoon vanilla**

Pastry:

- Melt shortening in the top of a double boiler.

- Add water and salt. Cool.

- When cool but not cold, add the flour and mix thoroughly.

- Cover and place in the refrigerator for several hours or until proper consistency to roll out.

- Roll out pastry to be fairly thin. Cut circles with cookie cutter to fit into miniature muffin cups.

- Line miniature muffin pans with the pastry circles. Place in freezer overnight or longer.

Filling:

- Prepare the filling before removing the pans from the freezer.

- Pour boiling water over the currants. Drain. Repeat with additional boiling water. Drain.

- Add remaining ingredients and beat with a spoon until foamy. After removing muffin pans from the freezer, fill each cup ⅔ full.

- Bake in a preheated 425° oven about 12-15 minutes. Remove from pans immediately to prevent sticking.

- Cool before serving, or store in refrigerator.

- Yield: 4 dozen tarts

Apricot Balls

¾ **cup dried apricots**
3 **ounces cream cheese,**
    softened
⅛ **teaspoon almond extract**
1 **cup flaked coconut, divided**
½ **cup sliced almonds, optional**

- Cook dried apricots in boiling water until tender, about 15 minutes. Drain well.

- Dice apricots. Combine apricots with the cream cheese and almond extract until well blended. Fold in half the coconut.

- Form mixture into small balls.

- Roll in remaining coconut. Can also roll in sliced almonds. Chill apricot balls until serving.

- Yield: 2 dozen balls

Trimmings

Plum Conserve

6 pounds fresh Italian plums
12 cups sugar
2 pounds raisins
4 large oranges
12 6-ounce jelly jars, sterilized
paraffin

- Pit and coarsely chop the plums. Place in a large saucepan. Bring to a simmer over medium heat.
- Slowly add sugar and raisins.
- Coarsely chop oranges by hand or in a food processor and add to plum mixture.
- Bring to a boil over medium heat, stirring constantly, for 10-15 minutes. Be careful as this burns easily.
- Fill all jars immediately to ½" of tops.
- Seal with paraffin according to package directions.
- Yield: 10-12 jars

Spiced Cranberry Sauce

2 cups fresh or frozen
  cranberries
1 cup sugar
½ cup water
½ teaspoon cinnamon
¼ teaspoon ground cloves
⅛ teaspoon ground nutmeg
½ cup sherry

- Heat water, sugar and sherry to boiling.
- Add cranberries. Boil rapidly until the cranberries burst skins. Add spices and cool.
- Yield: 3 cups

Microwave Raspberry Jam

1 pound frozen or fresh
  raspberries
2 Tablespoons lemon juice
2 cups sugar

- If raspberries are frozen, microwave them on high for 4 minutes.
- Add lemon juice and sugar, stirring well.
- Place in microwave on high for 5 minutes. Stir again.
- Return to microwave for 15 additional minutes on high, stirring occasionally.
- Place in jars and cover.
- Yield: 1½ pints

Microwave Strawberry Jam

½ tart apple, seeded and finely chopped with skin

4 cups fresh strawberries, hulled

1 cup sugar

1 teaspoon lemon juice

- Put apple in glass measuring cup. Microwave on high for 2 minutes.

- Place strawberries in a 3-quart dish with high sides. Gently mash. Stir in apple and sugar. Cover loosely with wax paper. Microwave on high 5 minutes. Stir. Remove cover.

- Microwave on high 15-20 minutes until jam becomes thick, skimming off foam and stirring every 3 to 5 minutes.

- Stir lemon juice into the berries. Cover and chill. Will keep up to 3 weeks.

- Yield: 1 cup

Lemon Curd

1 cup fresh lemon juice (4 to 6 lemons)

¼ cup finely shredded lemon peel

1¼ cups sugar

6 Tablespoons butter

3 eggs, lightly beaten

- In a medium saucepan, combine lemon juice, lemon peel and sugar.

- Bring to a boil and simmer 5 minutes. Add butter and stir until melted. Remove the mixture from the heat and cool to room temperature.

- Beat eggs into the lemon-sugar mixture until well blended, then place over low heat. Heat, stirring constantly 7-10 minutes, or until the mixture thickens and coats the spoon.

- Remove from heat and pour into 1 or 2 sterilized jars.

- Cool, cover and refrigerate.

- Yield: 2 cups

Blueberry-Lime Jam

3 pints blueberries
2 Tablespoons fresh lime juice
4 cups sugar
1 box pectin
½ teaspoon butter or margarine
6 6-ounce jelly jars, sterilized

- Remove stems from blueberries and crush.
- Pour fruit into a 6-8-quart pot. Add lime juice.
- Measure sugar and set aside.
- Add pectin and butter or margarine to fruit.
- Bring mixture to a full, rolling boil over high heat, stirring constantly.
- Quickly add sugar to the fruit mixture. Bring to a full, rolling boil again, stirring constantly and continue to boil 1 minute.
- Remove from heat. Skim off any foam with a large metal spoon.
- Fill all jars immediately to ⅛" of top. Carefully wipe jar rims and threads.
- Cover quickly with lids. Screw bands tightly.
- Invert jars for 5 minutes, then turn upright. After 1 hour, check seals.
- Yield: 1 quart

Peach Salsa

1 Tablespoon vegetable oil
1 medium onion, peeled and finely chopped
4 medium peaches
1 teaspoon sugar or to taste
juice of half a lemon
3 large tomatoes, peeled, seeded and sliced
1 hot chili pepper, seeded and finely chopped
salt to taste
2 Tablespoons chopped fresh mint or cilantro

- Heat oil in a skillet and cook onion for 5 minutes.
- Peel peaches by dipping them in boiling water for 30 seconds. Lift out and place in ice water.
- Peel and slice peaches and sprinkle with sugar and lemon juice.
- Add peaches to onions with tomatoes and chili pepper. Season with salt.
- Simmer mixture for 20 minutes, or until it begins to thicken.
- Pour mixture into serving bowl. Add mint or cilantro.
- Serve at room temperature with barbequed pork chops.
- Yield: 6

The manufacture of rum reached its height during the fifty years following the Revolution. Nearly all of it was made in Massachusetts. In 1783 there were 60 distilleries. In 1821 Salem alone had eight.
Successful shipping merchant Joseph Peabody (1757-1854) served his famous punch to the many guests he entertained in his home.

PEABODY PUNCH
1 bottle of the best dark rum
6 cups cognac
3 cups Madeira wine
1 dozen large limes
1 jar guava jelly
1 cup sugar

Should be made several days in advance, allowing it to mellow. Rub ⅓ cup of sugar on limes to get the essential oil diffused into sugar. Dissolve ⅔ cup of sugar into the tea. Then squeeze the limes and add juice to remaining impregnated sugar. Dissolve guava jelly in 1 pint of boiling water. Mix all these ingredients and adjust to required sweetness. Let it stand. One hour before serving, float a large lump of ice in the punch. This cools the punch and gives it a pleasant taste. Should there be leftovers, bottle for future use.

Sweet Yellow Squash Pickles

12 medium (12 cups) young, tender skin, yellow squash, in ¼" slices

36 small white onions, peeled and in ¼" slices (about 12 cups)

½ cup kosher salt

6 cups cracked ice cubes

3½ cups sugar

1 quart white vinegar

1¾ teaspoons ground turmeric

1¾ teaspoons celery seeds

1¾ teaspoons white mustard seeds

- Layer squash and onions alternately in a large mixing bowl. Sprinkle with kosher salt between layers.
- Pile cracked ice on top of squash and onions. Let stand, uncovered, at room temperature for 3 hours.
- Drain in colander and rinse in cold water.
- Drain again and press out all liquid.
- Sterilize 8 pint jars and tops. Keep hot.
- Bring sugar, vinegar, turmeric, celery and mustard seeds to a rolling boil over high heat in a large heavy stainless steel pot.
- Add squash and onions and stir gently. Bring to a boil, then pack into hot jars to ¼" of tops.
- Run a thin knife around edge of jars to release trapped air bubbles.
- Make sure onions and squash are covered with pickling liquid. Wipe rims clean and seal jars.
- Process 10 minutes in a boiling water bath. Remove. Cool to room temperature. Check seals, label and store in a cool, dark, dry place.
- Yield: 8 pints

Option: Use thinly sliced cucumbers instead of squash.

Garlic Spread for Bread

16 whole garlic bulbs, peeled

⅓ cup olive oil

3 Tablespoons white wine

1 Tablespoon butter

½ teaspoon salt

½ teaspoon thyme

1 Tablespoon chopped parsley

1 Tablespoon chopped celery leaves

¼ teaspoon allspice

freshly ground pepper to taste

- Place everything in a small ovenproof dish.
- Cover with tin foil and bake at 300° for 2 hours until soft and mushy.
- Spread on crusty French bread at the table.
- Yield: 6-8 portions

Tomato Chutney

1" peeled ginger root

2 Tablespoons vegetable oil

½ teaspoon fennel seeds

½ teaspoon cumin seeds

½ teaspoon mustard seeds

2 whole dried hot red chili peppers

6 cloves garlic, minced

1 pound tomatoes, chopped

1 teaspoon salt

2½ Tablespoons sugar

6 dried apricots, cut into ½" cubes

2 whole fresh hot green chili peppers

- Slice ginger and cut into fine slivers. Set aside.
- Heat oil in a heavy pan. When hot, add the fennel, cumin and mustard seeds. Let them sizzle and pop for a few seconds.
- Add red chili peppers to the seeds. Stir once. Then add ginger and garlic. Stir for 5 seconds.
- Add tomatoes, salt and sugar. Simmer 15-20 minutes until mixture begins to thicken.
- Add apricots and green chilies. Simmer for 10-15 minutes. Remove from heat.
- Serve at room temperature with Indian chicken, lamb or beef dishes.
- Yield: 6 portions

Cranberry Apple Relish

1 cup sugar

¼ teaspoon ground cinnamon

¼ teaspoon ground cloves

¼ teaspoon allspice

½ cup apple juice

1 pound fresh or frozen cranberries

2 medium sized tart apples, cored and coarsely chopped (about 2½ cups)

½ cup chopped walnuts

- Mix sugar, spices and apple juice in a deep 2-quart microwave safe casserole.
- Stir in cranberries and apples. Cover loosely with wax paper.
- Microwave on high 8-10 minutes, stirring twice until cranberries pop.
- Uncover and microwave 2-3 minutes more until slightly thickened.
- Stir in walnuts.
- Let cool before serving.
- Yield: 4½ cups

Mayonnaise and Variations

3 egg yolks
4 teaspoons lemon juice
1 teaspoon white wine vinegar
1 Tablespoon Dijon mustard
2¼ cups sunflower oil
1 scant teaspoon salt
freshly ground black pepper

▸ Aioli:
  2 cloves garlic, minced

▸ Herb Mayonnaise:
  1 cup chopped fresh dill, basil
    or cilantro
  1 Tablespoon lemon juice

- Put egg yolks, lemon juice, vinegar and mustard in a food processor and process until light and thoroughly combined.
- While machine is running, add the oil slowly, until all is emulsified.
- Add salt and pepper and adjust seasonings to taste.

Aioli:

- Add garlic to 1 cup mayonnaise and combine.
- Serve with poached seafood or steamed vegetables.

Herb Mayonnaise:

- Whisk into 1 cup of mayonnaise dill and lemon juice.
- Serve with steamed vegetables, seasoned, grilled meats or chicken.

Egg White Mayonnaise (Low Cholesterol)

2 large egg whites
2 teaspoons Dijon mustard
1 teaspoon red wine vinegar
salt
freshly ground pepper
1 cup safflower oil
½ cup extra virgin olive oil
¼ cup water

- Process the egg whites, mustard, vinegar, salt, pepper, and 3 tablespoons of oil in a food processor for 1 minute.
- With the machine running, add the remaining oil in a thin stream through the feed tube. The mixture will thicken.
- When all of the oil has been incorporated, with the food processor still running, slowly pour in the water.
- Cover tightly and refrigerate up to 2 weeks.
- Yield: 1½ cups

Acknowledgements

The Salem Hospital Aid Association is pleased to sponsor *Hospitality: A Cookbook Celebrating Boston's North Shore.*

Most of these recipes have been treasured by their donors for many years, in some cases for generations. Each dish has been thoroughly tested and we have attempted to present the instructions to satisfy both novice and experienced cooks. The collection was drawn from the more than one thousand recipes which were submitted for consideration. In some instances similar recipes were combined.

Hospitality was made possible through the efforts of many people, all of whom deserve our special thanks. The project would not have been possible without the assistance of many individuals, whose names appear on this and the following page, who graciously contributed recipes, tested and tasted, and assisted with countless project tasks.

We also offer our sincere appreciation to all those who will purchase the cookbook for the proceeds will be used to purchase life-saving and diagnostic equipment essential for patient care.

Angela Adams • Ruthann Alpern • Becky Anderson • Cora Felton Anderson • Diana Ashby • Margot E. Atwood • Sally Grant Aylward • Joan Bacall • Evelyn Baker • Mary Bannerman • Jan Barber • Diane Barbour • Donna Baribeau • Delena Barnard • Diana S. Barnes • Jamie Falk Barry • Joan M. Barry • Muriel C. Bates • Nancy Baxter • Sue Berey • Joyce A. Bergsten • Michele Bernet • Jim Bernstein • Gretchen Berrigan • Eileen Bertrand • Kathie Bertrand • Tammy Bevins • Ann Zoarski Birkner • Marcia Cunningham Bissell • Carole A. Bistrong • Gertrude M. Bixby • Grace Blanchard • Edith F. Blodgett • Helen G. Blount • Judy Boal • Susan Parker Boal • Nancy R. Boncore • Ruth Booth • Gaby Bradley • Mary Louise Bradley • Callie Brauer • Carol T. Bravos • Lynne D. Breed • Martha Bridge • Nancy E. Britz • Connie Brown • Ulla Brown • Nancy Bruett • Jean Budden • Irina T. Buras • Margaret R. Burke • Marjorie Burke • Betty Burns • Margaret P. Butler • Polly Caldwell • Marjorie I. Caliri • Patricia N. Camenga • Leslie Campbell • Marilyn Campbell • Marilyn Canton • Lee Carangelo • Esther B. Card • Judy Carpenter • Nancy T. Carvill • Lois Case • Elizabeth Cassidy • Marilyn Cassidy • Debbie Caulkins • Shirley Chaiken • Harvey Chamberlin • Jane V. Chamberlain • Joanna Chamberlin • Suzie Cheatham • Mary Clapp • Elaine Clark • Janice S. Cohen • Judy Cohen • Florence Coleman • Margaret Coleman • Sally Collier • Joan Collins • Marie K. Collins • Rita M. Collins • Rita J. Columbo • Barbara L. Conner, M.D. • Karen L.M. Connery • Donna M. Connolly • Marie R.G. Connolly • Jeanie Connor • Mary A. Connor • Joanne W. Cooke • Sally Cooke • Virginia Cooper • Lucy Coppola • Ginny E. Cote • Marcia Countie • Country Club Inn, Rangeley, Maine • Antoinette Cristoforo • Gail Cronin • Mary Culliton • Mrs. Bill Cunningham • Jeanne Cunningham • Suzanne I. Curran • Carol E. Curtin • Alison B. Curtis • Diane Cushman • Margaret H. Daley • Phyllis R. Davis • Claire C. Dembowski • Helen Dembowski • Joanne P. Devine • Joan Diamond • Joan Hammer Doan • Paula J. Dobrow • Mim Donaldson • Jack Donovan • Mary Donovan • Andrea Dorsey • Chris Dorsey • Lori G. Drumm • Gail E. Dudley • Margaret P. Duncan • Nancy S. Durkee • Kathleen M. Eagan • Virginia L. Eaton • LaMoyne Ebner • Margaret M. Eddy • Mary Jane English • Darlene Enscoe • Joyce Evans • Mary Ellen Falck • Jean Fallon • Nancy Fallon • Ruth Farwell • Katherine M. Fawson • Louise Finocchio • Eve Fitzgerald • Barry J. Follick • Muriel C. Follick • Theresa Fontaine • Mrs. Daniel L. Francescon • Phyllis Francis • Christine E. Franke • Susan Frary • Ann Fratini • Barbara Frawley • Judy Fredericks • Margot Galacar • Frances Gam • Gertrude C. Gam • Mary Louise Gannon • Kathleen Gauddreault • Dianne Geaney • Mike Geaney • Nancy E. Geaney • Gail H. Gibson • Bethany M. Gilboard • Elizabeth York Gingras • Mrs. Robert Girvin • Bernie Giuffrida • Barbara Gleason • JoAnn Gold • Alice Goldsmith • Mrs. Bertram M. Goldsmith • Darra Goldstein • Deanna Gollick • Camille Doan Goodby • Ellie Goodby • Betty Gordon • Anne Graciano • Jeanette Michaud Gray • Pearl Greenbaum • Gloria Wright Gutwirth • L. B. Haines • Barbara Hallowell • Joyce Hals • Gertrude Hammer • Ruth Hammer • Nancy Haskell • Sally Haskell • L. Blanche Hawes • Olive M. Hawkes • Mary C. Hayes • Barbara P. Healey • Patricia B. Healey • Audrey Frye Helzner • Mrs. Derek C. Hepworth • Janet Himmel • Wesley Hobbs • Helen Hodgden • Charlotte Hodges • Judy Hood • Philip E. Howard • Traci Howe • Lala Hrabovsky • Ann P. Huber • Marian P. Hubler • Elizabeth Humphrey • Marcia J. Hunkins • Pat Hurst • Florence L. Hyndman • Eileen Iskandar • Hettie Jackman • Sally Jackson • Bettie J. Jay • Helen C. Johnson • Joan Johnson • Christie-Ann Jones • Joan L. Jones • Erma W. Kaminski • Shirley Kaplan • D. L. Kaulbach • Emilie Kaulbach • Helen Kaulbach • Lisa Armstrong Kaulbach • Nordia Kay • Gloria Rose Kearney • Mark S. Keiler • Patti Kelley • Thelma B. Kenerson • Shirley Kenney • Anna Kenny, R.N. • Elaine R. King • Christine M. Kinney • Barbara Kittredge • Dorothy Kraft • Betty Ann Laidlaw • Edna Lail • Elizabeth M. LaLonde • Marcia Lambert • Alicia Lamkin • Donna M. Langburd • Jane Larivee • Joanne Larkin • Joanne Lavin • Bea Lazzaro • Anne M. Leach • Nell Leach • Nancy D. Lee • Alice R. Leidner • Dina K. Leonard • Joan Leonard • Susan B. Leonard • Stephanie McGrail Letendre • Sally Levine • Dottie Lider • Susan Lloyd • Sally Means Loring • Bernice P. Lucas • Joanne Lukens • Arthur Lund • Mrs. Harvey L. Macaulay • Betty MacDougall • Helen T. Macheras • Debbie MacLean • Joanne T. Macomber • Elizabeth Graham MaDan • Willie Mae • Marjorie Maclachlan Mahan • Adelaide Marquis • Adrienne E. Marscher • Barbara B. Martin • Lois Martin • Grace E. Mattson • Laura McCabe • Christina M. McCann • Kathy McCaughey • Lois McCormick • Carol C. McDowell • Caroline McGrail • Suzanne C. McGrail • Margo McGrath • Zelma McKay • Berenice McLaughlin • Bertha McLoon • Maureen McNeil • Lotte Mendelssohn • Jane S. Michon • Suzanne Milne • Nicky N. Moore • Mary Richardson Morley • Grace Morrison • Elsie S. Morse • Joyce Motta • Susan E. Moynihan, M.D. • Priscilla Munroe • Mary A. Murphy • Peter B. Napoli • Arline A. Nelson • Newbegin Family • Katharine C. Newhall • Suzanne Newhall • Jean Blake Nish • Jan Norris • Sigrid Novak • Sue Nye • Shelagh O'Dwyer • Robin C. Oliva • Joanne E. Olson • Boris Orkin, M.D. • Agnes Orlowski • Annie W. Ormiston

• Alison Ossatin • Dora Ossatin • Donna Ouellette • Lorraine Ouellette • Pat Paganis • Mary J. Palmer • Trish Patti • Christine Card Patton • Betsy Peffer • Ann Pierce • Kevin Pepper • Pat Pepper • Susan Pepper • Regina Ann Pevear • Carol S. Phillips • Janice Phillips • Richard Phippen • Marian G. Piro • Elizabeth Tenney Pittman • Joyce Pohlmeyer • Anthony Francis Politi, M.D. • Gladys H. Poor • Alice R. Pope • Marjorie Porosky • Barbara W. Porter • Jane Potter • Joanne Prives • Joan Quigley • Juanita Bethune Randall • Susan Redfield • Tricia Redrup • Peggy Reiley • Judy Remis • Jane Richardson • Marilyn Richardson • Ruth Earley Richardson • Ralph G. Richwagen • Martha G. Ritt • Sandra Roberts • Joan Robinson • Ann Rodgers • Mary Rogers • Stasia P. Roman • Alan Rosenfeld • Peggy Rothrauff • Mary Jo Rooney • Joan H. Rubel • Jeri Rugo • Mary Jane Russell • Lorraine Sadoski • Margie Satinsky • Denise A. Saulnier • Juanita Sayer • Norma M. Schribman • Mary Ann Schultz • Ann Scott • Anne Seaver • Scott Seaver • Ann Sellars • Ann Serafini • Gertrude M. Shaughnessy • Madeline Shavelson • Patsy Shevchuk • Lesllee Shlopak • Eleanor Short • Patti Shrum • Amy Jo Siden • Maggie Sides • Andy Sidford • Sylvia Sidman • Deborah J. Smith • Emily Greenleaf Smith • Jean Smith • Barbara Soleau • Bonnie J. Soleau • Betty Spooner • Bess Starr • Rosemary M. Stanek, • Marcia Lois Weinstein Steinbrook • Ginny Stocker • Mildred Stone • Judith Strenk • Carol Stuart • Sylvia Swain • Dorothy L. Swanson • Martha Tache • Beatrice Thenault • Kim Thistle • Alice U. Thompson • Flora Ruth Thompson • Alice M. Tierney • Anne L. Till • Brenda Till • Lillian Till • Dorothy Treadwell • Margaret H. Trevett • Edward R. Tufts • June E. Tufts • Mary Heath Tully • Barbara C. Uhl • Demetra Vallis • Brigitte N. Van Ringelestein • Wimmie Veenstra • Laurel Vincentio • Jean Viola • Carole A. Virtue • Bonnie Walker • Helane Walker • Brian L. Wallin • Gloria Wallis • Polly Wallis • Janel Walsh • Mrs. Paul L. Watson • Fran Waymouth • Lynne Weber • Cynthia K. Webster • Nancy J. Wegner • Hedy Weiss • Cottie Wellborn • Laurie Baker Wertz • Arlene Wheeler • Kay Hannon White • Linda K. Wiggin • Thelma E. Wiley • Lucile Willenbroh • Susan C. Williams • Yvette D. Williams • Martha B. Willis • Marilyn C. Winick • Trisha Wood • Roz Wosnick • Jane Yorge • Paula M. Zargaj

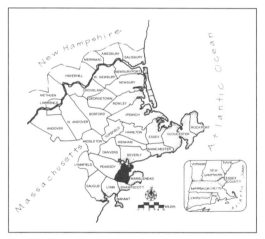

Map reproduced courtesy of the
U.S. Department of the Interior, National Parks Service.

Special appreciation is extended to the historical societies throughout Essex County who enthusiastically provided archival material and support for the project.

Andover Historical Society • Beverly Historical Society • Boxford Historical Society • Cape Ann Historical Association • Danvers Historical Society • Hamilton Historical Society • Ipswich Historical Society • Lynn Historical Society • Manchester Historical Society • Marblehead Historical Society • Peabody Historical Society • Sandy Bay Historical Society and Museum • Topsfield Historical Society • Wenham Historical Association and Museum

INDEX

A

ALMOND
Almond Cookies 182
Stephanie's Almond Rocca 193
Amaretto Rum Cream Pie 171
Anadama Bread 152
Angel Hair Pasta with Shrimp and Feta Cheese 122
Anise Cake 178
APPETIZERS
Artichoke Hearts au Gratin 126
Baba Ghanoush 4
Baguette Toppings
Curried Crab Spread 16
Garlic Spread for Bread 199
Leek, Sun-Dried Tomato and Goat Cheese Spread 16
Pesto with Mozzarella 16
Baked Brie Frangelico 18
Baked Brie with Figs and Raspberry Vinegar 18
Baked Caponata 10
Brussels Mussels 103
Cheese
Basil Torta 17
Mozzarella Milano 17
Dips
Baked Caponata 10
Crab, Artichoke and Jalapeño Dip 2
Smoked Salmon Pâté 5
Endive Leaves and Cherry Tomatoes with Crabmeat 2
Hen Cove Scallops 8
Leeks Vinaigrette 132
Lemon Cup Scallops 8
Oriental
California Rolls 3
Green Chile Won Tons 11
Indonesian Satay with Peanut Sauce 13
Pork Won Tons 13
Seasoned Oriental Mushrooms 12
Spinach Wrapped Chicken with Oriental Dip 12
Oysters on the Half Shell on Skiff 10
Savory Cheesecake with Saga and Bacon 15
Savory Cheesecake with Smoked Salmon and Leeks 15
Scallops Baked in Apples 108
Scallops Verde 105
Scampi alla Griglia 6
Seviche (Marinated Scallops) 97
Spicy Shrimp with Snow Peas 7
Summer Crab Mold 4
Tabouleh 40
Tartare of Marinated Salmon with Cucumber Salad 6
Terrines and Pâtés
Chicken and Vegetable Terrine 11
Pâté Maison Diamond 14
Shrimp and Artichoke Log 7
Smoked Oyster Log 9
Terrine de Trois Poissons 5
Tomato Concassé 14

Tomatoes Stuffed with Zucchini Pesto 129
Warmed Endive Vinaigrette 132
World's Best Clams Casino 9
APPLE
Apple Crisp Bars 188
Apple Sour Cream Pancakes with Apricot Butter 46
Apple Torte 172
Bolton Apple Muffins 142
Boxford Apple Cake 177
Chilled Curried Apple Soup 32
Deep Dish Apple Pie 168
APRICOT
Apricot Almond Shortbread 190
Apricot Balls 194
Apricot Cream Cheese Bread 142
Aromatic Game Hens 72
ARTICHOKES
Artichoke Hearts au Gratin 126
Brunch Eggs with Chèvre and Artichoke Hearts 47
Sautéed Chicken and Artichoke Hearts 60
ASPARAGUS
Asparagus in Provençal Mayonnaise 53
Autumn Pumpkin Bread 148
AVOCADO
Chilled Avocado and Grapefruit Soup 31
Awesome Oatmeal Chocolate Chip Cookies 185

B

Baba Ghanoush 4
Bahama Fish Supreme 89
Baked Brie Frangelico 18
Baked Brie with Figs and Raspberry Vinegar 18
Baked Caponata 10
Baked Halibut à la Grecque 92
Baked Pears 160
Baked Stuffed Lobster 108
BANANA
Banana Bran Muffins 143
Hawaiian Banana Bread 144
Microwave Bananas 164
Trade Winds Bread 146
Barbecued Boneless Leg of Lamb 83
Basil Torta 17
Beacon Hill Brownies 192
BEANS
Grandma Mariano's Escarole and White Cannellini Beans ... 131
Mexican Bean Salad 40
New England Baked Beans 126
Pasta e Fagioli 23
Red and Black Bean Salad with Lime Vinaigrette 36
Tasty Lentil Soup 31
Béchamel Raisin Sauce 91
Béchamel Sauce 111
Beef and Vegetables in Spicy Garlic Sauce 74
BEETS
Microwave Beets with Currant Sauce 127

Russian Beet Borscht 28
Berenice's Torte Verde 54
Bisteeya (Moroccan Chicken in Pastry) 62
Black and White Pecan Turtles 193

BLACKBERRY
Blackberry Cake 176

BLUEBERRY
Blueberry Brunch Cake 144
Blueberry Dessert Cake 177
Blueberry-Lime Jam 198
Dutch Blueberry Pie 169
New England Blueberry Muffins 145
Boiled Lobster 105
Bolton Apple Muffins 142
Boxford Apple Cake 177
Braised Cabbage 128
Brandied - Peach Chicken 58
Brandied Peaches 162

BREAD
Garlic Spread for Bread 199

BREADS
Anadama Bread 152
Blueberry Brunch Cake 144
Cinnamon Rolls 149
Currant Scones 150
Dilly Bread 151
Harvest Squash Rolls 148
Lemon Croissants 154
  Muffins
    Banana Bran Muffins 143
    Bolton Apple Muffins 142
    Corn and Red Pepper Muffins 146
    Glorious Muffins 143
    New England Blueberry Muffins 145
    Orange Date Muffins 145
Murphy's Crusty White Bread 150
Point Camp Corn Bread 144
Portuguese Bermuda Bread 154
Pumpernickel Bread 152
  Quick
    Apricot Cream Cheese Bread 142
    Autumn Pumpkin Bread 148
    Cranberry-Orange Bread 147
    Hawaiian Banana Bread 144
    Lemon Poppy Seed Teacake 147
    Trade Winds Bread 146
Sesame Semolina Bread 153
Brie and Bacon Brunch 51
Brisket of Beef with Fruit 79

BROCCOLI
Broccoli Salad 42
Broccoli with Cashew Nuts 127
Chicken, Broccoli and Ziti 61
Pasta with Roasted Garlic and Broccoli 117

BRUNCH
Apple Sour Cream Pancakes with Apricot Butter 46

Asparagus in Provençal Mayonnaise 53
Berenice's Torte Verde 54
Brie and Bacon Brunch 51
  Eggs
    Brunch Eggs with Chèvre and Artichoke Hearts 47
    Eggs Ranchero 48
    Festive Baked Eggs 47
    Harlequin Omelette 49
Mushroom Strudel 54
Mustard Brie Soufflé 50
Soufflé with Herbs and Mushrooms 48
Three Tomato Tart 53
Tomato and Pesto Quiche 51
Torta Rustica 52
Vegetable Strata 50
Brunch Eggs with Chèvre and Artichoke Hearts 47
Brussels Mussels 103
Buerre Blanc 104
Bundles of Sole with Sauce Mousseline 90
Butternut Squash with Cranberries and Apples 137

BUTTERS
Buerre Blanc 104
Chive-Cucumber Butter 113
Dill Lemon Butter 113
Lime Ginger Butter 113
Wasabi Butter 113

C

CABBAGE
Braised Cabbage 128
Spiced Red Cabbage 128

CAKES
Anise Cake 178
Blackberry Cake 176
Blueberry Dessert Cake 177
Boxford Apple Cake 177
Carrot Cake 176
Cheesecake Elegante 180
German Chocolate Cake 178
Holiday Bourbon Cake 181
Irish Cream Cheesecake 179
Macadamia Fudge Cake 179
Peach or Strawberry Shortcake 173
Walnut Meringue Gâteau 175
California Chicken Salad 38
California Rolls 3

CANDY
Apricot Balls 194
Stephanie's Almond Rocca 193
Cantonese Chicken 56
Cardinale Sauce for Poached Pears 160

CARROT
Carrot Cake 176
Carrots with Lemon and Honey 129
Cream of Carrot Soup 29
Glorious Muffins 143

Moroccan Carrot Salad 41
Catalan Sauce 96
Celery and Stilton Soup 31
Champagne Sauce for Fish 112
Chardonnay Sauce 106

CHEESE
Baked Brie Frangelico 18
Baked Brie with Figs and Raspberry Vinegar 18
Basil Torta 17
Brunch Eggs with Chèvre and Artichoke Hearts 47
Celery and Stilton Soup 31
Eggs Ranchero 48
Harlequin Omelette 49
Mozzarella Milano 17
Mustard Brie Soufflé 50
Parmesan Cheese Risotto 123
Savory Cheesecake with Saga and Bacon 15
Savory Cheesecake with Smoked Salmon and Leeks .. 15

CHEESECAKE
Cheesecake Elegante 180
Irish Cream Cheesecake 179
Chicken, Broccoli and Ziti 61

CHICKEN
Bisteeya (Moroccan Chicken in Pastry) 62
Brandied - Peach Chicken 58
California Chicken Salad 38
Cantonese Chicken 56
Chicken and Vegetable Terrine 11
Chicken, Broccoli and Ziti 61
Chicken Chili Rellenos 63
Chicken della Robbia 65
Chicken Galloupe 65
Chicken Persillade 57
Chicken Prunella 60
Chicken with Garlic, Goat Cheese and Sun-Dried Tomato Butter 57
Chili Yogurt Marinade 66
Fruited Herb Garden Chicken Salad with Orange Tarragon Dressing 39
Grilled Chicken Breasts Indonesia 59
Javanese Chicken 56
Linguine with Chicken Livers in Brandy 121
    Marinades
        Chili Yogurt Marinade 66
        Chive Sauce 66
        Dijon Mustard Marinade 66
        Honey-Ginger Marinade 66
        Peanut Marinade 66
New England Chicken Pie 64
Pasta Primavera with Chicken 119
Pâté Maison Diamond 14
Sautéed Chicken and Artichoke Hearts 60
Spiced Chicken Curry 58
Spinach Wrapped Chicken with Oriental Dip 12
Stir-Fry Chicken with Lime 61
Tandoori Chicken Barbecue 59
Chili Yogurt Marinade 66
Chilled Avocado and Grapefruit Soup 31

Chilled Curried Apple Soup 32
Chilled Strawberry and Wine Soup 32
Chinese Sesame Noodle Salad 37
Chive-Cucumber Butter 113
Chive Sauce 66

CHOCOLATE
Awesome Oatmeal Chocolate Chip Cookies 185
Beacon Hill Brownies 192
Black and White Pecan Turtles 193
Chocolate Dipped Strawberries 163
Chocolate Roulade with Raspberries 173
Chocolate Velvet 158
Elaine's Sinfully Rich Blacksmith Pie 170
German Chocolate Cake 178
Hot Chocolate Soufflé 174
Macadamia Fudge Cake 179
Marblehead Fudge Ecstacies 186
North End Cappuccino Bars 192
Truffle Sauce 163
White Chocolate Macadamia Nut Cookies 185
Chowder Mexicano 21

CINNAMON
Cinnamon Rolls 149

CLAMS
Clams au Buerre Blanc 104
Pier 4 Clam Chowder 22
World's Best Clams Casino 9
Cold Poached Salmon 92
Confetti Pasta Salad 35

COOKIES
Almond Cookies 182
Awesome Oatmeal Chocolate Chip Cookies 185
Cream Cheese Fancies 183
Diamond Cookies by Delphin 184
Filled Spritz Cookies 183
Granny Bissell's Old Fashioned Butter Cookies 182
Joe Froggers 187
Marblehead Fudge Ecstacies 186
Molasses Drop Cookies 187
Raspberry Heart Cookies 184
West Indies Cookies 186
White Chocolate Macadamia Nut Cookies 185

CORN
Corn and Red Pepper Muffins 146
Microwave Corn on the Cob 132
Point Camp Corn Bread 144
Court Bouillion 25

CRAB
California Rolls 3
Crab, Artichoke and Jalapeño Dip 2
Curried Crab Spread 16
Endive Leaves and Cherry Tomatoes with Crabmeat ... 2
Maryland Crab Cakes with Lobster and Cognac Sauce . 109
Soft-Shell Crabs with Ginger-Lime Beurre Blanc 104
Summer Crab Mold 4

CRANBERRY
- Cranberry Apple Relish 200
- Cranberry Cassis Sauce 94
- Cranberry-Orange Bread 147
- Spiced Cranberry Sauce 196
- Cream Cheese Fancies 183
- Cream of Carrot Soup 29
- Crème Brûlée Fruit Tart 164

CURRANTS
- Currant Scones 150
- Currant Tarts 194
- Curried Crab Spread 16
- Curry Tomato Coulis 102

D

- Deep Dish Apple Pie 168
- Delhi Style Lamb Curry 82

DESSERTS
- Anise Cake 178
- Apple Torte 172
- Baked Pears 160
- Blackberry Cake 176
- Blueberry Dessert Cake 177
- Bourbon Holiday Cake 181
- Boxford Apple Cake 177
- Brandied Peaches 162
- Carrot Cake 176
- Cheesecake Elegante 180
- Chilled Strawberry and Wine Soup 32
- Chocolate Dipped Strawberries 163
- Chocolate Roulade with Raspberries 173
- Chocolate Velvet 158
  - **Cookies**
    - Almond Cookies 182
    - Awesome Oatmeal Chocolate Chip Cookies 185
    - Cream Cheese Fancies 183
    - Diamond Cookies by Delphin 184
    - Filled Spritz Cookies 183
    - Granny Bissell's Old Fashioned Butter Cookies 182
    - Joe Froggers 187
    - Marblehead Fudge Ecstacies 186
    - Molasses Drop Cookies 187
    - Raspberry Heart Cookies 184
    - West Indies Cookies 186
    - White Chocolate Macadamia Nut Cookies 185
  - **Cookies/Bars**
    - Apple Crisp Bars 188
    - Apricot Almond Shortbread 190
    - Beacon Hill Brownies 192
    - Black and White Pecan Turtles 193
    - Fancy Nut Bars 191
    - Lemon Fingers 189
    - North End Cappuccino Bars 192
    - Orange Date Bars 190
    - Pecan Bars 189
    - Raspberry Walnut Bars 191

- The Best Hermits 188
- Currant Tarts 194
- German Chocolate Cake 178
- Hot Fruit Compote 165
- Irish Cream Cheesecake 179
- Lemon Snow with Grand Marnier Sauce 157
- Macadamia Fudge Cake 179
- Marinated Orange Slices 162
- Microwave Bananas 164
- Orange Cream 160
- Peach or Strawberry Shortcake 173
  - **Pies and Tarts**
    - Amaretto Rum Cream Pie 171
    - Crème Brûlée Fruit Tart 164
    - Deep Dish Apple Pie 168
    - Dutch Blueberry Pie 169
    - Elaine's Sinfully Rich Blacksmith Pie 170
    - Fruit Tart Toppings 167
    - Heavenly Fruit Cake 181
    - Incomparable Pumpkin Pie 169
    - Lattice Peach Tart 167
    - Pastry Cream for Tarts 168
    - Pear Maple Pie 172
    - Sweet Short or Basic Pastry for Pies or Tarts 166
    - Tangy Lemon Tart 166
  - **Puddings**
    - English Trifle 159
    - Exquisite Bread Pudding 156
    - Old English Christmas Pudding 158
    - Orange Pudding with Meringues 156
- Ricotta Fritters 165
  - **Sauces**
    - Cardinale Sauce for Poached Pears 160
    - Grand Marnier Sauce 157
    - Peach Sauce 161
    - Raspberry Sauce 161
    - Truffle Sauce 163
  - **Soufflés**
    - Frozen Daiquiri Soufflé 174
    - Hot Chocolate Soufflé 174
- Tangy Lemon Tart 166
- Tiramisù 159
- Velvet Cream with Sherried Oranges 161
- Walnut Meringue Gâteau 175
- Zabaglione Marnier Mary Ellen 157
- Diamond Cookies by Delphin 184
- Dijon Mustard Marinade 66
- Dill Lemon Butter 113
- Dill or Tarragon Mousseline 111
- Dilly Beans 44
- Dilly Bread 151

DUCK
- Duck Breast with 3-Peppercorn Sauce 68
- Roast Duckling with Orange and Cognac Sauce 68
- Sautéed Duck Breast with Autumn Berries 69
- Dutch Blueberry Pie 169

Dutch Herring Salad 34
Dutch Salad Dressing 44

E

Edgurdouce (Rabbit in Wine and Fruit) 72
Egg White Mayonnaise (Low Cholesterol) 201
EGGPLANT
    Baba Ghanoush 4
    Baked Caponata 10
    Minted Eggplant 131
Eggs Ranchero 48
Elaine's Sinfully Rich Blacksmith Pie 170
Endive Leaves and Cherry Tomatoes with Crabmeat ... 2
English Trifle 159
Exquisite Bread Pudding 156

F

Fabulous Sole with Béchamel Raisin Sauce 91
Fancy Nut Bars 191
Festive Baked Eggs 47
Fettucine alla Joanna 117
Fiddlehead Ferns Vinaigrette 41
Filled Spritz Cookies 183
Fourth of July Salmon with Egg Sauce 93
Friday Night Fish 96
Frozen Daiquiri Soufflé 174
FRUIT
    Crème Brûlée Fruit Tart 164
    Heavenly Fruit Cake 181
    Hot Fruit Compote 165
Fruit Tart Toppings 167
Fruited Herb Garden Chicken Salad with Orange Tarragon Dressing 39

G

GAME HENS
    Aromatic Game Hens 72
Garlic Roasted Potatoes 134
Garlic Spread for Bread 199
German Chocolate Cake 178
Glazed Veal Roast 81
Glorious Muffins 143
GOOSE
    Roast Goose with Fruit and Chestnut Stuffing 67
GRAINS
    Moroccan Couscous Pilaf 124
    Tabouleh 40
Grand Marnier Sauce 157
Grandma Mariano's Escarole and White Cannellini Beans 131
Granny Bissell's Old Fashioned Butter Cookies 182
GREEN BEANS
    Dilly Beans 44
    Green Beans with Basil and Orange 130
    Minted Green Beans and Peas 130
Green Chile Won Tons 11

Grilled Bluefish with Mustard Marinade 94
Grilled Chicken Breasts Indonesia 59
Grilled Marinated Shrimp 99
Grilled Swordfish with Catalan Sauce 96
Grilled Swordfish with Red Pepper Purée 97
Grilled Tuna Steaks with Avocado Salsa 95
Grilled Turkey Breast 69
Gruyère Salad 43

H

HALIBUT
    Baked Halibut à la Grecque 92
    Halibut Dijon 95
Harlequin Omelette 49
Harvest Squash Rolls 148
Hawaiian Banana Bread 144
Hazelnut Hollandaise 86
Hearty Mushroom Barley Soup 27
Heavenly Fruit Cake 181
Hen Cove Scallops 8
Herbed Roast Turkey 70
Holiday Bourbon Cake 181
Honey-Ginger Marinade 66
Hot Chocolate Soufflé 174
Hot Fruit Compote 165

I

Inaugural Fish Chowder 21
Incomparable Pumpkin Pie 169
Indonesian Satay with Peanut Sauce 13
Irish Cream Cheesecake 179
Italian Stuffed Swordfish 98

J

Jarlsberg Vegetable Bisque 26
Javanese Chicken 56
Joe Froggers 187
Julienne of Curried Sweet Peppers 136

L

Lafayette Onion Soup 30
Lamb, Corn and Pepper Hash 83
Lattice Peach Tart 167
Leek, Sun-Dried Tomato and Goat Cheese Spread 16
Leeks Vinaigrette 132
LEMON
    Lemon Croissants 154
    Lemon Cup Scallops 8
    Lemon Curd 197
    Lemon Fingers 189
    Lemon Poppy Seed Teacake 147
    Lemon Rice 122
    Lemon Snow with Grand Marnier Sauce 157
    Tangy Lemon Tart 166

Lemon Cup Scallops 8
Lemon Rice 122
LIME
    Lime Vinaigrette 36
Lime Ginger Butter 113
Linguine and Lobster 121
Linguine with Chicken Livers in Brandy 121
Linguine with Scallops 119
Linguine with Sun-Dried Tomatoes and Zucchini 118
LOBSTER
    Baked Stuffed Lobster 108
    Boiled Lobster 105
    Linguine and Lobster 121
    Lobster Stuffed Tenderloin 77
    Lobster and Corn Chowder 20
    The Absolute Best Lobster Newburgh 110
Lobster and Cognac Sauce 109

M

Macadamia Fudge Cake 179
Marblehead Fudge Ecstacies 186
MARINADES
    Chive Sauce 66
    Dijon Mustard Marinade 66
    Grilled Bluefish with Mustard Marinade 94
    Honey-Ginger Marinade 66
    Mustard Marinade 94
    Peanut Marinade 66
    Yogurt Marinade for Lamb 81
Marinated Orange Slices 162
Marinated Shrimp and Scallops with Curry Tomato Coulis 100
Maryland Crab Cakes with Lobster and Cognac Sauce ... 109
Massachusetts Seafood Chowder 22
Mayonnaise and Variations 201
McClain's Marblehead Seafood Casserole 106
MEATS
    Beef
        Beef and Vegetables in Spicy Garlic Sauce 74
        Brisket of Beef with Fruit 79
        Lobster Stuffed Tenderloin 77
        Spicy Beef Vindaloo 75
        Sukiyaki 74
        Tenderloin Salera 76
        Tenderloin of Beef Provençal 76
        Wickford Chili 78
    Lamb
        Barbecued Boneless Leg of Lamb 83
        Delhi Style Lamb Curry 82
        Lamb, Corn and Pepper Hash 83
        Roast Leg of Lamb with Herb Crust 82
        Roast Loin of Pork à la Boulanger 85
        Yogurt Marinade for Lamb 81
    Pork
        Pork Medallions with Hazelnut Holllandaise 86
        Pork in Squash Boats 84
        Smoke-Roasted Pork Tenderloin with Bourbon 85

    Southwestern Stir-Fry 84
    Sauces
        Mushroom Sauce for Tenderloin 78
        Roquefort Sauce for Tenderloin 75
        Sauce Aurora 77
    Veal
        Glazed Veal Roast 81
        The Veal Chop Special 79
        Veal Dijonnaise 80
        Veau avec Gin 80
Mediterranean Fish Soup 23
Mexican Bean Salad 40
Microwave Beets with Currant Sauce 127
Microwave Corn on the Cob 132
Microwave Raspberry Jam 196
Microwave Strawberry Jam 197
Microwave Bananas 164
Minted Eggplant 131
Minted Green Beans and Peas 130
Molasses Drop Cookies 187
Moroccan Carrot Salad 41
Moroccan Couscous Pilaf 124
Mozzarella Milano 17
Murphy's Crusty White Bread 150
MUSHROOMS
    Hearty Mushroom Barley Soup 27
    Mushroom Casserole 133
    Mushroom Sauce for Tenderloin 78
    Mushroom Strudel 54
    Seasoned Oriental Mushrooms 12
    Soufflé with Herbs and Mushrooms 48
MUSSELS
    Brussels Mussels 103
    Mussels Provençal 103
Mustard Brie Soufflé 50
Mustard Marinade 94

N

Nancy's Mustard Sauce 114
Nantucket Scallops with Spring Vegetables and Chardonnay Sauce 106
New England Baked Beans 126
New England Blueberry Muffins 145
New England Chicken Pie 64
Normandy Sauce 112
North End Cappuccino Bars 192
North Shore Fish Cakes 102

O

Old English Christmas Pudding 158
ONION
    Lafayette Onion Soup 30
    Roasted Onions with Sage 129
ORANGE
    Marinated Orange Slices 162
    Orange Cream 160

Orange Date Bars 190
Orange Date Muffins 145
Orange Pudding with Meringues 156
Orange Rice with Currants, Zucchini and Red Onion 124
Orange Tarragon Salad Dressing 39
Velvet Cream with Sherried Oranges 161

OYSTERS
Oysters on the Half Shell on Skiff 10
Smoked Oyster Log 9

P

Pâté Maison Diamond 14
Parmesan Cheese Risotto 123
Parsnip and Onion Soup 27
PASTA
Angel Hair Pasta with Shrimp and Feta Cheese 122
Chicken, Broccoli and Ziti 61
Chicken
Linguine with Chicken Livers in Brandy 121
Pasta Primavera with Chicken 119
Chinese Sesame Noodle Salad 37
Confetti Pasta Salad 35
Fettucine alla Joanna 117
Linguine with Scallops 119
Linguine with Sun-Dried Tomatoes and Zucchini 118
Pasta e Fagioli 23
Pasta Provençal 118
Pasta with Roasted Garlic and Broccoli 117
Seafood
Linguine and Lobster 121
Seafood Lasagne 120
Shrimp and Scallop Primavera 98
Spinach Pasta with Gorgonzola 116
Stir-Fry Pasta and Vegetables 116
Szechwan LoMein 36
PASTRY
Sweet Short or Basic Pastry for Pies or Tarts 166
Pastry Cream for Tarts 168
PEACH
Brandied - Peach Chicken 58
Brandied Peaches 162
Lattice Peach Tart 167
Peach Salsa 198
Peach Sauce 161
Peach or Strawberry Shortcake 173
Peanut Marinade 66
PEAR
Baked Pears 160
Cardinale Sauce for Poached Pears 160
Pear Maple Pie 172
PECAN
Pecan Bars 189
Pesto with Mozzarella 16
Pier 4 Clam Chowder 22
PLUM
Plum Conserve 196

Three Plum Island Salad 38
Poached Salmon Fillet 93
Point Camp Corn Bread 144
PORK
Indonesian Satay with Peanut Sauce 13
Pork in Squash Boats 84
Pork Medallions with Hazelnut Holllandaise 86
Pork Won Tons 13
Portuguese Bermuda Bread 154
POTATO
Garlic Roasted Potatoes 134
Potato Salad Française 42
Potatoes Baked in Parchment 133
Potatoes with Sesame Seeds 134
The Great Potato Cake with Goat Cheese and Leeks 135
Zucchini Potato Pie 138
POULTRY
Stuffings
Stuffing Befitting a Celebration (For Poultry) 70
Pumpernickel Bread 152
PUMPKIN
Autumn Pumpkin Bread 148
Incomparable Pumpkin Pie 169
Spicy Pumpkin Soup 30

R

RABBIT
Edgurdouce (Rabbit in Wine and Fruit) 72
RASPBERRY
Microwave Raspberry Jam 196
Raspberry Heart Cookies 184
Raspberry Sauce 161
Raspberry Walnut Bars 191
Red and Black Bean Salad with Lime Vinaigrette 36
RICE
Lemon Rice 122
Moroccan Couscous Pilaf 124
Orange Rice with Currants, Zucchini and Red Onion 124
Parmesan Cheese Risotto 123
Rice Salad 35
Risotto Florentine 124
Spiced Basmati Rice 123
Ricotta Fritters 165
Risotto Florentine 124
Roast Duckling with Orange and Cognac Sauce 68
Roast Goose with Fruit and Chestnut Stuffing 67
Roast Leg of Lamb with Herb Crust 82
Roast Loin of Pork à la Boulanger 85
Roasted Garlic Vinaigrette 43
Roasted Onions with Sage 129
Roasted Red Pepper Dressing 44
ROLLS
Cinnamon Rolls 149
Harvest Squash Rolls 148
Roquefort Sauce for Tenderloin 75
Russian Beet Borscht 28

SALAD

Broccoli Salad	42
California Chicken Salad	38
Chinese Sesame Noodle Salad	37
Confetti Pasta Salad	35
Dilly Beans	44

Dressings

Orange Tarragon Salad Dressing	39
Roasted Garlic Vinaigrette	43
Dutch Herring Salad	34
Dutch Salad Dressing	44
Fiddlehead Ferns Vinaigrette	41
Fruited Herb Garden Chicken Salad with Orange Tarragon Dressing	39
Gruyère Salad	43
Mexican Bean Salad	40
Moroccan Carrot Salad	41
Potato Salad Française	42
Red and Black Bean Salad with Lime Vinaigrette	36
Rice Salad	35
Roasted Red Pepper Dressing	44
Seafood Salad Oriental	34
Sesame Snow Pea Salad	42
Szechwan LoMein	36
Tabouleh	40
Three Plum Island Salad	38
Warm Goat Cheese Salad with Roasted Garlic Vinaigrette	43

SALMON

Cold Poached Salmon	92
Fourth of July Salmon with Egg Sauce	93
Poached Salmon Fillet	93
Smoked Salmon Pâté	5
Tartare of Marinated Salmon with Cucumber Salad	6

SAUCES

Béchamel Raisin Sauce	91
Béchamel Sauce	109
Bundles of Sole with Sauce Mousseline	90
Catalan Sauce	96
Champagne Sauce for Fish	112
Chardonnay Sauce	106
Cranberry Cassis Sauce	94
Curry Tomato Coulis	100
Dill or Tarragon Mousseline	111
Fabulous Sole with Béchamel Raisin Sauce	91
Grilled Swordfish with Catalan Sauce	96
Hazelnut Hollandaise	86
Lobster and Cognac Sauce	109
Maryland Crab Cakes with Lobster and Cognac Sauce	109
Mushroom Sauce for Tenderloin	78
Nancy's Mustard Sauce	114
Normandy Sauce	112
Roquefort Sauce for Tenderloin	75
Sauce Aurora	77
Scrod with Orange Madeira Sauce	88
Souffléed Tartar Sauce	114

Sweet

Cardinale Sauce for Poached Pears	160
Grand Marnier Sauce	157
Peach Sauce	161
Raspberry Sauce	161
Truffle Sauce	163
Tuna with Cranberry Cassis Sauce	94
Sautéed Chicken and Artichoke Hearts	60
Sautéed Duck Breast with Autumn Berries	69
Savory Cheesecake with Saga and Bacon	15
Savory Cheesecake with Smoked Salmon and Leeks	15

SCALLOPS

Hen Cove Scallops	8
Lemon Cup Scallops	8
Linguine with Scallops	119
Nantucket Scallops with Spring Vegetables and Chardonnay Sauce	106
Scallops Baked in Apples	107
Scallops Verde	105
Seviche (Marinated Scallops)	97
Shrimp and Scallop Primavera	98
Scallops Baked in Apples	108
Scallops Verde	105
Scampi alla Griglia	6

SCROD

Scrod with Orange Madeira Sauce	88
Scrod with Tomato Buerre Blanc	89
Scrod with Orange Madeira Sauce	88
Scrod with Tomato Buerre Blanc	89

SEAFOOD, FISH

Bahama Fish Supreme	89

Butters

Chive-Cucumber Butter	113
Dill Lemon Butter	113
Lime Ginger Butter	113
Wasabi Butter	113

Clams

Clams au Buerre Blanc	104

Crab

Curried Crab Spread	16
Maryland Crab Cakes with Lobster and Cognac Sauce	109
Soft-Shell Crabs with Ginger-Lime Beurre Blanc	104
Friday Night Fish	96
Grilled Bluefish with Mustard Marinade	94

Halibut

Baked Halibut à la Grecque	92
Halibut Dijon	95
Inaugural Fish Chowder	21

Lobster

Baked Stuffed Lobster	108
Boiled Lobster	105
The Absolute Best Lobster Newburgh	110
Massachusetts Seafood Chowder	22
McClain's Marblehead Seafood Casserole	106
Mediterranean Fish Soup	23

Mussels

Brussels Mussels	103

Mussels Provençal	103
North Shore Fish Cakes	102
Salmon	
Cold Poached Salmon	92
Fourth of July Salmon with Egg Sauce	93
Poached Salmon Fillet	93
Sauces	
Béchamel Sauce	111
Champagne Sauce for Fish	112
Dill or Tarragon Mousseline	111
Nancy's Mustard Sauce	114
Normandy Sauce	112
Souffléed Tartar Sauce	114
Scallops	
Nantucket Scallops with Spring Vegetables and Chardonnay Sauce	106
Scallops Baked in Apples	108
Scallops Verde	105
Seviche (Marinated Scallops)	97
Scrod	
Scrod with Orange Madeira Sauce	88
Scrod with Tomato Buerre Blanc	89
Seafood Diablo	101
Seafood Lasagne	120
Shrimp	
Grilled Marinated Shrimp	99
Marinated Shrimp and Scallops with Curry Tomato Coulis	100
Seafood Salad Oriental	34
Shrimp and Scallop Primavera	98
Spicy Cajun Shrimp	102
Stillington Shrimp	100
Stir-Fry Shrimp with Asparagus and Pea Pods	99
The Ultimate Shrimp Curry	101
Sole	
Bundles of Sole with Sauce Mousseline	90
Fabulous Sole with Béchamel Raisin Sauce	91
Sole Stuffed with Crab	88
Swordfish	
Grilled Swordfish with Catalan Sauce	96
Grilled Swordfish with Red Pepper Purée	97
Italian Stuffed Swordfish	98
Terrine de Trois Poissons	5
Tuna	
Grilled Tuna Steaks with Avocado Salsa	95
Tuna with Cranberry Cassis Sauce	94
Seafood Diablo	101
Seafood Lasagne	120
Seafood Salad Oriental	34
Seasoned Oriental Mushrooms	12
Sesame Semolina Bread	153
Sesame Snow Pea Salad	42
Seviche (Marinated Scallops)	97
SHRIMP	
Angel Hair Pasta with Shrimp and Feta Cheese	122
Grilled Marinated Shrimp	99
Marinated Shrimp and Scallops with Curry Tomato Coulis	100

Rice Salad	35
Scampi alla Griglia	6
Shrimp and Artichoke Log	7
Shrimp and Scallop Primavera	98
Spicy Cajun Shrimp	102
Spicy Shrimp with Snow Peas	7
Stillington Shrimp	100
Stir-Fry Shrimp with Asparagus and Pea Pods	99
The Ultimate Shrimp Curry	101
Smoke-Roasted Pork Tenderloin with Bourbon	85
Smoked Oyster Log	9
Smoked Salmon Pâté	5
Soft-Shell Crabs with Ginger-Lime Beurre Blanc	104
SOLE	
Bundles of Sole with Sauce Mousseline	90
Fabulous Sole with Béchamel Raisin Sauce	91
Sole Stuffed with Crab	88
Soufflé with Herbs and Mushrooms	48
Souffléed Tartar Sauce	114
SOUPS	
Celery and Stilton Soup	31
Chilled Avocado and Grapefruit Soup	31
Chilled Curried Apple Soup	32
Chilled Strawberry and Wine Soup	32
Chowder Mexicano	21
Court Bouillion	25
Cream of Carrot Soup	29
Hearty Mushroom Barley Soup	27
Inaugural Fish Chowder	21
Jarlsberg Vegetable Bisque	26
Lafayette Onion Soup	30
Lobster and Corn Chowder	20
Massachusetts Seafood Chowder	22
Mediterranean Fish Soup	23
Parsnip and Onion Soup	27
Pasta e Fagioli	23
Pier 4 Clam Chowder	22
Russian Beet Borscht	28
Spicy Pumpkin Soup	30
Sweet and Sour Soup	26
Sweet and Sour Tomato Basil Soup	29
Tasty Lentil Soup	31
Won Ton Soup	25
Zucchini Minestrone	28
Zuppa di Sposalizio/Abruzzi Wedding Soup	24
Southwestern Stir-Fry	84
Spaghetti Squash with Cheese	138
Spiced Basmati Rice	123
Spiced Chicken Curry	58
Spiced Cranberry Sauce	196
Spiced Red Cabbage	128
Spicy Beef Vindaloo	75
Spicy Cajun Shrimp	102
Spicy Pumpkin Soup	30
Spicy Shrimp with Snow Peas	7

SPINACH
Berenice's Torte Verde 54
Gruyère Salad 43
Spinach Pasta with Gorgonzola 116
Spinach Roulade 139
Torta Rustica 52
Spinach Wrapped Chicken with Oriental Dip 12
SQUASH
Butternut Squash with Cranberries and Apples 137
Harvest Squash Rolls 148
Pork in Squash Boats 84
Spaghetti Squash with Cheese 138
Sweet Yellow Squash Pickles 199
Stephanie's Almond Rocca 193
Stillington Shrimp 100
Stir-Fry Chicken with Lime 61
Stir-Fry Pasta and Vegetables 116
Stir-Fry Ratatouille 136
Stir-Fry Shrimp with Asparagus and Pea Pods 99
Stir-Fry Snow Peas 135
STRAWBERRY
Chilled Strawberry and Wine Soup 32
Chocolate Dipped Strawberries 163
Microwave Strawberry Jam 197
Stuffed Sweet Peppers Apulia 137
STUFFINGS
Roast Goose with Fruit and Chestnut Stuffing 67
Stuffing Befitting a Celebration (For Poultry) 70
Sukiyaki 74
Summer Crab Mold 4
Summer Vegetable Platter 140
SWEET PEPPER
Julienne of Curried Sweet Peppers 136
Stuffed Sweet Peppers Apulia 137
Sweet Short or Basic Pastry for Pies or Tarts 166
Sweet Yellow Squash Pickles 199
Sweet and Sour Soup 26
Sweet and Sour Tomato Basil Soup 29
SWORDFISH
Grilled Swordfish with Catalan Sauce 96
Grilled Swordfish with Red Pepper Purée 97
Italian Stuffed Swordfish 98
Szechwan LoMein 36

T

Tabouleh 40
Tandoori Chicken Barbecue 59
Tangy Lemon Tart 166
Tartare of Marinated Salmon with Cucumber Salad 6
Tasty Lentil Soup 31
Tenderloin Salera 76
Tenderloin of Beef Provençal 76
Terrine de Trois Poissons 5
The Absolute Best Lobster Newburgh 109
The Best Hermits 188
The Great Potato Cake with Goat Cheese and Leeks 135

The Ultimate Shrimp Curry 101
The Veal Chop Special 79
Three Plum Island Salad 38
Three Tomato Tart 53
Tiramisù 159
TOMATO
Sweet and Sour Tomato Basil Soup 29
Three Tomato Tart 53
Tomato Chutney 200
Tomato Concassé 14
Tomato and Pesto Quiche 51
Tomatoes Stuffed with Zucchini Pesto 129
TOPPINGS
Savory
Curried Crab Spread 16
Garlic Spread for Bread 199
Leek, Sun-Dried Tomato and Goat Cheese Spread 16
Pesto with Mozzarella 16
Sweet
Fruit Tart Toppings 167
Torta Rustica 52
Trade Winds Bread 146
TRIMMINGS
Blueberry-Lime Jam 198
Cranberry Apple Relish 200
Egg White Mayonnaise (Low Cholesterol) 201
Lemon Curd 197
Mayonnaise and Variations 201
Microwave Raspberry Jam 196
Microwave Strawberry Jam 197
Peach Salsa 198
Plum Conserve 196
Spiced Cranberry Sauce 196
Sweet Yellow Squash Pickles 199
Tomato Chutney 200
Truffle Sauce 163
TUNA
Grilled Tuna Steaks with Avocado Salsa 95
Tuna with Cranberry Cassis Sauce 94
TURKEY
Grilled Turkey Breast 69
Herbed Roast Turkey 70
Turkey Roast 71
Turnip and Apple Purée 136

V

Veal Dijonnaise 80
Veau avec Gin 80
Vegetable Curry 140
Vegetable Strata 50
VEGETABLES
Artichokes
Artichoke Hearts au Gratin 126
Beans
Grandma Mariano's Escarole and White Cannellini Beans 131
New England Baked Beans 126

Beets
    Microwave Beets with Currant Sauce 127
Broccoli
    Broccoli with Cashew Nuts 127
Cabbage
    Braised Cabbage 128
Carrot
    Carrots with Lemon and Honey 129
Corn
    Microwave Corn on the Cob 132
Eggplant
    Baked Caponata 10
    Minted Eggplant 131
Endive
    Warmed Endive Vinaigrette 132
Green Beans
    Green Beans with Basil and Orange 130
    Minted Green Beans and Peas 130
Leeks
    Leeks Vinaigrette 132
Mushrooms
    Mushroom Casserole 133
Onion
    Roasted Onions with Sage 129
Potato
    Garlic Roasted Potatoes 134
    Potatoes Baked in Parchment 133
    Potatoes with Sesame Seeds 134
    The Great Potato Cake with Goat Cheese and Leeks 135
    Zucchini Potato Pie 138
Ratatouille
    Stir-Fry Ratatouille 136
Red Cabbage
    Spiced Red Cabbage 128
Snow Peas
    Stir-Fry Snow Peas 135
Spinach
    Spinach Roulade 139
Squash
    Butternut Squash with Cranberries and Apples 137
    Spaghetti Squash with Cheese 138
Summer Vegetable Platter 140

Sweet Pepper
    Julienne of Curried Sweet Peppers 136
    Stuffed Sweet Peppers Apulia 137
Tomato
    Tomatoes Stuffed with Zucchini Pesto 129
Turnip
    Turnip and Apple Purée 136
Vegetable Curry 140
Vegetable Strata 50
Zucchini
    Tomatoes Stuffed with Zucchini Pesto 129
Velvet Cream with Sherried Oranges 161
VINAIGRETTE
    Dutch Salad Dressing 44
    Lime Vinaigrette 36
    Orange Tarragon Salad Dressing 39
    Roasted Garlic Vinaigrette 43
    Roasted Red Pepper Dressing 44

W

Walnut Meringue Gâteau 175
Warm Goat Cheese Salad with Roasted Garlic Vinaigrette 43
Warmed Endive Vinaigrette 132
Wasabi Butter 113
West Indies Cookies 186
White Chocolate Macadamia Nut Cookies 185
Wickford Chili 78
Won Ton Soup 25
World's Best Clams Casino 9

Y

Yogurt Marinade for Lamb 81

Z

Zabaglione Marnier Mary Ellen 157
ZUCCHINI
    Zucchini Minestrone 28
    Zucchini Potato Pie 138
Zuppa di Sposalizio/Abruzzi Wedding Soup 24

The Salem Hospital Aid Association thanks you for purchasing **HOSPITALITY: A Cookbook Celebrating Boston's North Shore**

Proceeds from sales will provide funds for the purchase of diagnostic and life-saving equipment.

Please send _____ **copies of Hospitality at $19.95 each** _____

Make check payable to Salem Hospital Aid Association/Hospitality, 81 Highland Avenue, Salem, MA 01970.

Hospitality

Name _____

Address _____

City _____ State _____ Zip _____

Daytime telephone number _____

Gift from _____

Please mail gift to _____

Address _____

City _____ State _____ Zip _____

Massachusetts residents add 5% sales tax _____
Shipping and handling $2.00 each   _____
Gift Wrap and mailing $2.00 each   _____
                          TOTAL   _____

- -

The Salem Hospital Aid Association thanks you for purchasing **HOSPITALITY: A Cookbook Celebrating Boston's North Shore**

Proceeds from sales will provide funds for the purchase of diagnostic and life-saving equipment.

Please send _____ **copies of Hospitality at $19.95 each** _____

Make check payable to Salem Hospital Aid Association/Hospitality, 81 Highland Avenue, Salem, MA 01970.

Hospitality

Name _____

Address _____

City _____ State _____ Zip _____

Daytime telephone number _____

Gift from _____

Please mail gift to _____

Address _____

City _____ State _____ Zip _____

Massachusetts residents add 5% sales tax _____
Shipping and handling $2.00 each   _____
Gift Wrap and mailing $2.00 each   _____
                          TOTAL   _____

The Salem Hospital Aid Association thanks you for purchasing **HOSPITALITY: A Cookbook Celebrating Boston's North Shore**

Proceeds from sales will provide funds for the purchase of diagnostic and life-saving equipment.

Please send _____ copies of Hospitality at $19.95 each _____

Make check payable to Salem Hospital Aid Association/Hospitality, 81 Highland Avenue, Salem, MA 01970.

Hospitality

Name _____

Address _____

City _____ State _____ Zip _____

Daytime telephone number _____

Gift from _____

Please mail gift to _____

Address _____

City _____ State _____ Zip _____

Massachusetts residents add 5% sales tax _____
Shipping and handling $2.00 each   _____
Gift Wrap and mailing $2.00 each   _____
TOTAL _____

The Salem Hospital Aid Association thanks you for purchasing **HOSPITALITY: A Cookbook Celebrating Boston's North Shore**

Proceeds from sales will provide funds for the purchase of diagnostic and life-saving equipment.

Please send _____ copies of Hospitality at $19.95 each _____

Make check payable to Salem Hospital Aid Association/Hospitality, 81 Highland Avenue, Salem, MA 01970.

Hospitality

Name _____

Address _____

City _____ State _____ Zip _____

Daytime telephone number _____

Gift from _____

Please mail gift to _____

Address _____

City _____ State _____ Zip _____

Massachusetts residents add 5% sales tax _____
Shipping and handling $2.00 each   _____
Gift Wrap and mailing $2.00 each   _____
TOTAL _____